BURNT BY DEMOCRACY

Youth, Inequality, and the Erosion of Civic Life

Burnt by Democracy traces the political ascendance of neoliberalism and its effects on youth. The book explores democracy and citizenship as described in interviews with over forty young people – ages 16 to 30 – who have either experienced homelessness or identify as an activist, living in five liberal democracies: Canada, Australia, New Zealand, the United States, and the United Kingdom.

Highlighting significant cuts to social and affordable housing, astronomical increases in the costs of higher education, and the transformation and erosion of state benefits systems, Jacqueline Kennelly argues that democracy's decline is not occurring because young people are apathetic, or focused on informal politics, or unaware of their civic duties. Rather, it is because of collective misunderstanding about how democracy is actually structured, how individuals learn to participate, and how growing wealth inequality has undermined the capacity of those at the bottom to meaningfully advocate for changes that might improve their conditions.

Against a vivid and often heart-breaking backdrop of stories from young people struggling to survive and thrive under conditions of ever-expanding state retrenchment and inequality, *Burnt by Democracy* makes a timely and impassioned plea for protecting and strengthening democracy by truly levelling the playing field for all.

JACQUELINE KENNELLY is a professor in the Department of Sociology and Anthropology and Director of the Centre for Urban Youth Research at Carleton University.

Burnt by Democracy

Youth, Inequality, and the Erosion of Civic Life

JACQUELINE KENNELLY

UNIVERSITY OF TORONTO PRESS
Toronto Buffalo London

© University of Toronto Press 2024
Toronto Buffalo London
utorontopress.com
Printed and bound by CPI Group (UK) Ltd, Croydon, CR0 4YY

ISBN 978-1-4875-4847-6 (cloth)   ISBN 978-1-4875-5900-7 (EPUB)
ISBN 978-1-4875-5164-3 (paper)   ISBN 978-1-4875-5542-9 (PDF)

Library and Archives Canada Cataloguing in Publication

Title: Burnt by democracy : youth, inequality, and the erosion of civic life / Jacqueline Kennelly.
Names: Kennelly, Jacqueline, author.
Description: Includes bibliographical references and index.
Identifiers: Canadiana (print) 20230442447 | Canadiana (ebook) 20230442676 | ISBN 9781487548476 (cloth) | ISBN 9781487551643 (paper) | ISBN 9781487559007 (EPUB) | ISBN 9781487555429 (PDF)
Subjects: LCSH: Youth – Social conditions – 21st century. | LCSH: Neoliberalism. | LCSH: Democracy. | LCSH: Equality.
Classification: LCC HQ796.K46 2023 | DDC 305.235–dc23

Cover design: Louise OFarrell
Cover images: iStock.com/AntiMartina; iStock.com/Komthong Wongsangiam

We wish to acknowledge the land on which the University of Toronto Press operates. This land is the traditional territory of the Wendat, the Anishnaabeg, the Haudenosaunee, the Métis, and the Mississaugas of the Credit First Nation.

University of Toronto Press acknowledges the financial support of the Government of Canada, the Canada Council for the Arts, and the Ontario Arts Council, an agency of the Government of Ontario, for its publishing activities.

  Canada Council   Conseil des Arts
for the Arts   du Canada

To my phenomenal children and dedicated partner

and

To all the young people who participated in this project

and

To young people everywhere who feel burnt by democracy.

Contents

Acknowledgments   ix

Introduction   3

1 The Growth of Inequality across (Neo)liberal Democracies   24

2 Democratic Dispositions in the Twenty-First Century   53

3 Democratic Biographies: Pathways towards a Democratic Disposition   77

4 Democracy's Failures/Failures of Democracy   106

5 The Social Distribution of Democratic Knowledge   143

6 Belonging to the State: Citizenship as Symbolic Power   167

Conclusions: When I Say the Word "Democracy," What Comes to Mind?   197

Appendix 1: Youth Participants by Country   207

Bibliography   209

Index   225

Acknowledgments

This book would not exist without the truly extraordinary research support of Cihan Erdal. Cihan's primary task was to recruit young activists, which he did with his usual care and attention to detail. But he also did so much more, from reviewing the manuscript to pulling together the bibliography to helping me work through complex ideas to providing necessary moral support as my work life was going sideways, for reasons separate from this project. When his partner, Ömer Ongun, texted to tell me that Cihan had been arrested in his home country of Turkey for his former political and activist work there, I was devastated. Thankfully, due to the herculean efforts of Ömer, strategic legal defences in both Turkey and Canada, and a global network of supporters, Cihan was first released from detention (although remaining under house arrest), and then was able to flee Turkey to come home to Canada. As I note in chapter 3 of this book, Cihan's experience brought me face to face with the importance of the rights that continue to exist in liberal democracies such as Canada, and the duty we carry to fight for protecting and expanding those rights. Freedom of expression, freedom to dissent, freedom from arbitrary arrest, and freedom from police violence are not nearly as universal as they ought to be even in countries like Canada that claim to maintain such rights.

I am intellectually indebted to a number of colleagues and friends, who have provided key scholarly interventions or supports throughout the development of this manuscript. Beau Clarke helped me find resources and statistics about neoliberalism's effects on the five countries under study here, as well as reading early chapters and letting me know that my writing struck a chord even with a non-academic reader. Firoze Manji alerted me to Domenico Losurdo's work on liberalism very early on, while Daniel McNeil kindly reviewed chapter 6 and pointed me towards important literature on citizenship that I had missed. Steve Threadgold and David Farrugia invited me to participate in their online seminar with the Newcastle Youth Seminar in Australia, early in the writing of the project. David Farrugia and Karen Nairn organized well-attended and extremely enjoyable in-person events to discuss the book in Australia and New Zealand, when I traveled there in the summer of 2023. Cihan Erdal (again) has organized two seminar series as part of his work as coordinator of my research centre, the Centre for Urban Youth Research, and has kindly reserved places for me to speak about this work in both the 2022 and 2023 virtual series. Megan Rivers-Moore, Carolyn Ramzy, Jamie Liu, Miranda Brady, and Azar Masoumi are scholar-friends who helped protect and nurture a supportive online co-writing space while the pandemic wrought havoc in all of our personal lives. Three successive Chairs of the Department of Sociology & Anthropology – Aaron Doyle, Blair Rutherford, and Carlos Novas – have been supportive of my work and have helped me navigate the workplace challenges that emerged while writing this book, with care and empathy. My Faculty Dean, Pauline Rankin, has also stood by me, to the extent that she was able, throughout this challenging time. I am grateful for her ongoing support.

The research project on which this book is based would have been impossible without my six in-country research assistants: Fiona Carey (Australia), Piero Corcillo (UK), Brian Ristow (New Zealand), Peyton Wilson (US), Cassandra Eng (US), and Chloé Samala (US). Many thanks to colleagues from all four of these countries for helping me find suitable RAs: Jennifer Patico (US), Paul Watt (UK), Bronwyn Wood (NZ), and Juliet Watson (AU).

At University of Toronto Press, Jodi Lewchuk has provided me with the finest editorial experience I have had with book publishing to date. Prompt, professional, friendly, and kind, Jodi has taught me what is possible in academic publishing – and it is so much more than others have offered before this! So many thanks.

Alex Campbell, my life partner and number one fan (even when I'm grumpy and distracted), read every word of this manuscript and helped me work through what in the world I could possibly have left to say by the time I was writing the Conclusions. He also picked up the slack, walked the dogs, took care of the kids, and massaged my tight shoulders, alongside so many other small and large gestures of love and support. As Hawksley Workman tells us, this is the ground we stand on. All my love.

Kai Duong and Diana Campbell, you are my treasures and my reason for living. Thank you for teaching me, bugging me, teasing me, hugging me, antagonizing me, waking me up in the middle of the night, and allowing me to watch you both grow into phenomenal humans.

Last, but certainly not least, my heartfelt thanks to all of the participants in this project, who shared your stories with me, a perfect stranger, and trusted me to treat them with the dignity and care they deserve. I hope you find in these pages that I have taken that trust deeply to heart and tried to work with the collective knowledge you offered to produce something of value to the world. Your courage, honesty, and insights were and are humbling and inspiring.

BURNT BY DEMOCRACY

Introduction

> Democracy does not require absolute social and economic equality, but it cannot withstand large and fixed extremes of rich and poor that undermine the very possibility of legislating our lives in common.
>
> –Wendy Brown (2011, p. 20)

What does it mean to be burnt by democracy?

Stephanie (USA, age twenty-one) describes democracy as "the façade of equity." She attributes her critical views to her liberal arts education at a progressive university, where she is now doing a graduate degree. Like most of the young people interviewed for this book, she recalls little education about democracy from her K–12 schooling, which for Stephanie happened in a private Catholic school. That same private Catholic school influenced her as a teenager to be deeply religious and politically conservative, so much so that her first protest was an anti-abortion rally, and she thought she would train to become a nun. Now she attends Black Lives Matter rallies and organizes for sex workers' rights. Her complex history includes adoption from a country in the Global South and multiple forays in and out of the American foster system. Starting at age fifteen, her adoptive family began sex trafficking her. At age eighteen, Stephanie cut all ties with her abusive adoptive family, left the foster system, and immediately became homeless, a fate shared by many young people leaving care in Western liberal democracies. Although she has been housed since starting university, it has required her to continue doing sex work despite it being "really triggering." She would stop if she could, "but it's so hard because of the money. Even when I have other jobs and have great opportunities and stuff, it's like but, I can get the same amount for a week's work [in other jobs] in like two hours [of sex work]. So how am I ever going to let this go?" With tuition at American universities such as hers topping USD 30,000 per year for students from outside of the state – and that doesn't include fees, books, rent, food, and other living expenses – her dilemma is understandable.

Stephanie's undergraduate thesis was a research project on the "mandatory reporting"[1] rules that ought to have protected her as a child but did not; her graduate work is looking at the resources that can be accessed by survivors of sex trafficking and how to improve them. "I used to be really angry at the system," she told me, "until I did the research and realized they're underfunded." When I asked her to tell me more about how the system had failed her, she responded:

> Well, what ways have they not failed me? I guess like the biggest system that's failed me is the foster system. So many kids just fall through the cracks. With that mandatory reporting – this is something I put in my research – I actually interviewed a coach of mine and I used to be really upset because I would come to school visibly not okay. And I was always upset because I was like, "okay, I know these people care about me. Like, why is nothing being done?" And I remember I found out, a bunch of teachers were really trying, but the principal and like a local police officer that the principal knew kept sweeping it under the rug because they didn't want a bad name for the private school. So I guess in that sense, it started opening my mind and perspective to the fact that it's a systemic issue. It's not on the individual.

Stephanie is one of very few participants in this research to have both experienced homelessness and been enmeshed in activist work and communities. As she observes: "I have noticed that as someone who's had lived experience, that most of the people who are activists are not the people who have experienced these things. So, for example, I have a bunch of friends who are housing insecure, a bunch of friends who have also been in the foster system, and most of the time, they are not in activist roles." Straddling both of these worlds gives Stephanie unique insights into the limits and possibilities of democratic participation, through activism and otherwise. She is clear that she has been able to engage in activism, "because I have that privilege of that education that was different from most people [in the foster system]." She is also keenly aware of the flaw this introduces to supposedly democratic systems, contributing to the "façade of equity": "I think that is actually the source of where these systems are failing. Because they're [victims, survivors, or marginalized communities] not invited to the discussion. They're not kept in direct dialogue when decisions are being made, and like how are you going to try to improve things without including the people that are going to benefit from them? So that's actually one of the biggest parts of how the system has failed me." As experienced by Stephanie, to be burnt by democracy is to be told repeatedly that you live in a democratic system in

---

1 Mandatory reporting refers to the requirement for teachers and other adults who work with children under age eighteen to report signs of child abuse to the relevant agency, such as Children's Aid Societies in Canada or Child Protective Services in the United States.

which your voice and opinions matter, and yet to encounter systems failure after systems failure and be unable to do anything about it. It is to live in a society in which being able to actively engage in democratic work that may improve conditions for the most marginalized requires access to education and networks that are class-delimited and typically exclude those who have been negatively affected by the broken systems in question. It is to be misinformed about the structures and logic of formal liberal democracy, so that you may eventually come to believe it is your own fault if you cannot make the systems work in your favour and/or you give up entirely on achieving a comfortable and secure life. It is to learn that democracy is somehow the domain of the individual – one's individual capacity to vote, to pay taxes, to earn an income – rather than being embedded within a relational web of connections to one another, which structure our capacities, beliefs, and abilities to participate meaningfully under current systems and to envision more effective alternatives for the future. To be burnt by democracy is to be stuck in the system as is, which claims to be democratic and yet becomes less and less so as inequality grows.

Democracy, Activism, Homelessness

The study on which this book is based encompasses the thoughts and experiences of forty-six young people (ages sixteen to thirty) who have either experienced homelessness or identify as an activist, living in five liberal democracies: Canada, Australia, New Zealand, the United States, and the United Kingdom. These five countries have distinct geographies, histories, political leadership, and education systems, yet they share broadly similar approaches to government, shaped first by British liberalism exported to the colonies, then later by British neoliberalism taken up by those same former colonies. My central argument is that these shared ideological premises, built upon similar political histories and strengthened by the globalization of neoliberal common sense, or doxa, generates a specific set of conditions that shape the possibilities and proscriptions, the points of access and barriers, to participate meaningfully in civic life. By conducting comparative qualitative research across five (neo)liberal democracies, I was able to discern the patterns that transcended national location, allowing me to offer a more powerful and hopefully persuasive argument about the specific characteristics of liberal democracy under neoliberalism in the twenty-first century.

I chose these two groups of young people because they represent, in my experience, the extremes of democratic engagement and democratic disengagement. Although I have interviewed young activists and youth who have experienced homelessness, the focus of the book is neither activism nor homelessness. Rather, it is about how democracy is lived and experienced, with exemplars from both ends of the spectrum of political engagement to illustrate the contours of liberal democracies after forty years of neoliberalism. I believe the experiences of young activists – with unusually high access to and knowledge of democratic practices and possibilities – and homeless young people – who have been repeatedly failed by the state and yet have little to no access to the knowledge and networks needed to change it – can tell us a lot about the young people who fall between these two extremes. The book uses these exemplar cases of youth engagement and disengagement to illustrate the dynamics of inequality that structure the access of the one group, and the barriers for the other. These same dynamics play out across the entire range of young people who fall in the middle, depending on the intersecting conditions of parental dispositions towards political life, stability of housing and income, access to higher education, networking opportunities, and the barriers and enablers created by class, race, gender, sexuality, and dis/ability more generally. One of the core arguments of the book is that the current structures of inequality are inexorably contributing to a destructive disjuncture between knowledge and action, leaving our democratic ideals in tatters. If those at the bottom of the opportunity structures are unable to express their fundamental needs and insights through existing democratic processes, then those processes are *not* actually democratic. Instead, liberal democracy has become yet another structure to maintain the division between the haves and the have-nots.

When we look beyond restrictive formal definitions, such as are emphasized in contemporary civics curriculum, there are in fact many different ways of understanding democracy. One of the simplest, described by many of the young activists I have spoken with, is a system of government where everyone's interests are heard and everyone's essential needs are met. This can happen in many different ways, but the activist youth I spoke with were almost universal in feeling that it does not happen through current representative, liberal democratic structures. For young people who had experienced homelessness, democracy was a word they did not recognize, or an abstract concept that meant little to their everyday lives. The base condition necessary for democracy to even be possible is equality; that is, equality of access to opportunities, wealth equality, educational equality, housing equality, and equality in health care. Under neoliberalism, which has held sway for forty years in each of the national sites in which this research was conducted, such equality is impossible.

Meaningful participation in civic life is more than just voting. Indeed, as Pierre Bourdieu argues, voting signifies the bare minimum of democracy and can even become anti-democratic in that it individualizes and atomizes the members of a polity. Democracy is a *relational* process; it cannot be shaped by individuals in isolation from one another. The activists I have spoken with all vote, or will when an election comes and they are at the voting age. They all feel it is important, if only as a protest against some of the more terrifying political actors on offer at the polling station. But they do not *only* vote; indeed, every one of them indicated that voting was a necessary but not sufficient ingredient to their own contributions to the polis. They believe themselves to be political people because they *think*, and they *learn*, and they *act in concert with others*. This conception of politics and public life closely matches that described by Hannah Arendt, as a *space of appearances* where plural actors come together at a *shared table* to form a *web of relations* that shapes the political space that they all inhabit. It is a capacity carried by every human person, simply by being born, and thus being of the world. This does not mean that every human will participate, however. Pierre Bourdieu helps us understand how every person might carry the potential, and yet not have the capacity to enact that potential under conditions of extreme inequality, such as exist in each of the study countries.

My interviews with twenty-four activist youth across these five liberal democratic/neoliberal countries have allowed me to sketch the contours of a democratic disposition, or habitus, the homologous fields through which it is produced, and the blind spots inherent to those fields. Each have been shaped by neoliberal and liberal democratic doxa that induces young activists to misapprehend their own conditions of access, and thus misconceive the possibilities for others to similarly engage. This is not their fault; rather, it speaks to the deeply sedimented *illusio* that is generated by the state most directly through its education systems but also indirectly through political decisions and media discourse. This illusio – or investment in the rules of the game – includes the belief that it is their willingness, their empathy, their desire to do good, or, put differently, their inherent qualities unique to them as individuals, that drives their activism and engagement. This is part of the liberal and also neoliberal story, which locates the will to act within the individual, and, under neoliberalism, flips this very easily into a blame game for those who do not act.

After speaking with young activists, I interviewed twenty-two young people who had experienced homelessness in the same five countries. I asked them similar questions about democracy, social change, and their role in the polity. With a few important exceptions, every one of these young people was lacking a basic understanding of liberal democratic structures, such as systems of parliament and how to vote, and were generally not engaged in social change work designed to make the systems they dealt with more just. They viewed formal electoral politics as a combination of incomprehensible, corrupt, and meaningless. Simultaneously, they articulated insightful, unique, and relevant analyses of the complex systems they were forced to navigate – such as housing supports, the foster care system, and the failures of public education – which had generally worsened their circumstances as already impoverished and marginalized young people. Were their opinions and experiences to inform public debate and policy decision-making, I believe that these systems could quickly become streamlined and effective.

Capitalism, Liberalism, Democracy

Saskia Sassen (2006) argues that globalization is located not only in international institutions – such as the IMF and World Bank – nor primarily in the fluid financial transactions and trade deals that have forced open borders and lessened national autonomy over social citizenship and the welfare state. It also, importantly, resides *within* the nation-state, confined by borders that have become more porous to finance but less porous to (most) people. Globalization and its ideological companion, neoliberalism, is nurtured, reproduced, and enabled within the nation-state, creating the conditions for global capital to move more freely. This occurs not only through financial mechanisms but also through the cultural conditioning of its citizenry, who are educated both implicitly and explicitly into a version of democracy that mimics the ideological tenets of capitalism. Under capitalism, people must be seen as autonomous units, as individuals making "rational" choices that then shape their particular place in the world, whether that be as a factory worker or member of the managerial class. Under capitalism, citizens must be invested in the idea of a meritocracy, that those who work the hardest get their just rewards (and vice versa). Under capitalism, the notion of collective desires, conditions, decision-making, or organizing is incommensurable, unintelligible. Capitalism exists for and through the individual, just as does liberal democracy.

It is no secret that liberalism arose alongside and intertwined with capitalism; as Domenico Losurdo points out, "liberal thought has vigorously insisted on the need for competition between individuals in the market, in order to develop social wealth and the productive forces" (2014, p. 343). It likewise was built upon a foundation of exploitation of the poor and the racialized, with an ideology of white, male, heterosexual, able-bodied, propertied European supremacy that went largely unmarked and unchallenged – at least from within the power structures of the time – for centuries (Losurdo, 2014). What I am attempting to show, through empirical investigation, are the consequences of this genealogy in the present day: how does the past live on and get reproduced through the everyday experiences of young activists and homeless youth, who are either contesting the state or being catastrophically failed by it? The social structures of democracy in the contemporary moment are shaped by this past and the present, while also being challenged, converted, immobilized, or transformed by those actors who cannot help but act with the knowledge they have been given from the world they live in, a world which thankfully also contains the seeds of resistance, counter-knowledge, and possibility that emerge through what Arendt calls *thinking*, and Bourdieu (via Wacquant, 2004) characterizes as the *dissolution of doxa*.

According to Losurdo (2014), liberalism as the promise of universal rights has historically come into perpetual conflict with liberalism as the protection of private property and hard limits on interference by the state. It has been struggles for the expansion of inclusion under the umbrella of universal rights that has pushed liberalism, and liberal democracy, forward into the twentieth century with increased recognition for labour, women, people of colour, LGBTQ2S+ communities, and, eventually but far too late, Indigenous peoples. Many of these struggles were generated through social movements that were led by the people most impacted: by workers through general strikes, by suffragettes struggling for the vote (or at least the vote for white, middle-class women), by African Americans for civil rights, by queer and trans folx for LGBTQ2S+ rights. In other words, historically, progressive social change has often come from those most impacted, led by those who have been marginalized by the liberal state. What Losurdo's historical analysis leaves out, perhaps because it is too recent a phenomenon, is the rise of neoliberalism and the manner in which this has shaped the specific individualizing and meritocratic discourse of liberalism into a high art form while simultaneously entrenching and expanding wealth inequality.

In my effort to understand the role of capitalism, liberalism, and the state in shaping our current ideas about democracy, I begin with neoliberalism – which has married capitalism and liberalism into an ideological stew that converts all social value into economic value and all social goods into economic commodities – and Pierre Bourdieu's theory of the state. Chapter 1 outlines the rise of neoliberalism in all five countries examined in this research, emerging more or less simultaneously in the 1980s and early 1990s, and its impact on social infrastructure that used to protect against rampant inequality, such as reasonable welfare benefits, access to higher education, and affordable housing. We must appreciate these material impacts in order to better understand the ideological effects of neoliberal policymaking, which valorizes the individual and downplays the role of the state.

Ironically, as neoliberalism pretends to diminish the state, it relies on what Bourdieu describes as the "three fundamental qualities" of the state in order to ensure compliance with its logic. The first of these is "one of the most general functions of the state," which is "the production and canonization of social classifications" (2014, p. 9). Put differently, we can understand that all people "are quantified and coded by the state; they have a state identity" (2014, p. 10). Schooling is one of the major modes of classification wielded by the state; the sorting role of schooling has been well established in the sociology of education, where schooling serves as an arbiter of the pathways available to its pupils, established through educational streaming, programs of applied versus academic learning, and the kinds of opportunities that are offered to students who might wish to transcend their (often class-based) social location in the school. As we shall see in chapters 2, 3, and 4, access to high-quality schooling and postsecondary education plays a key role in the development, or not, of democratic skills and capacities.

The second key quality of the state, as described by Bourdieu, is to be the authorizer of acts and identities, which "goes back step by step to an ultimate site, like Aristotle's god: the state. Who guarantees the teacher? What guarantees the teacher's judgement?" (2014, p. 11). etc. The ultimate arbiter of legitimacy is the state, and the hands of the state are felt particularly keenly in the realm of education in liberal democracies, where even in private schools, the credentials required to teach are authorized through the granting of degrees that come from universities which are accredited and funded through the state, and the curriculum must still meet state guidelines. The importance of this will become particularly relevant in chapter 6, when I discuss civics curriculum and its effects on young people in all five countries.

The third quality of the state is its phenomenal existence as a "well-founded illusion, this place that exists essentially because people believe it exists" (Bourdieu, 2014, p. 10). From Bourdieu: "It is something that you cannot lay your hands on, or tackle in the way that people from the Marxist tradition do when they say 'the state does this,' 'the state does that'" (ibid.). Rather, he argues, we must focus on the "acts of state," such as the authorizations produced by the state that then shape the everyday lives and beliefs of people living within it. The state, essentially, is the ultimate producer of *doxa*, which is a "particular point of view, the point of view of the dominant, which presents and imposes itself as a universal point of view – the point of view of those who dominate by dominating the state and who have constituted their view as universal by constituting the state" (1998, p. 57). The fundamental project of this book is to peel back the layers of attitudes, experiences, and perspectives, as expressed by young people in five liberal democratic countries, in order to come to an understanding about the dominant, state-imposed view of democracy and its possibilities and limits in contemporary twenty-first-century neoliberal states.

Arendt and Bourdieu on Public Space and Democracy[2]

In contrast to the ideologies perpetuated by liberalism and neoliberalism, this book relies on the political philosophy of Hannah Arendt, as well as the cultural sociology of Pierre Bourdieu. Arendt's concept of the public sphere marks a radical departure from Western philosophical traditions of liberalism in a number of ways. For Arendt, the public is the realm of *action*, and it is through action that one's *whoness* can be revealed in what Arendt calls the *space of appearances*. Arendt was a phenomenologist, trained by Martin Heidegger, and this

---

2 I first developed this theoretical framing in an article entitled "Envisioning Democracy: Participatory Filmmaking with Homeless Youth," published in 2018 by the *Canadian Review of Sociology* 55, no. 2: 190–210.

sensibility permeates her political philosophy. The space of appearances is a deeply phenomenological concept, referring as it does to the means by which we come into visibility to others, not as objects but instead as perceiving and perceived subjects who always exist in relation to others. In other words, the space of the public is a space of *relations, a web of relations,* as Arendt (1998) calls it. We act within the public always in relation to others, and it is among others with whom we reveal our *whoness* through actions and speech. Arendt contrasts the public with the "social," which she identifies as the realm of care, nurturance, and housekeeping, also known as the private sphere. She sees this as the realm of *whatness*, the maintenance of the biological self that has little to do with each individual's human uniqueness, or plurality. Arendt (1998) understands that the social is necessary to everyday life, but she identifies one of the problems of modern society as being that the social has come to be conflated with the political, and with the state.

Arendt's definition of the public is distinct from the common perception of the public realm under liberal democracies, which is seen as belonging to the space of political structures – joining political parties, or voting, or writing letters to politicians. Arendt's concept is much broader than that and is marked by the fact that all humans must come together at a shared table, a metaphor Arendt uses to denote a common space of interests that bind us together and yet also keep us separate (1998). Under this definition, the public is made up of "the organization or constitution of the power people have when they come together as talking and acting beings" (Young-Bruehl, 2009, p. 84), as opposed to our conventional understanding of politics, deeply entrenched in liberal Western traditions, as the "domination of some people (one or a few or many) over other people, requiring the threat or use of violence" (Young-Bruehl, 2009, p. 84).

Arendt's political philosophy is inherently egalitarian; as Young-Bruehl notes, "[Arendt began with] the idea that action is open to all people, in all their diversity or plurality; it requires no special talents (although in many situations it requires the virtue of courage) because it arises from ('is ontologically rooted in') the human condition of natality, the condition of being born" (2009, p. 86). Arendt paints a picture of potentials, of the possibility for all to participate in the public as their birth-right, and that public as a much broader space than the narrow liberal democratic definitions with which we are currently familiar. Yet questions remain: in contexts of enormous inequality, where conditions of poverty, police violence, abuse, exploitation, trauma, addiction, and disempowerment are lived daily, the potential for people to reveal their *whoness* to others at a shared table of common concern is severely curtailed. Even if Arendt's conception of the public is accurate, she provides no guidance to illuminate the process by which people might escape the clutches of the social and its dehumanizing capacity, and instead participate in the public as equals. Hers is an ideal form, and it does not account for inequality of access and opportunity. It is here that I turn to the work of Pierre Bourdieu, whose concepts describe the *processes* by which inequality is reproduced. Bourdieu's work is motivated by a deep concern with the constraints that inhibit the capacities and opportunities of those who were not born into the elite classes. His work helps us understand how those who are born into poverty often remain in poverty, and also can help us think through what this means for participating in a public realm such as that described by Arendt.

Like Arendt, Bourdieu was deeply committed to democratic politics, and intervened in the political stage throughout his career, both through his intellectual work and also through activism, media, and education. But he was also sceptical of claims made by political scientists that the public sphere is available to everyone; as Loïc Wacquant points out, Bourdieu's general principle of political engagement involved, "first to acknowledge that the conditions of access to political expression are not universally granted *a priori* to all … but that, on the contrary, they are socially determined and differentially allocated; and then to work to universalize the ability and the propensity to act and think politically, that is, to universalize realistic means of gaining access to that particular historical embodiment of the universal that is democratic politics as we know it" (Wacquant, 2005, p. 21). Bourdieu's theorizing thus highlights that *first* we must appreciate that people are constrained in participating in the public, *then* we must work out how to lift those constraints. What Wacquant refers to as the "historical embodiment of the universal" refers to the *political dispositions* necessary to take part in the public sphere, the *habitus* of political engagement that has shaken off the effects of symbolic violence long enough to see that there is potential for change in acting politically. Bourdieu uses *habitus* to refer to the "sense of the game," always existing in relation to the *field*, one of his other key concepts: "A field consists of a set of objective, historical relations between positions anchored in certain forms of power (or capital), while habitus consists of a set of historical relations 'deposited' within individual bodies in the form of mental and corporeal schemata of perception, appreciation and action" (Bourdieu & Wacquant, 1992, p. 16). In other words, acting politically – participating in the public sphere, in Arendt's language – does not come easily and naturally to all, though Bourdieu would agree with Arendt that we all carry the potential for it. But such potential can be displaced by the embodied dispositions of acquiescence or refusal or avoidance or simply of absorbing the dominant circulating discourses of oneself as incapable of political thought or political intervention. It can manifest in a sense of fatalism, that nothing matters because nothing can change, an experience that has been unfortunately borne out over and over, particularly in the lives of young people who have experienced homelessness.

Bourdieu understands democracy, "not as an affirmative state – of formal equality, equal capacity, or shared freedoms – but as a historical process of active negation of social negation, a never-ending effort to make social relations *less* arbitrary, institutions *less* unjust, distributions of resources and options *less* imbalanced, recognition *less* scarce" (Wacquant, 2005, p. 21). In other words, democracy is not a given, but rather a constant act of taking back public space from the incursions of inequality. Arendt would agree with this, although in *The Human Condition* she conceives of the public in a more positive light. But as Elizabeth Young-Bruehl notes, Arendt was primarily concerned with the question "What elements can preserve freedom or help people achieve freedom?" (2009, p. 79). Like Bourdieu, she understood democracy not as a given but as a process, as an ongoing effort to stave off totalitarianism, inequality, brutality, and violence.

Taking Arendt and Bourdieu together, what we have is a vision of democracy and its potential as much broader than that typically on offer through liberal democratic doxa. Democracy is also constantly under threat, not least because of the embodied and incorporated dispositions that make meaningful action seem impossible for those at the bottom of the opportunity structure. When combined with the manner in which they are responded to by dominant groups, the result is multiple barriers preventing the dominated (the marginalized, the disadvantaged, etc.) from taking up space at the shared table of the public sphere.

Speaking Back to Social Movements

One political task that I see for this book, as for my previous ethnography of young Canadian activists (Kennelly, 2011a), is to expand the horizons through which social movements and their democratic potential are understood, not only by scholars but by activists themselves. Activists are *made*, not born; activists in liberal democratic states are predominantly created through access to specific forms of cultural and social capital that are not broadly available to all. This lack of availability is in part due to the limited space given to activism or other forms of meaningful civic engagement within public education, coupled with the problematic and biased reporting of activism in corporate media. The cultural and social capital needed to become an activist in liberal democracies is instead acquired through close relationships with others who are in the know. These others are most commonly direct family members – nine out of twenty-four activists in this study (or 38 per cent) describe their first activist experience as happening alongside their parents, who brought them to a demonstration or to organizing meetings from an early age. If we divide these numbers by class, the difference is even more stark: eight out of sixteen (or 50 per cent) of middle-class activists were directly politicized by their families, whereas only one out of eight (or 13 per cent) of working-class activists received this kind of family politicization. Working-class activists were more likely to be politicized through higher education or another adult mentor. In other words, the acquisition of the political skills required to become an active civic participant (such as an activist) are extremely class-bound and not available to everyone.

These findings exactly mirror those of my 2007–8 ethnography of young activists in Canada (Kennelly, 2011a), despite the current research being conducted thirteen years later and across five countries (including Canada). Between 2007 and 2020 there has been an explosion of youth-led social movements globally, from the Arab Spring and Occupy in 2011 to the Quebec Student strikes (Maple Spring) in 2012 to the UK anti-austerity strikes in 2015 to the March for Our Lives gun control rallies in the United States in 2018 to the global Student Strikes for Climate in 2019 to Black Lives Matter protests happening all over the world in 2020, as I began writing this book. Some of these movements have played important roles in the politicization of participants in this project; however, those who were able to gain access to those opportunities shared biographical pathways into activism that were class-delimited and often relied on either being born to a politically engaged family or encountering mentors to bring one into activism. As shall be discussed in more detail throughout, what I am calling the development of a *democratic disposition* is intricately tied to social structures and what Bourdieu calls the "field of power" (Wacquant, 2013). In other words, not just anybody can become an activist, under contemporary liberal democracies. It is not in the state's interest to develop activist citizens that can challenge the state's legitimacy. Not surprisingly, public education contains little or no information on how to meaningfully engage in such civic work (see Kennelly & Llewellyn, 2011; Erdal & Kennelly, under review).

The importance of this for social movements is twofold: firstly, it provides an essential counter-narrative to the still dominant view from within movements that activism is a noble act of sacrifice belonging to a moral subject who has "chosen" to position themselves against the evil currents of capitalism, sexism, racism, etc. We see this current in ongoing debates over the role of "professional activists" who are derided by certain movement actors for being "paid" to do activism, and in the radical rejection of strategies other than those offered by specific movements themselves, who believe in a purity of action that can only exist within a bubble that ignores all structural forces and their impact (or, in a bubble that makes invisible the privileges acquired through gender, race, class, etc.) (See Samuel, 2017, for a theoretically sophisticated discussion of these dynamics; also see Shotwell, 2016, on the limits of purity thinking for social change).

Secondly, it offers clear pathways towards effectively building movements. By recognizing that movement actors come to activism because they have been mentored into it, either by family or other trusted adults and/or opportunities frequently found in postsecondary schooling, movements seeking to expand their membership and engagement can develop strategies that have such mentorship and support built in. The School Strikes for Climate were politicizing for many participants across all five countries because they were entirely youth-run, with the support of adult-led organizations. Young people were thrown quickly into leadership positions and had to learn on-the-run about how to speak to media, how to manage relations with police, how to negotiate with other movement actors, etc. This offered a political education by fire for many of the participants in this project, who credit the learning they did through the School Strikes as the beginning of their active politicization. Of course, not just anybody could step into those roles and thrive; the pre-existing dispositions that allowed some young people to take up that invitation into an active leadership role remains relevant.

Speaking Back to Democratic Theorists and Youth Political Participation Literature

Another project of this book is to challenge the vast majority of democratic theory, generally developed from within political science, and in particular the way political scientists and other scholars have undertaken to make sense of youth political participation. The shared preoccupation in such attempts is generally to demonstrate that youth are, indeed, political, even if they are not voting, joining political parties, or otherwise participating in elements of public life that have traditionally been considered "political." One paradigmatic analysis suggests that young people participate politically through "alternative" means, such as through recycling, engagement on social media, or by signing online petitions (e.g., Harris, Wyn, & Younes, 2010; Smith et al., 2005; Torres, Rizzini, & Del Rio, 2013). The problem, according to this line of reasoning, is not with young people but with our narrow perceptions of democratic engagement. Other scholars concerned with youth democratic engagement focus on the importance of re-engaging youth in formal political processes, and suggest that civic education could help counter this deficit (e.g., Martin, 2012). In both approaches, "youth" is taken to be a more or less homogeneous category, with little or no attention paid to distinctions in young people's experiences on the basis of class, gender, race, or other social categories. Even in studies where such distinctions are the centre of focus, conclusions replicate rather than extend beyond the above dichotomy of "youth participation is more diverse than we acknowledge" and/or "young people need to be better engaged in existing political structures" (e.g., O'Toole & Gale, 2013).

The political participation literature keeps "youth" as their primary focus of attention: how do youth behave, respond, think, and participate under liberal democracies? In doing so, the structures of that democracy fade from view, with youth foregrounded as the relevant foci of scholarly attention. By contrast, democratic theorists typically foreground the object called "democracy," and yet separate it from the experiences of those who live within these structures. Bourdieu points to the different political philosophers who are given supremacy in the Anglo-Saxon tradition (Hume, Locke) versus in the French (Kant, Descartes): this demonstrates how "political philosophy," as he explains, "is generated in political action, in political work, and that it forms part of the object itself" (2014, p. 269). Educated as I was within Anglo-Saxon Canadian higher-education institutions, political philosophy was introduced to me through the writings of John Locke, John Stuart Mills, Jeremy Bentham, and the like through a second-year undergraduate course non-self-consciously entitled "Western Thought." Even then, I was struck by how much of these philosophers' work *just made sense* – not because they were inherently sensible, but because everything I had learned to that moment about politics and the law matched these thinkers' orientations to the world. I gained in this moment some partial insight into how the structures in which I had grown up had been shaped by and were reflected in these founding political traditions of liberalism. This experience reflects the degree to which the *doxa* of liberalism pervaded my consciousness; Bourdieu tells us that the state is an "unthinkable object" because of "the fact that our thinking, the very structures of consciousness by which we construct the social world and the particular object that is the state, are very likely the product of the state itself" (2014, p. 3).

In contemporary approaches to political philosophy, democracy is presented in its ideal form under liberalism with varying emphases: Habermasian calls for deliberative democracy tempered by feminist interpretations of the limits to who can deliberate (e.g., Iris Marion Young, Carole Pateman); Rawlsian calls for the veil of ignorance that presupposes all ought to be treated equally without knowing their own social conditions of natality (e.g., Amartya Sen); the argument that market economies are necessary to democratic development while also endangering said democracies (e.g., Dahl & Shapiro, 2015); and many others. Whether I agree or disagree with this wide range of democratic theorists is irrelevant: what I seek to do here is fundamentally different. Rather than beginning from a theory of democracy and considering how individuals (in this case, young people) act within it, I instead seek to understand how democracy *is experienced and understood* by young people, and what this tells us about contemporary liberal democratic states under conditions of growing wealth inequality facilitated by the expansion of neoliberal politics. In doing so, I seek to skirt the problems of political science identified by Bourdieu, who queries whether "it tends to legitimate [current structures] by giving it the appearance of scientificity and by treating political questions as matters for specialists which it is the specialists' responsibility to answer in the name of knowledge and not of class interests" (1991, p. 177).

I will add here a speculative note about whether and how this work will be taken up outside of youth studies. I think many child and youth scholars will recognize the suspicion I carry that our work is considered of lesser importance to the "rest" of the scholarly world because it is concerned with a supposedly small subgroup of human experience – a subgroup of human experience that belongs traditionally to women (as mothers and caretakers), to boot. In other words, a book with "youth" in the title, authored by a woman, may immediately be dismissed by scholars who feel themselves to actually be interested in "other" topics, like democracy, the state, or social movements (coded as masculine within the cultural context in which Western scholarship exists). This implicit bias prevents non–youth studies academics from appreciating that *young people grow up* and become the adults involved in politics, social movements, and the state. I have even considered publishing this book under a masculinized name, to protect against this (although I opted against it in the end). I have always considered the study of young people to be a "canary in the coal mine" approach to social theorizing, seeing their experiences as signifiers both of wider strands within contemporary cultural and political contexts, as well as portents of things to come. My work is never really about "young people" as a social category. Rather, it is about the worlds in which young people find themselves, as a lens through which the rest of us might understand and appreciate the broader structures of those worlds. As I wrote above, this is fundamentally a book about *democracy*. I hope it is taken up as such.

On Recruitment: Operationalizing "Homelessness" and "Activism"

In March of 2020 the World Health Organization declared that COVID-19 had reached pandemic status, effectively shutting down travel, face-to-face interactions, and every qualitative research project in the world. My hopes of travelling to the four study countries outside of Canada (where I live) – Australia, New Zealand, the United States, and the United Kingdom – to conduct interviews during my upcoming sabbatical were dashed. As experienced by researchers everywhere, I was able to pivot rapidly to use video-conferencing technology to conduct my interviews. What I lost from in-person interactions, I gained in being able to reach young people from across their home countries, rather than being restricted to the one or two cities to which I could have reasonably travelled in each country. I was assisted in my recruitment efforts by several research assistants; while one RA assisted with recruiting young activists in every country, I hired country-specific RAs to recruit young people experiencing homelessness. I reasoned that young activists are more easily located through remote means, such as finding them through activist organizations or on Twitter, whereas recruiting young people who had experienced homelessness would require boots to the pavement. This proved true, and it is reflected in the uneven numbers of young people recruited from each category. While in the end I was able to speak with roughly even numbers of young people who self-identified as activists (twenty-four) and young people who had experienced homelessness (twenty-two), they are not evenly distributed across the study countries. Most notably, I was able to recruit and interview eight youth who had experienced homelessness in Canada, entirely because I was able to attend a youth drop-in at an organization with which I had worked previously. By contrast, in the United States I was only able to interview two young people who had experienced homelessness, despite hiring two RAs in two different states to try to drum up recruitment. By the time US recruitment of young people experiencing homelessness began, in early 2021, the COVID-19 pandemic had ripped through that country and was still wreaking havoc with service providers and individuals. I strongly suspect this was the reason for the low success rate in recruiting youth who had experienced homelessness in the United States.

Despite these variations, I was able to speak with between eight and thirteen young people from each study country, when counted across both categories (see Appendix 1). Recruitment criteria for activists was self-described: if a young person considered themselves an activist, and responded to the call for participants as such, I would interview them. Recruitment for young people who had or were experiencing homelessness was slightly more complex. I directed country-specific RAs to use the definition created by the Canadian Observatory on Homelessness:

> Homelessness describes a range of housing and shelter circumstances, with people being without any shelter at one end, and being insecurely housed at the other. That is, homelessness encompasses a range of physical living situations, organized here in a *typology* that includes 1) **Unsheltered**, or absolutely homeless and living on the streets or in places not intended for human habitation; 2) **Emergency Sheltered**, including those staying in overnight shelters for people who are homeless, as well as shelters for those impacted by family violence; 3) **Provisionally Accommodated**, referring to those whose accommodation is temporary or lacks security of tenure, and finally, 4) **At Risk of Homelessness**, referring to people who are not homeless, but whose current economic and/or housing situation is precarious or does not meet public health and safety standards. It should be noted that for many people homelessness is not a static state but rather a fluid experience, where one's shelter circumstances and options may shift and change quite dramatically and with frequency.
>
> (Gaetz et al., 2012, p. 1)

To find young people who fit within this typology, RAs used a number of strategies including postering in local service agencies, reaching out through their own networks, posting on social media, and/or contacting staff of drop-ins or shelters. RAs were of course hampered in this work by the ongoing pandemic; for instance, my Melbourne-based RA was limited to travel only within her own neighbourhood for prescribed times while recruiting for the project. Another major challenge of recruiting for homelessness is that some young people who fit the broad definition above would not consider themselves to have been homeless, as the social consensus sees homelessness solely in terms of option 1 in the definition, that is, as unsheltered or street homeless. Thus, young people who had lived in a shelter or had been "couch surfing" with family or friends might not recognize themselves as having experienced homelessness. Nonetheless, country-specific RAs were able to recruit a range of participants with diverse experiences. As I shall describe in more detail in chapter four, I believe that the participants from Canada were ultimately from the most disadvantaged end of the spectrum of poverty and homelessness, as they were young people who happened to be at the drop-in centre the two days I attended. Youth from other countries had to respond to an advertisement or to the prompting of a youth worker; this in itself requires the stability and capacity to plan ahead that is often impossible for youth who are still entrenched in the most difficult periods of homelessness. This means that among my Canadian sample, none of the eight participants had completed, or even attended, postsecondary schooling, although at least two had intentions to start or return. Of the remaining fourteen participants from other countries, five had completed a university degree, and two were intending to start university in the coming year. This is not typical of young people who have experienced homelessness (Villagrana et al., 2020; Braver & Jenvey, 2012), and I believe reflects the differences in sampling techniques.

In contradistinction to the myth of homelessness as confined only to the unsheltered, there is another myth that claims that "anyone can become homeless." While this may be true in the most abstract sense, the reality in (neo) liberal democracies is that homelessness is overwhelmingly an experience of the already poor (Giano et al., 2020). That is, young people who come from impoverished families are more likely to become homeless than those from nonimpoverished families, and the majority of young people experiencing homelessness grew up in poor or working-class families, including those with recent migration histories. This was borne out in this study; across all five countries, parental employment history for youth who had experienced homelessness was typically working class and/or manual labour (e.g., forestry, driving for Uber, trucking, cleaning); pink-collar work for women (e.g., secretary, managing a grocery store); or services and retail (e.g., waitressing, hairdressing, childcare). Several parents of participants were long-term unemployed, and/or living on disability benefits. Many participants who had experienced homelessness had parents who had not finished high school. A few participants had one or both parents in middle- or upper-middle-class professions; in these cases, pathways to homelessness included family estrangement and/or parental abuse. (Chapter three details the biographical pathways and class backgrounds of activist participants.)

Working across five countries, with a limited sample of participants from each, opens this work to critique from those conditioned to understand generalizability as inextricable from representative sampling, and validity as a feature only of studies which can be replicated by others. Such approaches to research have their place, and I support my arguments by drawing on research designed from within this paradigm, particularly in chapter one, where I explore the growth of neoliberalism across all five countries. Indeed, it is the support of such studies – which make an irrefutable case for rising wealth inequality in all five of these countries as the result of very similar political and policy decisions regarding higher education, housing, and social benefits – that provides the backbone for the qualitative comparison being made throughout the rest of the book. Some distinctions related to geography, biography, and localized political contexts are inevitably present in the qualitative data. But what is striking to me, and what will hopefully become clear to readers, are the *similarities* across national sites. For young people who have experienced homelessness, the similarities reside in the failures of the state to offer appropriate services and supports, and the consequences for youth who are then deprived of education, stability, health, and employment options. Among young activists, it is the shared trajectories into political engagement, shaped by class-bound access to activist dispositions and political education, that is most notable. Also shared across all five countries are the experiences of young people with civics education, which is almost universally found to be unhelpful and alienating from meaningful political engagement. Last but not least, the articulation by young people of "citizenship" as a concept linked primarily to belonging and bureaucracy, shared across all five national sites, distinctively marks the symbolic reproduction of state-driven ideologies about the rights of the citizen under neoliberalism. These are the patterns, uncovered through qualitative interviewing and close sociological analysis, that empirically support my wider assertion about the damage being wrought to democracy via the growth of wealth inequality that has been accelerated and exacerbated by neoliberal policymaking and ideology. It is qualitative research with relatively small samples of participants that can provide this kind of close comparison and analytical depth.

What Is to Come: Chapter Outlines

In the chapters that follow, I begin by providing a detailed overview of the descent of each country into neoliberalism since the 1980s, and the impact this has had on three of the social arenas that most affect young people: postsecondary education, housing, and state benefits. The latter is of particular relevance to young people who have grown up impoverished, with families who rely on such benefits and/or are relying on these benefits themselves. This chapter sets the scene for the analysis to come, providing context and history by which to understand how neoliberalism has increased inequality in each country, and the ways in which this is then lived out by young people growing up two or three decades after these policies were first introduced. Chapter 1 also makes the case for recognizing that the effects of neoliberal retrenchment and the expansion of wealth inequality is being felt most keenly by the young, particularly so by the young and poor.

Chapter 2 begins the dive into the empirical qualitative data in order to trace the views that young people have developed about what it means to "be political," and from here to define what I mean by a "democratic disposition." This is the start of identifying links between class background and biographical pathways, demonstrating how approaches to politics and political action can be understood structurally and also as a marker of distinction, following Bourdieu. In other words, young activists are able to mark who is also "in" the category of being an activist by their views on being political – that is, as being about "everything" – but misapprehend this as meaning that anyone who does not see politics this way must be coming from a position of privilege. By contrast, young people who have experienced homelessness almost universally mark "being political" as connected to formal politics, with which they understandably feel little affinity. The exceptions to this are young people who have received some political socialization from activists or other advocacy groups. Thus, young people who come from extreme disadvantage feel themselves to be "not political," not because of their privilege but because of the dissemination of the liberal ideal of politics as confined to formal systems.

Chapter 3 focuses primarily on the biographies of young activists, breaking down their experiences by class background and finding three major pathways into activism, which are bound and structured by social class in specific ways: the most frequent pathway of young activists, particularly middle-class activists, was to be introduced to activist organizing through their parents or immediate families; next were young activists who had been politicized directly through postsecondary education and/or exposure to student- or youth-led movements; and finally there were the young people, almost exclusively from working-class backgrounds, who were mentored into political activism by a trusted adult outside of the family. This chapter also notes the universally shared pathway into postsecondary, specifically into university, experienced by young activists, no matter their class origins, which distinguishes them from young people who have experienced homelessness.

Chapter 4 shifts the focus from activists to young people who have experienced homelessness, using their stories to illustrate how liberal democracy's unwillingness to engage these youth in meaningful ways means that failing systems remain broken. Instead of tapping into the rich sources of knowledge from people who are forced to live with the inequities and contradictions of systems broken by neoliberalism – such as housing, welfare benefits, and access to high-quality public and postsecondary schooling – the liberal democratic state has taught youth who have experienced homelessness to see themselves as outside of the arena of political insight and thus unable to influence the systems through which they suffer. The second half of the chapter provides more detailed examples of systems failures, wrought by and exacerbated through neoliberal policymaking, and the impact these have had on young people's capacities and opportunities in life.

In chapter 5, I make the analytical link between activism and more formal political engagement, identifying similar structures within each which require similar dispositions and capacities. In other words, young activists, while often fighting unjust systems, are also learning in great detail about how to work within those same systems in order to influence change. This creates what Bourdieu might call a homological relationship between activism and formal political involvement, opening further pathways for young activists into political influence and social change. While not all activists follow such a path, the connections between the two are striking, not least because they demonstrate how activist organizing provides much more effective civic education than do formal civics courses provided in public schooling. Also striking in this relationship between activism and formal political involvement is the current class-based parallels between the two; in other words, these linkages emphasize the middle classness of both activism and formal political involvement, a connection which is often disguised or elided in popular discourse. Although this is currently the case, and it has arguably been exacerbated by the entrenchment of inequality, it does not have to remain the case. Secure housing, coupled with universal high-quality public education and affordable postsecondary schooling could transform who is able to access the realm of formal politics within one generation.

Chapter 6 provides empirical evidence for the argument made implicitly throughout the book about the problem with current approaches to civics education across all five study countries. As discussed particularly in chapter three, biographical pathways into activism, and thus into a set of skills and relationships that can lead to formal political involvement, are most influenced by class-based access, such as family of origin or being exposed to movements and knowledge through postsecondary schooling. When asked about the effect of formal public school civics training on their activism, young activists were universal in feeling it to be irrelevant, or even counter-productive. Young people who had experienced homelessness, on the other hand, particularly if they had not completed high school, sometimes had no conception whatsoever of democracy or formal politics. If they had been exposed to some minimal civics training through high school, their concept of politics remained confined to the realm of the formal and felt irrelevant to their lives, as discussed in chapter two. This suggests that broad-based reform to public schooling's approach to civics education could actually have an impact on young people's capacity to engage politically, in the broader sense. Such reforms would need to emphasize the connections between people's everyday lives and the political decisions that have been made to shape them as such, as well as providing concrete examples and opportunities to engage in meaningful advocacy work to make the systems they encounter more just. By contrast, civics curricula currently remains entrenched in neoliberal ideological approaches that emphasize the responsibility of the citizen *to* the state – rather than the inverse – and the role of the citizen as limited to formal and individual engagement (through voting) and economic productivity (by paying taxes and consuming goods).

Chapter 6 also provides insight into the hidden curriculum of citizenship in all five liberal democracies. Despite the connection that the state appears to want made between citizenship and democratic participation, via civics curriculum, young people almost universally separated out the concept of "citizenship" from that of "democracy." Instead, they linked the former to affective experiences of belonging, or not, to the nation-state. Belonging was experienced most viscerally through the categories of class and race, whereas to "belong" unconditionally to the five liberal democratic nation-states in this study was to be white, middle class, and housed. Indeed, it was only the few participants who experienced this unmarked belonging who made the connection between citizenship and democracy in the way that civics curriculum appears to intend it.

The concluding chapter draws together the insights that have come before in order to reflect on the implications of these findings for democracy and its potential to be realized. I end with recommendations on how we might move ahead collectively to create countries that can truly realize their democratic potential, in which those most affected by systems are able to influence their shape. Importantly, democracy requires equality; as noted by Wendy Brown in the quote that opens this book, it does not have to be "absolute social and economic equality," but it cannot withstand the effects of deep and ever-increasing inequality. Unfortunately, this is the road on which all five of these countries have been set since the introduction and expansion of neoliberal policymaking and ideology in the 1980s and 1990s. Transforming the role of the state from reinforcing inequality to ameliorating it is the first step towards strengthening and enhancing truly democratic spaces.

1 The Growth of Inequality across (Neo)liberal Democracies

The history of the distribution of wealth has always been deeply political, and it cannot be reduced to purely economic mechanisms.
– Thomas Piketty (2017, p. 27)

It is a bad time to be young.
What's left to us can't be undone
Without it riding on our backs
When young and poor go hand in hand.
– Rheostatics, "Bad Time to Be Poor"

In the late 1990s and early 2000s, with the visible emergence of the anti-globalization movement characterized by massive protests against global financial institutions and trade agreements – such as the WTO protests in Seattle in 1999 and the Free Trade Area of the Americas protests in Quebec City in 2001 – Pierre Bourdieu used his status as a public intellectual to decry the ravages of neoliberalism in two small books, *Acts of Resistance* and *Firing Back*. Both denounce the travesty of neoliberalism's exaltation of the market at the expense of the welfare state, and applaud the emerging anti-globalization movement for exposing and fighting this hypocrisy. Bourdieu passed away not long after the ascendance of these movements, in 2002. Twenty years later, neoliberalism's retrenchment of the welfare state continues, absorbing global recessions, such as that of 2008, through massive bailout packages for banks and corporations, while imposing austerity on the general population across the liberal democracies that are part of this study. Throughout this period, from welfare retrenchment to austerity, from Thatcherism to whatever term we want to use for the bizarre reign of Donald Trump, inequality has grown. Differential access to financial resources, higher education, and secure housing all signal that the net impact since the explosion of neoliberalism in the early 1980s has been ever-increasing inequality.

Inequality is a relatively benign description for what has happened to those at the bottom of the opportunity structure. Saskia Sassen (2014) calls it "expulsions"; Judith Butler and Athena Athanasiou (2013) call it "dispossession"; Loïc Wacquant (2009) calls it "advanced marginality." I agree with all of these descriptors. My task for this chapter is to trace the advancement of marginality, dispossession, and expulsions in each of the five liberal democracies being examined here, all of which have been powerfully shaped by neoliberalism since the 1980s. This seemingly inexorable march of ever-growing inequality provides the backdrop for the stories and experiences of the young people with whom I have spoken across these five countries, all of whom were born in the 1990s or the early 2000s, a decade or more into the first fierce corrosion of the welfare state under neoliberalism. They have thus grown up in a period shaped by neoliberal retrenchment, with parents who may have vague memories of a time when housing was more affordable, when higher education did not guarantee a lifelong weight of student debt, and when state benefits were available for those who fell into severe financial need, and the amounts paid were high enough to actually live on. By contrast, the world into which these young people were born is marked by continued lip service to the platitudes of universal access to human rights and democracy, while elites continually undermine the foundations upon which such access could be built. The result, at a macro level, is that young people born into the 1990s and early 2000s in every one of the liberal democracies included in this study are, as a cohort, significantly poorer than their parents (Joyce & Xu, 2019; Sawhill & Pulliam, 2019; Cokis & McLoughlin, 2020; OECD, 2014; Workman, 2020). At a micro level, the manner in which their financial circumstances are entrenched and reinforced is both representative of their individual biographies as well as telling the story of the structural failures that are one of the key legacies of neoliberalism.

Take Daraja, for instance. Daraja fled an abusive family situation in her home country of Nigeria, and, through familial support and great resourcefulness on her part, was able to travel to the United Kingdom where she claimed refugee status. She immediately set about building up her credentials in order to be able to work and contribute to her new country. In the meantime, she bore two children to a man who did not keep up his obligation to support her and her babies. Currently "housed" in a bachelor flat with her six-month-old son and four-year-old daughter, Daraja does her best to continue her studies to become a nurse while caring for her children. She is chronically underslept, having to share her single fold-out couch with her two young children, studying at night in the bathroom, which is the only room separate from where the children sleep in the living area. She has been advocating with the local council for more appropriate accommodations but was getting nowhere until she joined an activist group demanding better housing in East London.

Or there is Scarlett. Scarlett grew up in extreme poverty in a large city in Australia, with a father whose violence was the organizing element of the houshold. Scarlett was taken from her family home at age fourteen by Child Protective Services and placed in foster care. Although her first foster home was a positive experience, she was soon moved into a group home where she was introduced to drugs, sex work, and shop lifting. She aged out of the care system at eighteen, coming out as trans shortly after. When I spoke to her at age twenty-four, she was a few months into her first permanent housing situation since she had left care. Between eighteen and twenty-four, she spent the majority of her time rough sleeping or staying in youth shelters, facing homophobic and transphobic violence among many other struggles to survive.

In Canada, where I live, the myth of our strong social safety net and egalitarian values continues to circulate both within and outside of our borders. This is belied by stories of people like Dominic. Born on an Inuit reserve in the far north of Canada, his Inuit mum lost a custody battle to his white dad, who took Dominic to live in Montreal and then Ottawa. Dad was an abusive alcoholic, so Dominic left home to live with a friend at age fifteen and was then taken in by the Children's Aid Society (Child Protective Services) at age sixteen. Rather than try to find him a foster family at that age, CAS put him in the Young Men's Shelter in Ottawa, a transitional housing program for homeless young people. They then found him a subsidized unit through Ottawa Community Housing, where he has been living ever since. The building is riddled with bed bugs, police and ambulances come at all hours of the night, and his social housing landlord is unresponsive to his concerns. Dominic left high school when he left home, unable to keep up with the demands of education while dealing with his complicated personal life. He told me that the school had tried to set him up with a counsellor, but all they would offer were drugs (presumably anti-depressants), which he didn't think would really address his circumstances. When I met him at age eighteen, he was a year and a half away from finishing his high school diploma through a special program run by a local youth service provider, with the intention of applying to a Health Sciences program at university upon completion.

What links these three stories, across three neoliberal/liberal democracies, is the phenomenal resilience of young people who have faced tremendous barriers, and the palpable desire of each to better their circumstances. Also linking them are state failures that can be attributed to neoliberal welfare retrenchment policies, an utter lack of national efforts to maintain affordable housing stock in each country, and inadequate or unhelpful responses from the systems that have survived retrenchment and austerity. What might have happened if Daraja had received suitable housing that allowed her to study for her chosen profession of nursing? What if Scarlett had received appropriate mental health and addiction supports from the state, possibly saving her from six years of homelessness after leaving the care system? Or if the group home she'd lived in, run by the state, had not introduced her to drugs and shoplifting in the first place? Imagine a system in which Dominic could continue schooling while being supported into a better living situation, while receiving meaningful mental health support instead of only pharmaceuticals. Think of how much faster he could progress towards his goal of attending university if he were not trying to find laundry solutions that would rid him of bed bugs in his state-funded social housing unit.

In what follows, I sketch the contours of the growth of inequality in each study country, alongside an account of the neoliberal political priorities ushered in by successive governments, with startling commonalities across all five sites. In each section, I focus on three main policy arenas that have particular impacts for young people as a group, and for impoverished, housing precarious or homeless young people specifically: cuts to social and affordable housing, increases in the individual costs of higher education, and the transformation and erosion of state benefits systems. My intention here is to set the scene for the larger argument I am making throughout the book, about the decline of democracy under neoliberalism: not because young people are apathetic, or focused on informal politics, or unaware of their civic duties, but rather because of our deep collective misunderstanding of how democracy is actually structured, how individuals learn to participate, and how growing wealth inequality and welfare state retrenchment has undermined the capacity of those at the bottom to participate in any meaningful way in democratic processes that might improve their conditions and those of their families.

The Ascendance of Neoliberalism

I am probably not alone when I say that I am tired of telling the story of neoliberalism. It was the structure that shaped my own anti-globalization activism in the 1990s and early 2000s, alongside environmental decline and animal rights; it was the context in which both my master's (completed, 2001) and doctoral work (completed, 2008) were analysed and discussed. Although I did not know it then, it was part of the story of my childhood poverty, with a single mother who moved us to Toronto from Winnipeg in 1984 and could only find inadequate housing in a one-bedroom apartment with cockroaches and ant infestations. It chased me through my university degrees, as I watched tuition jump 300 per cent under the Mike Harris Conservatives in Ontario between the first and fourth years of my undergraduate degree, and then witnessed the same increase in tuition and cuts to supports under the British Columbia Liberals during my doctorate. Because I was born in the 1970s instead of the 1990s, I am among the last generation to do better than our parents did. Now I am parenting children who may not have that privilege. Yes, I am heartily sick of telling the story of neoliberalism; and yet, it remains the story that must be told so as to make partial sense of life conditions for those of us living under its influence.

First, what is neoliberalism? Wendy Brown (2019, p. 17) adroitly points out that although neoliberalism carries "no settled definition," and that there is "now a substantial academic literature arguing about its constitutive characteristics," the fact that there is disagreement about its specifics "does not vitiate [its] world-making power." At its most basic, neoliberalism is the ideological belief that the "free market" ought to be left to its own devices to shape society, unfettered by state interference. In practice, it has typically taken shape as "a bundle of policies privatizing public ownership and services, radically reducing the social state, leashing labour, deregulating capital, and producing a tax- and-tariff friendly climate to direct foreign investors" (Brown, 2019, p. 18). Also relevant is the cultural effect of neoliberalism, described by Foucault (2008) and others who have used his work (Rose, 1993; Brown, 2005, 2017) as a form of self-governance that gives precedence to individualism, self-efficacy, and responsibilization – in other words, generating citizen-subjects who are expected to rely less on the state and more on themselves (see also Kennelly, 2011a).

Pierre Bourdieu analyses this effect of the state in broader terms, not specific to neoliberalism but certainly relevant to its dispersal. Instead of seeing within neoliberalism something unique because it becomes incorporated into the very being of the people it governs, he attributes this "symbolic power" to all state ideologies: "Throughout my work, I have sought to reintroduce this paradox of symbolic force, symbolic power, the power that is exercised in such an invisible way that people are unaware of its very existence, and those subject to it are the first among these, since the very exercise of this power depends on this lack of awareness" (Bourdieu, 2014, p. 163). This power exercised by the state is that of generating *doxa*, the "common sense" that becomes the dominant version of what is seen through that lens and that upholds the interests of the state. Neoliberalism and its market logic has undoubtedly become the doxa of contemporary times in liberal democratic countries that have adopted its ideological approach to governance. Of the five Anglo-American liberal democracies I include in this study, each leapt aboard the neoliberal ship at about the same time, starting in the 1980s.

The United Kingdom

The rise of Thatcherism in the United Kingdom is generally seen as the first instance of neoliberalism's global political ascendance. Coming to power as the first female prime minister in 1979, and governing with a Conservative party majority until her resignation in 1990, Margaret Thatcher was strongly influenced by the thinking of Friedrich Hayek and Milton Friedman, both architects of neoliberal ideology in their economic and political written works. At least one historian (Evans, 2004) claims that "Thatcherism" is the only eponymous political category referencing a prime minister in the twentieth century; proponents of "Reaganomics" in the United States and "Rogernomics" in New Zealand might disagree. Not surprisingly, Thatcherism precisely overlaps the basic tenets of neoliberalism, including "individual rights; private enterprise within a free market; firm, perhaps authoritarian, leadership; low levels of personal taxation; union and vested interest bashing; simple patriotism" (Evans, 2004, p. 3). The first budget under her leadership, in 1979, set as its main goals "to cut public spending and increase personal incentives by reducing direct taxation" (Reitan, 2003, p. 30), a set of policies that unabashedly benefited the wealthy with the intention of "encouraging entrepreneurship and innovation" (ibid.). This same budget saw the first in what would become a series of deep cuts to public spending, particularly in housing, local government, and education (ibid.).

In 1979, the year of her election to prime minister, Britain's public housing stock was one of the largest in the world, standing at about 6.5 million homes and "providing the least expensive and most secure shelter for around a third of the population as a mainstream tenure of choice" (Hodkinson, Watt, & Mooney, 2013, p. 4). In 1980, the Thatcher government introduced the Housing Act (England and Wales), and the Tenancy Rights, Etc. (Scotland) Act, giving housing council and local authority tenants the "right to buy" their social housing units for a vastly reduced price. This spearheaded the privatization of British social housing, which continued well into the 1990s under the "New Labour" government of Tony Blair. By the time the Conservatives were defeated by the Labour Party in 1997, the construction of public housing in the United Kingdom had fallen from 75,000 units per year to only 1,540; by this time, over 1.8 million council homes (or one in four) had been purchased and thus removed from the supply of public housing (Hodkinson, Watt, & Mooney, 2013).Unfortunately, neoliberal housing policies continued under New Labour, which focused on forced "regeneration" schemes for working-class urban neighbourhoods, transferring these areas into the hands of middle-class gentrifiers and private landlords (ibid.). Currently, social housing makes up about 18 per cent of overall housing stock in the United Kingdom (OECD, 2020), dropping from around 30 per cent in 1980 (Hodkinson, Watt, & Mooney, 2013). This puts the United Kingdom behind OECD countries now considered to have "large social housing stock" of over 20 per cent, such as Austria and Denmark, although still far ahead of the other countries in this study – Australia, New Zealand, the United States, and Canada – which are clustered together as having between 3 and 5 per cent social housing stock as of 2018 (OECD, 2020).

The loss of affordable housing in the United Kingdom has been a major driver of wealth inequality both within and between generations. As noted in a study by the non-partisan IPPR Commission on Economic Justice, "The next generation is set to have less wealth, largely due to housing inequalities … Every generation since the post-war 'baby boomers' has accumulated less wealth than the generation before them had at the same age" (Roberts & Lawrence, 2017, p. 2). Thatcherism's attack on unions and regressive taxation policies, which shifted tax revenue away from income and towards commodities, has also generated a knock-on effect that is disproportionately affecting those born in the 1990s and later. The result has been stagnant wages, more insecure jobs and higher levels of self-employment, alongside a widening gap between those with access to inherited wealth and those without (Roberts & Lawrence, 2017). This has meant that average incomes for young people (between ages twenty-two and thirty) fell by 7 per cent between 2007/08 and 2014/15, while returns on capital (such as for housing, stocks, and bonds) has increased on average by 7 per cent *annually* since the 1980s (ibid.). As younger people are less likely to own a home or have invested in the stock market, this fuels the disparities in wealth acquisition between young people and the generations that have preceded them. It also increases disparities between young people born into a family with less wealth and those born into a family with more: as Roberts and Lawrence (2017, p. 9) point out, "It is becoming increasingly hard for younger cohorts to share in the UK's wealth without substantial support from family, which not everyone has."

Higher education is one means by which individuals might successfully shift their access to wealth and status, if they are born to families without (Piketty, 2017). This is certainly part of my own biography, and it figures in the stories of a number of participants, for both themselves and their parents. All of the liberal democracies under study saw a massive expansion of their postsecondary education systems from the 1960s onwards, creating more enrolment opportunities for their populations. In the United Kingdom, higher-education expansion stalled under Thatcher, but restarted again in the 1990s. Until 1998, postsecondary tuition was covered entirely by taxpayers rather than being charged directly to students; despite this, participation in higher education remained extremely stratified by social class, with those from the poorest backgrounds being one-quarter as likely to enrol in higher education as those from the wealthiest backgrounds, and one-sixth as likely to enrol in a degree program leading to a university credential (Boliver, 2011). Put differently, for every four students from a wealthier background, only one from a poorer background would enrol in higher education (including both degree-granting and non-degree-granting institutions), and for every six students from a wealthier background enrolled in a degree program at a university, there would be only one from a poorer background enrolled. This disparity is even more marked when looking at enrolment in the more prestigious "Old" universities in the United Kingdom (e.g., Cambridge, Oxford), which were established prior to the post–Second World War expansion of higher education (Boliver, 2011).

After 1998, class stratification in higher education in the United Kingdom became even more pronounced. The Teaching and Higher Education Act introduced up-front tuition fees for students of £1200 per year for all degree programs, and eliminated maintenance grants (a non-repayable form of support that had been common prior to this period) (Dearden, Fitzsimons, & Wyness, 2011). Although the grants were re-introduced in 2004, postsecondary students saw another increase in fees in 2006/07, to £3000 per year. Under the Liberal Democrat-Conservative Coalition government, tuition fees skyrocketed to £9000 per year in 2012, precipitating massive student strikes (which would play a politicizing role in the lives of some of this project's participants). One statistical analysis has shown that every £1000 increase in tuition results in a 3.9 percentage point decrease in university participation, while every £1000 increase in maintenance grants results in a 2.6 percentage point increase in participation (Dearden, Fitzsimons, & Wyness, 2011). Although this study does not disaggregate these findings by social class, the persistence of hierarchies and stratification in the higher-education sector has been established by others (Croxford & Raffe, 2015), and concerns about student debt and the rising cost of higher education are being raised even by Conservative politicians, such as former party leader Theresa May (Mason & Adams, 2019). As we shall see in the accounts of participants, this disparity in social class and higher-education participation was felt keenly by those from poorer families, should they have been lucky enough to attend university at all.

One of the major planks of any neoliberal approach to government is the reduction of welfare benefits, which includes supports paid directly to people living in poverty and/or living with a disability to help them afford costs of living, such as housing, groceries, and utilities. Unsurprisingly, cuts to welfare benefits in the United Kingdom began under the Thatcher Conservatives in the 1980s and '90s, levelled off during the late 1990s and early 2000s under New Labour, and then accelerated in the 2010s under the Liberal-Democrat and Conservative coalition (Béland & Waddan, 2012). In 2013, the government introduced an arbitrary "cap" on the amount of welfare benefits that a given family could receive, lowering this cap further in 2016 (Human Rights Watch, 2019). They introduced a benefits "freeze" in 2016 that lasted until 2020, essentially leaving recipients at the same level of benefits despite the steadily increasing cost of living (Holloway, 2018). These cuts have disproportionately impacted single mothers and their children, who have the highest poverty rates in the United Kingdom (ibid.); the overall rate of those living in poverty has hovered around 21 to 22 per cent of the population since 2004 (ibid.).

A Universal Credit (UC) system began to be rolled out in 2012, to replace six so-called legacy benefits; the UC system shifted the payment of benefits to occur *after* assessment, resulting in a potentially disastrous waiting period for those relying on its income. UC also introduced a punitive system of sanctions that can result in benefits being withheld if recipients have not provided the required information, generally to do with their efforts to find employment (Human Rights Watch, 2019). As we will see in the sections below on the American, Australian, and Canadian welfare systems, this is an unfortunate example of neoliberal policy borrowing, emulating the punitive workfare systems introduced under the Australian Labour Party in the 1980s, and under President Bill Clinton in the United States and Premier Mike Harris in Ontario, Canada, in the 1990s.

The impact of such cuts on the everyday lives of the poorest in the United Kingdom can be seen in the 5,146 per cent increase in the distribution of food parcels between 2008 and 2018, as documented by the country's largest food bank charity, Trussell Trust (Human Rights Watch, 2019). It can also be seen in the 21 per cent increase in psychological distress for individuals making use of the Universal Credit system as it was rolled out across the United Kingdom, as measured in a study published in the *Lancet* in March 2020 (Wickham et al., 2020).

The United States

The next global power to enthusiastically wave the neoliberal flag was the United States of America, which ushered in a Republican government under the leadership of Ronald Reagan in 1981. "Reaganomics" was the eponymous description assigned to his government's neoliberal approach to governance, which, like Thatcherism, involved cuts to taxes and public spending as well as economic deregulation, in order to provide more freedom to the so-called invisible hand of the market. This initiated a period of financial capital growth that Saskia Sassen (2014, p. 76) identifies as "a strengthening of dynamics that expel people from the economy and from society," which "are now hardwired into the normal functioning of these spheres." Reaganomics and its subsequent neoliberal offspring have generated perverse economic consequences, such as financial assets being valued at 450 per cent of the US GDP in 2006, before the economic crisis precipitated by the sub-prime mortgage fiasco of 2008 (Sassen, 2014, p. 136). While the economic collapse that followed resulted in 9 million Americans losing their jobs, and at least 10 million losing their homes, the market bounced back quickly – for those who were still in it. GDP, or gross domestic product, is a rough estimate of the "productivity" of an economy, measuring the value of goods and services produced within a country in a given period of time. Although it has many flaws, it is typically used to measure the strength of a country's economy in any given year. In 2019, US GDP growth was 2.16 per cent according to the World Bank; over the previous ten years, the maximum GDP growth in a given year had been 4.75 per cent and the lowest was −2.53 per cent in 2009, after the financial crash (The World Bank Data, 1961–2021). This is considered a reasonably healthy economy by global standards, with modest but sustained growth. By contrast, in 2019 the return on investments (stocks, bonds, and real estate) was 31.5 per cent, with an average between 2010 and

2020 of 13.6 per cent growth (Knueven & Houston, 2022). In other words, after the economy crashed and 10 million Americans lost their homes, those who managed to stay in the housing market and those with investments became at least 13.6 per cent richer, while the economy grew no more than 4.75 per cent in a given year for everyone else. As economist Thomas Piketty (2017, p. 34) has argued, "If ... the rate of return on capital remains significantly above the growth rate for an extended period of time ... the risk of divergence in the distribution of wealth is very high." The impact has been a massively expanding gap between rich and poor in the United States, accompanied by increased difficulty for those living in poverty to find their way out (Sassen, 2014).

Unlike the United Kingdom, the United States has never had a particularly strong portfolio of public housing. What little was available has been decimated since the 1980s. The federal Department of Housing and Urban Development (HUD) was established in 1965 to provide housing subsidy programs that would help combat poverty and racial injustice (Sisson, Andrews, & Bazeley, 2020). Under the Reagan administration, HUD's rental-assistance programs were drastically cut, a move that housing advocates identify as the root of the American homelessness problem that started to emerge in the 1980s and continues today (ibid.). Also under Reagan and the subsequent Clinton administration – which could be seen as the American answer to Tony Blair's "neoliberal light" UK Labour Party of the 1990s – funds for the construction of affordable public housing were reduced such that only existing units were being replaced, and no new public housing was being built (ibid.).

Long before the emergence of neoliberalism in the 1980s, US federal policy privileged private homeowners and mortgage holders over renters and the construction of public housing. In 1913, the mortgage-interest tax deduction (MID) was introduced. Just like it sounds, this tax deduction, which exists to this day, allows homeowners to deduct the amount of interest paid on their mortgage from their income taxes. According to Sisson, Andrews, and Bazeley (2020, para. 12), "the Congressional Joint Committee on Taxation predicts that in 2020 the MID will save homeowners (and cost the federal government) $30.2 billion in lost revenue. This annual federal tax expenditure is more than the funding of all rental subsidies and public housing, and benefits mostly middle-class and wealthy homeowners because renters don't benefit at all and the more expensive a home is the more the owner benefits." In other words, public funds in the form of tax exemptions are flowing, via tax refunds to individual citizens, to private banks and other lenders to offset debts incurred by homeowners through their mortgages. The consequence of these policies, beginning in the early twentieth century and intensifying from the 1980s onwards, is a massive crisis in affordable housing and ever-increasing homelessness within the United States. By 2019, before the COVID-19 pandemic hit, 62 per cent of households in the lowest income bracket – earning less than US$25,000 per year – were paying *more than half* their incomes for housing, typically in the form of rent (Joint Centre for Housing Studies of Harvard University, 2020). According to the United Nations, housing should cost no more than 30 per cent of a household's income to be considered reasonable and sustainable. The housing affordability crisis disproportionately affects those who are young and non-white. Whereas the median net worth of families with a head of household age sixty-five or older *increased* by 68 per cent between 1989 and 2016 in the United States, over the same period the median net worth of families headed by individuals thirty-five or younger *decreased* by 25 per cent (Sawhill & Pulliam, 2019). As of 2016, Black households had $43,262 less wealth than white households, even while controlling for other factors such as education. This gap has increased from $29,966 in 1989 (Gale, Gelfond, & Fichtner, 2018).

Neoliberalism and its market logic has also had a massive impact on higher education in the United States. By 1985 under the Reagan administration, higher-education budgets had been slashed by about 25 per cent, particularly in the area of student aid. Criteria for accessing student grants narrowed precipitously while most grants were transformed into loans, and low-cost, low-interest loans were limited to families who made $32,000 or less, regardless of family size (Fergus, 2014). Individual state spending followed the federal lead so that state higher-education funding on a per-student basis is substantially lower than it was in 1980, and all states but one (North Dakota) reduced higher-education spending per student even further after the financial crash of 2008 (ibid.). During the same period, tuition fees have risen rapidly, as well as becoming ever more stratified by status of the postsecondary institution. Overall, tuition increased by 260 per cent between 1980 and 2014, an increase that more than doubles the rise in the Consumer Price Index at 120 per cent (Jackson, 2015) – the weighted price of an imaginary "basket" of consumer items meant to roughly represent the increase or decrease in the cost of living for the average consumer. This indicates that the rise in tuition costs is because of cuts made by government, not inflation. In 2015–16, the average tuition per year for a "public" or state university was just over US$19,000; for selective or "private" universities, it was over $40,000 per year. The average across all four-year institutions was $104,480 for a four year bachelor's degree in 2015–16, whereas a four-year degree in 1989 cost an average of $26,902 (or $52,892 when adjusted for inflation) (Maldonado, 2018). Combined with the drop in funding for student grants, the result is a student debt load that is now second only to housing debt in the United States and is, unsurprisingly, far higher for those born in the 1990s and later.

As cuts to higher education have advanced, the impact of social class and socio-economic status (SES) on access to university degrees has become even more apparent. The US postsecondary education system is "institutionally heterogenous" (Andrew, 2017, p. 31), consisting of community colleges which offer more affordable two-year "associate degree" programs that students can then use as a jumping off point to enter a "regular" or public, non-selective four-year degree-granting institution. These "regular" institutions require sufficient secondary school grades or test results for students to gain entry, but they are easier to gain admission into than "selective" (or private, elite) institutions, which include Harvard, Yale, and Stanford. In a statistical analysis of data on tuition and enrolment at all American public four-year colleges and universities between 1991 and 2007, Hemelt and Marcotte (2011, p. 444) found that "a $100 increase in tuition and fees would lead to a decline in enrolment of approximately 25 students, or a little more than 0.23%," with larger effects at Research I (higher-status) universities. Jackson and Holzman (2020) analysed US statistics for income inequality in relation to collegiate inequality (that is, inequality in enrolments and completions) from across the twentieth century, concluding that there is a strong correlation between the two; unsurprisingly, the period of highest collegiate inequality is for those born in the 1980s and later. Andrew (2017) analysed postsecondary routes by socio-economic status and in relation to achievement (grades and test scores) in the United States. She found that high academic achievement is correlated with the completion of a four-year bachelor's degree and with "moving forward" in the hierarchical postsecondary system in the United States; however, those from low-SES backgrounds with high academic achievement are much less likely to attend elite institutions, thus losing out on the benefits that accrue to those with degrees from more highly regarded universities. This is one of many ways in which economic inequality in the United States reproduces educational inequality and stratifies opportunities for higher-paying jobs.

The Reagan administration ushered in cuts to welfare (social assistance) payments that rivalled those of the Thatcher government, with an explicit and unapologetic claim that welfare benefits were harming the poor, and – more alarmingly, according to the logic of conservative neoliberals with a strong Christian base – the family. In a 1982 radio address, President Reagan stated: "We're in danger of creating a permanent culture of poverty as inescapable as any chain or bond; a second and separate America, an America of lost dreams and stunted lives. The irony is that misguided welfare programs instituted in the name of compassion have actually helped turn a shrinking problem into a national tragedy" (Reagan, 1986). In an effort to fix these supposedly "misguided" welfare programs, Reagan introduced the new Omnibus Budget Reconciliation Act (OBRA) in 1981, seven months after he took office. Under the OBRA, he introduced a new Aid to Families with Dependent Children (AFDC) program, with stricter eligibility requirements that resulted in 408,000 families losing eligibility altogether, and another 299,000 having their benefits reduced (Stoesz & Karger, 1993, p. 620). The OBRA also reduced federal expenditures on social services significantly, including fund-matching programs that formerly induced state governments to support social programs, and funding for non-profit agencies that had been filling in some of the gaps in state-run programs (ibid.). To "replace" welfare benefits, the Reagan administration introduced a series of tax cuts and tax rebates, including increasing the eligibility threshold for the Earned Income Tax Credit (EITC) that had been introduced by the previous administration in 1975. The EITC allowed low-income families, particularly single mothers, to claim back a portion of the income taxes they otherwise would have owed (Meyer & Sullivan, 2004). However, the rebates that poor people received through the EITC failed to make up for the benefits they had lost (Stoesz & Karger, 1993). Rich Americans also benefited from tax cuts, increasing inequality even further between rich and poor during this period; between 1980 and 1990, the federal tax burden dropped by 5.5 per cent for the richest quintile, while increasing by 16.1 per cent for the poorest (ibid., p. 621).

In 1996, Democratic President Bill Clinton signed into law the Personal Responsibility and Work Opportunity Reconciliation Act (PRWORA), a "so-called reform of public aid," according to Loic Wacquant (2009, p. 78), that "essentially *abolished the right to assistance* for the country's most destitute children, which had required a half century of struggle to fully establish, and replace it with *the obligation of unskilled and under-paid wage labor* for their mothers in the short run" (italics in original). Recycling the arguments used by Reagan – "that welfare support is too generous, that it saps the will to work of its beneficiaries, and sustains a 'culture of dependency'" (Wacquant, 2009, p. 84) – the new Act set out to achieve one major goal: reduce the number of people receiving welfare by increasing their engagement in employment and reducing out-of-wedlock births (Chamlin & Denney, 2019). While the goal was (sort of) achieved – by 2016, the number of people receiving welfare benefits dropped by 80 per cent (Chamlin & Denney, 2019) – this occurred because of the increased stringency and punitive nature of the welfare bureaucracy, rather than because of access to employment or reduced births by single women (ibid.). Despite the fact that the new welfare regime required recipients to demonstrate that they were seeking employment, there were no measures introduced to improve employment options or conditions facing workers, and no budget for job training or job creation (Wacquant, 2009). As Wacquant (2009, p. 86) points out: "The new legislation never addresses the dearth of jobs, the subpoverty wages, the instability of employment, and the lack of protection and ancillary supports such as transportation at the bottom of the labor market. It concentrates on making public aid beneficiaries 'work ready' while disregarding the fact that the jobs that single mothers find or need are themselves not 'mother ready.'"

The rise of low-paying and insecure work in the context of neoliberalism has a perverse consequence in the United States (and elsewhere) when it comes to social assistance. In a 2020 report produced by the United States Government Accountability Office (2020), Walmart and McDonald's are identified as the top two employers with employees receiving either or both of SNAP (Supplemental Nutrition Assistance Program) and Medicaid (government subsidized medical insurance). SNAP, formerly known as the Food Stamp Program, was included and revised as part of the 1996 welfare reforms captured in the Personal Responsibility and Work Opportunity Reconciliation Act introduced by the Clinton administration. Medicaid is a separate, means-tested program for low-income Americans that runs parallel to PRWORA. The implication of this is that massive corporations with US$129.359 billion (Walmart) and $9.752 billion (McDonald's) in profits in 2020 (Macrotrends, 2021) are receiving state subsidies for their employees through government welfare programs. Rather than pay their staff a living wage and provide them with medical insurance, these extremely profitable businesses can keep their employees in poverty and benefit from the state subsidy that allows their staff to eat and receive health care, so that they can continue to work and generate profits for their massive employers.

New Zealand

New Zealand, like Canada, has a reputation for being a social welfare utopia that largely escaped the ravages of neoliberalism, particularly when compared to their larger and better-known neighbour, Australia (Canada enjoys a similar relationship to the United States). While six years (2017–23) under Left-centrist and proudly feminist Labour Prime Minister Jacinda Ardern shifted the country somewhat away from overtly neoliberal policy measures, the legacies of neoliberalism continue to be felt through the country's affordable housing shortage and resulting homelessness crisis, the high rate of child poverty, as well as the growth in student debt and decline in tertiary education enrolments. Like every other country in this study, income inequality in New Zealand has risen substantially since the 1980s; by 2010, the top 10 per cent of New Zealand's income bracket owned almost 60 per cent of the wealth (Rashbrooke, Rashbrooke, & Molano, 2021) and 2017/18 data show the wealthiest 1 per cent of New Zealanders hold sixty-eight times the wealth of the average middle-class individual (Rashbrooke, 2020).

New Zealand's answer to British Thatcherism and American Reagonomics was a home-grown model of neoliberal reforms that came to be known as "Rogernomics" after then Finance Minister Roger Douglas. Introduced in 1984 under a Labour government, Rogernomics mimicked the British and US versions of neoliberalism, but with a speed and intensity that earned them the dubious distinction of being known as the Western country that took neoliberal economic reforms the furthest and fastest (Nairn, Higgins, & Sligo, 2012). Beginning with the corporatization of state-run enterprises in order to "increase efficiency and accountability" (neoliberal catchphrases that continue to resonate powerfully today), government economic policy under the ostensibly left-leaning Labour party evolved towards deregulation of state enterprises followed by privatization and internationalization – or rather, the opening up of former state-run enterprises to international investors – in the 1990s under the right-leaning National Party (Larner, 1997).

Although Labour began the neoliberal economic reforms, it was the National Party in the 1990s that began to apply neoliberal logic explicitly to housing. The state-run housing group, alternately called Housing Corporation of New Zealand (1974), Housing New Zealand Corporation (2001), Housing New Zealand (2018), and currently Kāinga Ora (2019), has been the main landlord in the social rented sector for decades (Murphy, 2020). The first impact of neoliberal policy reforms on state-run housing was transforming it into a profit-generating enterprise, which led to the introduction of market rents and the sell-off of substantial stock to the private market (Murphy, 2003). Between 1992 and 1999, Housing Corporation of New Zealand (HCNZ) rents rose by 106 per cent, compared to a 23 per cent increase in the private rented sector (Murphy, 2003); tenant movement and evictions within HCNZ rose in this period, indicating a loss of security of tenure for those in the lowest income bracket (ibid.). Social rented housing in New Zealand experienced a slight reversal of these neoliberal policies in the 2000s under a Labour-Alliance coalition government, during which time rent-geared-to-income was reintroduced and the sale of social housing stock was halted (ibid.). However, state-run social housing remains less than 5 per cent of the overall stock of housing in New Zealand, leaving those in the lowest income brackets more vulnerable as housing prices in the private market across New Zealand have skyrocketed (OECD, 2020).

Despite the current Labour government making a commitment to tackling housing and homelessness as a major issue, the housing crisis in New Zealand is deepening. The cost of housing in New Zealand has grown much more rapidly than average earnings (Nunns, 2021), and the proportion of New Zealanders spending more than 30 per cent of their income on rent has risen from just over 10 per cent in 1988 to hover around 31 per cent of the population since the early 2000s (Te Tūāpapa Kura Kāinga, 2020; Webb, 2017). In other words, about one in three New Zealand households are living in housing that is considered unaffordable for their income bracket. In January 2020, the Demographia International Housing Affordability Survey analysed eight housing markets across New Zealand and ranked them all as "severely unaffordable" (The Borgen Project, 2020). The rising cost of housing is contributing to a growing homelessness crisis across the country, which currently numbers almost 1 per cent of its population among the homeless (Stats NZ, 2020). The authors of a report on homelessness in New Zealand in 2018 acknowledge that the use of census data, which is the basis for the 1 per cent estimate, is highly likely to undercount those who are homeless or housing insecure (Amore, Viggers, & Howden-Chapman, 2021). This is true of most homelessness measurements, typically missing those who are "couch surfing," trading sex for housing, or living in overcrowded and unsuitable accommodations (Collins, 2010). Young people tend to be disproportionately represented among these missing statistics. As in other settler-colonial liberal democracies, the Indigenous peoples of New Zealand (the Māori) are over-represented among those who are most precariously housed or homeless, as are people from the colonized Pacific Islands that surround New Zealand, often referred to as Pasifika or Pacific Islanders (The Borgen Project, 2020; Radio New Zealand, 2016).

In New Zealand, as in every other Anglo-American liberal democracy that is part of this study, an individual's family income and the location of their housing is highly predictive of the quality of public elementary and secondary education they receive, as well as the likelihood that they will go on to attain a university degree. Until early in 2023, New Zealand divided its schools into "deciles" to indicate the socio-economic position of a school's local community in relation to all of the other schools in the country.[1] The range of deciles is between 1 and 10, where a decile 1 school is among the poorest 10 per cent of communities, and decile 10 is among the wealthiest 10 per cent (Te Tāhuhu o te Mātauranga, no date). In other words, the lower the decile, the poorer the surrounding community. In 2019, 70 per cent of the school leaver cohort from deciles 9 and 10 enrolled in tertiary education, while only 48.3 per cent of school leavers from deciles 1 and 2 enrolled (Government of New Zealand, 2019). Among those from the lowest two deciles who enrolled in tertiary education, 33.5 per cent of these enrolled in non-degree granting programs and only 14.8 per cent enrolled in bachelor's and above; by contrast, only 17.3 per cent of school leavers from deciles 9 and 10 enrolled in non-degree-granting tertiary education programs, and 52.7 per cent enrolled in bachelor's and above in 2019 (ibid.).

The higher or tertiary education sector has also been shaped by neoliberal policy reforms in ways that will be familiar to those who have read the above sections on educational reforms in the United Kingdom and the United States in the 1980s: ending government grants and the transformation of student assistance into loans; increasing tuition fees in the face of substantial cuts in government funding; and an increasing focus on students as "customers" and education as a private investment rather than as a right and necessity for all in a democratic nation (Shore, 2010). As of 2016, median student loan debt upon leaving a bachelor's degree in New Zealand was NZ$32,300, an increase of $13,300 from a decade prior (Nissen, Hayward, & McManus, 2019). New Zealand's students are seventh among OECD countries for student debt; they carry similar student debt loads to those in Australia and Canada (ibid).

After economic reform in New Zealand came welfare reform. Treasury briefing papers in 1990 argued that the only way to manage rising inflation and unemployment was to cut wages and welfare benefits (Nairn, Higgins, & Sligo,

---

1 The ruling Labour Party promised to abolish the decile system in Education, over longstanding concerns about its stigmatizing effects on lower-decile schools. As of January 2023, the decile system was replaced with an Equity Index (EQI), used to "determine a school's level of equity funding" (NZ Ministry of Education, 2023).

2012). Prior to this time, New Zealand was understood by its own citizens and others in the world as a country with a strong welfare state. The Royal Commission on Social Security in 1972 and the Royal Commission on Social Policy in 1988 affirmed that the role of the welfare state in New Zealand was to ensure that all citizens, regardless of socio-economic background, were able to feel a "sense of participation in and belonging to the community" (as cited in Boston, 1993). Despite this ethos and their reputation, New Zealand was in fact relatively low among OECD countries in social spending compared to other countries during this period: in 1975, New Zealand spending on cash benefits and health care was 11.8 per cent of their GDP, the lowest when compared to the other countries in this study: Australia (12.7 per cent), Canada (15.4 per cent), Britain (15.6 per cent), and the United States (14.5 per cent). Even at their zenith of social spending in the 1970s, all five of these liberal democracies fell well below the spending of countries such as the Netherlands (29.6 per cent), Sweden (21.2 per cent), and West Germany (27.1 per cent) (Boston, 1993).

New Zealand's welfare benefits thus started behind the pack when the neoliberal cuts began in the 1980s, and then were decimated with ferocious rapidity over the course of the 1980s and '90s. In 1991, the government under the leadership of the National Party instituted a 10 per cent cut to welfare benefits across the board, among a number of other changes (Dodson, 2006). In 1988, rates of child poverty nationally were at 12 per cent; by 1994, this number had risen to 35 per cent, an increase that commentators link directly to the cuts to welfare benefits for families (Wilson et al., 2013). Although some of the worst of the neoliberal welfare reforms were ameliorated slightly by the return to power of the Labour Party in 1999, the subsequent re-gaining of parliament by the right-wing National Party in 2008 introduced even more draconian welfare reforms, which emphasized reducing welfare "dependency," and shifted from a focus on income adequacy to getting recipients into paid employment, with accompanying sanctions and increased surveillance of benefits recipients (Wilson et al., 2013). Despite commitments made by the current Labour government to revise the welfare system, change has been slow and uneven. The ruling Labour Party convened a Welfare Expert Advisory Group (WEAG) to conduct consultations and then generate a report and recommendations; the report was published in 2019. The WEAG recommended a complete overhaul to the current system, arguing that: "The current system is based on conditionality including sanctions and is tightly targeted, with inadequate support to meet even basic needs. The experience of using the system is unsatisfactory and damaging for too many of the highest need and poorest people. We heard overwhelmingly during our consultation that the system diminishes trust, causes anger and resentment, and contributes to toxic levels of stress. There is little evidence in support of using obligations and sanctions (as in the current system) to change behaviour; rather, there is research indicating that they compound social harm and disconnectedness" (Welfare Expert Advisory Group, 2019, p. 7). The report includes forty-two recommendations for welfare reform directed at the Jacinda Ardern–led Labour government, which won a majority parliament in the October 2020 election, after ruling as part of a coalition government since 2017. In November 2020, the Child Poverty Action Group condemned the Ardern government for "unjustifiably slow" reform to the welfare benefits system, claiming that only seven of the recommendations have been "partially" implemented with a further thirteen "minimally" implemented (Small, 2020).

Australia

In a report published shortly after the beginning of the COVID-19 pandemic, Australia's income and wealth inequality were summarized with the following statistics: for income, the top 20 per cent of earners brought home six times as much income as the bottom 20 per cent; and for wealth (which includes assets such as investments and real estate), the top 20 per cent held *ninety times* the wealth of the bottom 20 per cent (Davidson et al., 2020). The growth of wealth inequality in Australia is a story about young people, as it is in our other study countries. A 2017 report notes that wealth shifted from younger people to older people between 2004 and 2016; the same report points out that wealth inequality *between* young people increased the most rapidly during this same period (Davidson, Saunders, & Phillips, 2018). In other words, young people as a group in Australia are getting poorer compared to older Australians; but also, wealthier young people are pulling away from poorer young people within their own generation. By this point in the chapter, this will be a familiar story. Australia's adoption of neoliberal economic and governance principles mirrors that of the other countries we have examined thus far; like those other countries, the consequence of forty years of neoliberalism has been huge and growing levels of inequality. As in Britain, the United States, and New Zealand, here we will look specifically at the impacts of neoliberalism on housing and homelessness, higher education, and social-assistance levels (welfare benefits).

Housing affordability and homelessness in Australia emerged as key issues in the early 2000s, as the cost of housing began to rise precipitously, much higher than the rate of average income growth. Between 2001 and 2011, the median Australian house price increased by 147 per cent, while median after tax incomes increased by 57 per cent (Nicholls, 2014). Many scholars identify the expansion of neoliberal policymaking in the housing sector as one of the key contributors to the loss of affordable housing in Australia (e.g., Beer et al., 2016; Beer, Kearins, & Pieters, 2007; Nicholls, 2014; Dodson, 2006). Before the "neoliberal turn" in the 1980s, social housing had emerged in post-war Australia with a clear focus on providing adequate dwellings for Australian families (particularly, in the immediate post-war period, for returned servicemen and their families) (Yates, 2013). However, the role of the state in providing social housing was to be relatively contained and devolve earlier than in the other countries in this study, with the selling off of social housing stock beginning as early as the 1950s and 1960s in order to meet operating deficits due to under-funding (ibid.). Shifts in eligibility requirements and the calculation of rents (moving from a needs-based to market-based assessment) in the 1970s combined with a focus on using social housing for those most vulnerable to eventually create large and poorly maintained housing estates with a concentration of the most marginalized families and individuals (ibid.). By the 1990s, housing policy had shifted away from supply-side subsidies that could be used to maintain or build new social housing and towards demand-side subsidies, such as rent supplements for individual renters; this resulted in a decline in social housing stock as a percentage of overall housing stock from a high of 6 per cent in the early 1990s to a fifty-year low of 4 per cent by 2008 (ibid.).

With the election of a Labour government in 2007, national funding for social housing re-emerged as a key policy issue, and a AU$5.6 billion investment was the largest to go towards social housing since the 1980s (ibid.). Funding was also allocated towards stimulus of the private and not-for-profit sector to provide affordable housing, geared towards low- and moderate-income households. The allocation of funds was insufficient to overcome many decades' worth of disinvestment, and the devolution of government provision towards the private, community, and not-for-profit sector did not realize its aims of increasing housing for those in greatest need (Pawson, Milligan, & Yates, 2020). By 2018, available social housing stock was still at its low 2008 levels, hovering at 4.2 per cent (ibid.). As a direct consequence of this and other factors, such as the loss of private market affordable housing and the casualization of labour, homelessness in Australia increased by 30 per cent between 2001 and 2016 (ibid.).

In the tertiary (postsecondary) education sector, neoliberal reforms in Australia began in 1987–9, during which time public funding was restructured to encourage institutions to compete with one another for research, training, and consultancy funds, and to seek non-government support (Western et al., 2007). The government share of funding for postsecondary institutions declined from 91 per cent in 1983 to just over 60 per cent in 1994, and to just under 44 per cent by 2003 (ibid.). Student fees have risen in lockstep with the reductions in government funding (Connell, 2015). University fees had been abolished in order to make university more accessible to the middle and working classes in 1974; in 1989, under the Hawke Labour government, a flat fee of $1800 was introduced (Glavin, 2019). This flat fee was replaced with a three-tier fee structure by the Howard Coalition government in 1996; this was later converted into grants for selected students only, on the basis of secondary school grades (called Commonwealth Supported Places, or CSP) (Glavin, 2019). The Howard government also increased fees overall by 40 per cent and allowed universities to open up full fee-paying places for the first time in Australian higher-education history

(Heath, 2017). In 2017, fees increased again in response to a 2.5 per cent across-the-board cut to tertiary education funding (Glavin, 2019). As of this writing in 2021, the Australian higher-education sector is again facing extreme budget cuts and fee increases; some of the young people I spoke with were involved in activism against these changes, while others were wondering what the changes would mean for their own futures in higher education. In the fall of 2020, the Morrison centre-right Coalition government increased fees for degrees they considered to be leading towards less remunerative careers, such as a 113 per cent increase to tuition fees for the humanities and communications, while reducing fees for those they considered to be more in need of workers, such as teaching (cut of 42 per cent), agriculture (cut of 59 per cent), and maths (cut of 59 per cent). In real numbers, this means that, as of 2021, a humanities degree will cost AU$14,500 per year, while a maths degree will cost AU$3950 (Visentin, 2020). This is highly consistent with neoliberal logic that understands tertiary education as a means towards creating an economically productive citizen-consumer, rather than an educated democratic citizen with the capacity to effectively engage in the public sphere.

Although neoliberal thinking in Australia about reducing government spending on social benefits originated with a conservative government led by Malcolm Fraser in the late 1970s and early 1980s – the Fraser government introduced cuts to unemployment benefits "under the dubious theory that this would create work incentives" (Weatherley, 1994, p. 157) – it was the Bob Hawke Labour Party, elected in 1983, that moved Australia firmly onto the path of neoliberal logic with respect to many issues, including social spending. Under the Hawke government throughout the 1980s, welfare benefits shifted away from universal access and towards emphasizing the compliance of recipients, with increased monitoring and scrutiny to catch potential "fraud" (Weatherley, 1994). In 1991, they introduced the Newstart program, which required those who had received unemployment benefits for twelve consecutive months to actively negotiate an "agreement" with a Commonwealth Employment Service representative in order to remain eligible for benefits (ibid.). Such "agreements" included active plans for job seeking, volunteer work, and/or retraining that must be undertaken as a condition for continuing to receive government support.

In 1996, the Liberal-National coalition led by John Howard was elected to government. This centre-right coalition would deepen and entrench neoliberal policies throughout government over the course of their four-term reign, ending in 2007. In 1998, the Howard government replaced the Commonwealth Employment Service and the Newstart program with the "Job Network" and "Centrelink" – although, confusingly, the benefit payment continued to be called the Newstart Allowance (or NSA) until March 2020, when it was renamed the Job Seeker Payment (JSP) (Government of Australia 2021). Centrelink is the government agency that administers benefit payments, while the Job Network (which was renamed Job Services Australia in 2009 and then became the Jobactive Program in 2015) is a network of private, community, and not-for-profit agencies that are tasked with moving those on benefits towards employment. The case managers of the Job Network, many of them social workers, have limited discretion in terms of deciding whether a person is capable of work or not, and instead have performance benchmarks to reach of the number of people they move from benefits into employment, no matter the structural, institutional, and personal barriers such individuals face (Mcdonald and Chenoweth 2006). The orientation of the case managers towards unemployment is largely to view it as an individual problem, to do with motivation and aptitude, rather than a problem of diminishing employment opportunities and/or increasingly casualized, unsafe, and unpleasant workplaces (ibid.).

The 1998 changes to employment benefits introduced a new euphemism for Australian income support, namely, "mutual obligation." The Government of Australia (2021, para. 3) defines this as follows: "Mutual obligation requirements are based on the principle that it is fair and reasonable to expect unemployed people receiving activity tested income support to do their best to find work, undertake activities that will improve their skills and increase their employment prospects and, in some circumstances, contribute something to their community in return for receiving income support." As Parker and Fopp (2004) argue, the concept of mutual obligation emerged on the basis of at least three overlapping assumptions about the unemployed: firstly, that they had, as a group, become "dependent" on welfare benefits; secondly, that such dependence had rendered them incapable of seeking employment; and thirdly, that this so-called welfare dependence was the cause of long-term unemployment. The overall logic echoes Reagan's assertion about welfare dependence in the United States in the 1980s: "the [Australian] government asserts that for many unemployed people 'working is almost more trouble than it's worth'; the previous system was a disincentive to work. It removed the motivation to work and increased the attraction of welfare" (Parker & Fopp, 2004, p. 263). McKeever and Walsh (2020) identify this as rooted in the concept of "moral hazard," which has "a history as old as the idea of state relief itself" (p. 74). The moral hazard is "the need to ensure that individuals do not see or experience life on benefits as more attractive than a life of independent paid labour" (ibid.). Unfortunately, as McKeever and Walsh (2020) highlight, the mutuality of mutual obligations is questionable at best. If the obligations were indeed mutual, then in exchange for the efforts of recipients they would be ensured a provision of state benefits that allow for an adequate standard of living to be maintained. This is not the case. In a review of research on the health effects of direct-payment social welfare benefits in countries with advanced welfare systems, including all five countries that are the subject of this chapter as well as several other Western European and Nordic countries, the authors found that "social assistance programs are not … associated with positive health outcomes" (Shahidi et al., 2019, p. 8). Although they acknowledge that there may be confounding factors that contribute to the poor health of income-assistance recipients regardless of the benefits systems, they argue nonetheless that, "the scope and generosity of existing social assistance programs are insufficient to offset the negative health consequences of the severe socioeconomic disadvantage that renders one eligible for such programs" (ibid.). They further note that US studies with a strong randomized experimental design demonstrate that, "When benefits were reduced and work conditionalities were intensified [as a result of welfare reform], there were observable declines in the health status of the socioeconomically disadvantaged groups who tend to be the principal recipients of welfare; namely, poor and low-educated single mothers" (Shahidi et al., 2019, p. 8). Despite evidence about the poor outcomes associated with welfare reforms such as those undertaken in Australia – and every other Anglo-American liberal democracy that is included in this book – the Australian government continues down this pathway of cuts to welfare benefits, even in the midst of the global COVID-19 pandemic. While the national government increased employment benefits temporarily at the start of the pandemic, as of 1 January 2021 they had reduced them again, with the intention to bring them back to the (insufficient) levels they had been at pre-pandemic by the end of March 2021 (Henrique-Gomez, 2020). In dollar amounts, this means that recipients would go from a high of AU$1115 a fortnight to AU$715.70 a fortnight after the first set of cuts, then to AU$565 a fortnight after benefits returned to pre-pandemic levels (ibid.). With average 2020 rents ranging from a low of AU$340 per week (AU$680 per fortnight) in Adelaide to a high of AU$600 per week (AU$1200 per fortnight) in Canberra (Granwal, 2022), it is difficult to understand how the government justifies such low levels of benefit payments. As one commentator observes, "The Australian government's decision to cut benefits is based on feelings, not facts" (Denniss, 2020).

Canada

Canada's federal descent into neoliberalism began with the election of Conservative Prime Minister Brian Mulroney in 1984. I was in grade four at the time, and not paying too much attention to Canadian or global politics. I do remember the fight over the Canada–US free trade agreement five years later; my grade nine geography teacher was involved with protests against it and took the time to explain the issues to us. I remember his outrage more than his explanation, but once I was into my graduate degrees I began to understand what he had been upset about. The Canada–US agreement was a precursor to the North American Free Trade Agreement (NAFTA), which opened up the borders to finance and trade (but not people) between Mexico, the United States, and Canada. These were among the first major sallies of globalized trade and deregulation of finance in the Global North, initiated by US President Ronald Reagan. In an analysis of the effects of these free trade agreements on the Canadian manufacturing sector, overall economy, and social programs, Jim Stanford (2014) argues that the neoliberal logic embedded in these trade deals ultimately permeated all levels of Canadian political and economic decision-making, resulting in a "race to the bottom" with the United States that saw massive cuts to government spending on social programs alongside tax cuts to corporations and higher-income earners. About a decade before Stanford's analysis, Wendy McKeen and Ann Porter (2003, p. 111) described the process as a complete transformation of the Canadian welfare state: "Not only has the welfare state in Canada been restructured, it has been transformed.... [T]he transformation taking place is one from a more generous system to what neoliberals have described as a 'tough love' social welfare system that aims to help welfare 'dependents' kick their habit. The result has been an increasingly punitive model; increased poverty, inequalities, and hardship among certain groups; and the downloading of responsibility for meeting social needs to individuals and to the home."

As in all countries examined here, neoliberal economic and policy changes happened under both right- and left-leaning political parties. While neoliberalism in Canada gained a foothold under the right-wing Mulroney Conservatives, it was the centrist-left Jean Chrétien Liberals who undertook the most substantial welfare state restructuring, particularly with the 1995 federal budget under then Finance Minister Paul Martin. It was at this time that the structure and content of federal transfer payments to provinces were substantially changed, with the introduction of the Canada Health and Social Transfer. Under these new conditions, funds transferred to the provinces from the federal government had fewer conditions attached – meaning provinces did not need to maintain specific social benefits that had been previously required – and also provided significantly less funding (McKeen & Porter, 2003). In Canada, which is essentially a federation of diverse provinces and territories across a massive tract of land, it is the provincial and territorial governments that manage housing, education, and social assistance programs, with both federal and provincial or territorial funds. Federal to provincial and territorial transfers fell from $18 billion annually in the 1980s to $12.5 billion in the mid-1990s; in Ontario, Canada's most populous province, federal transfers that had covered 17 per cent of provincial revenues between 1980 and 1986 dropped to only 9 per cent of revenues by 1996–2001 (Suttor, 2016, p. 128). The significant cuts to federal funds being transferred to the provinces and territories in the mid-1990s accelerated the retrenchment of social assistance benefits (Luxton, 2010) and became part of the rationale for cuts to higher education, resulting in rising tuition fees for students across the country (Lang, 2005). Simultaneously, the federal government completely withdrew financial support for building new public housing by 1993, with the exception of new builds on First Nations reserves; this historic shift marked the end of fifty-two years of federal involvement in public housing production (Suttor, 2016) and is widely considered to mark the beginning of the homelessness crisis in which Canada continues to be embroiled (Gaetz et al., 2013).

Provincially, neoliberalism had already made its ideological imprint in the Western provinces decades earlier, beginning with the Social Credit government in British Columbia during the late 1970s and early 1980s, followed by Conservative wins in Saskatchewan and Alberta (Carroll & Little, 2001). In 1995, Ontario voters ushered in an explicitly neoliberal provincial government by electing the Mike Harris Conservatives under their so-called common sense revolution. I was in the second year of my undergraduate degree at the time and had not yet encountered the work of Pierre Bourdieu. If I had, I might have noticed the un-ironic use of common sense by the Mike Harris Conservatives, employed to reproduce and reinforce a *doxa* (or state-imposed logic) that was not, in fact, common sense up to that point. As Meg Luxton (2010, p. 163) explains: "the success of neoliberalism rests on widespread acceptance that households must absorb more of the work necessary to ensure their subsistence and the livelihoods of their members.... This perspective was articulated quite explicitly in Ontario by the Conservative Harris government when, in 1995, as part of their efforts to create a climate of public opinion supportive of their neoliberal program, they urged people in Ontario to rely less on government services and more on families, friends, neighbours and their communities." When combined with federal cuts to housing, Ontario's "common sense" approach resulted in the decimation of what had once been the strongest public housing portfolio in Canada, which occurred alongside a significant decline of social and affordable housing across the rest of the country (Suttor, 2016). Canadian officials had been carefully observing their neighbours to the south (the United States) and their former colonial master and Commonwealth partner (Britain). According to a past president of the federal housing organization (Canada Mortgage and Housing Corporation, or CMHC), the selling off of large amounts of social housing by the United Kingdom in the 1980s had an influence on "the thinking of senior politicians and public servants, both at the federal and provincial level" (Suttor, 2016, p. 132). While Canada did not have much public housing to begin with – nowhere near the number enjoyed by the United Kingdom prior to the Thatcher era, nor even after the massive sell-off under Thatcher – the logic of neoliberalism as applied to housing made its way across the Atlantic.

From the beginning of Canada's post-war commitment to building social housing in 1949 to the complete halt called for by the Chrétien Liberals in the 1990s, Canada built only 545,000 units of social housing, including public, co-op, and non-profit housing. Since the minor re-engagement of the federal government in building affordable housing between 2001 and 2017, only 50,000 more units were added; most of these are not considered "deeply affordable," with rents set between 80 per cent and 100 per cent of average market rents and limited rent supplements available. Taken together, this comprises less than 5 per cent of all housing in Canada (Pomeroy, 2017, p. 2–3). Although the Justin Trudeau Liberals introduced a long-awaited National Housing Strategy in 2017 that promises to reduce homelessness by 50 per cent and make significant investments in affordable housing, so far the impacts have not been widely felt. According to the Government of Canada's website, over 58,900 new affordable housing units are currently being planned or built, and a further 68,000 existing units are being upgraded or repaired (Government of Canada, 2022). Their stated goal is to build 150,000 new units of affordable housing over ten years. The Canadian Alliance to End Homelessness (2021, para. 13) points out that in order to make a real dent in homelessness, the National Housing Strategy needs "to build at least 300,000 new deep subsidy, permanently affordable and supportive housing units and ensure those units are specifically prioritized to people experiencing or at greatest risk of homelessness." In the meantime, global investment companies are financializing the low-income private rental sector and converting it into "luxury" accommodations and condominiums, resulting in a net loss of 322,600 affordable units between 2011 and 2016, an average annual loss that far outstrips the modest 15,000 affordable units per year planned for the first decade of the National Housing Strategy (Pomeroy, 2020). In other words, Canada has a long way to go to make affordable housing a widespread reality, in a country where housing prices have risen over 25 times faster than those of the United States since 2005 (Punwasi, 2021).

Federal funding for postsecondary education is even less coherent than that for housing, with no national body overseeing higher education in Canada. Instead, provinces and territories transfer funds to colleges and universities, which are themselves typically legally independent institutions. As Daniel Lang (2005, p. 2) explains, "In many other jurisdictions, the status of Canadian universities would be classified as private or perhaps as charter. They are funded through what Canadian governments almost universally describe as *transfer payments*. They are not regarded as line-items in the governments' budgets." Nonetheless, Canadian universities and colleges depend on government funding for their survival and are regulated by provincial and territorial rules that are increasingly linked to such funding. When federal transfer payments to provinces and territories were reduced in the 1990s, it was students who paid the price: between 1993 and 1999 – the precise period in which my own undergraduate degree occurred – tuition fees across the country nearly doubled, and in some cases tripled (Lang, 2005). According to Lang (2005, p. 2), "Since governments in Canada closely control tuition fees, the cause and effect relationship between reductions in public funding and increases in tuition fees is not a coincidence."

As Canadian tuition fees have increased, so too have student debt loads. Prior to the wave of tuition increases in the 1990s, 45 per cent of students graduated with some student debt – on average just over CA$8000 ($14,482 in 2021 dollars)[2]. By 2000, 53 per cent of students were graduating with student debt, and the average debt load had more than doubled to CA$20,500 ($30,435 in 2021 dollars) (Junor & Usher, 2004). This number has held more or less constant since that time, although debt loads by professional degree and by province vary dramatically (Government of Canada, 2020). As is true in the other countries described in this chapter, the increase in student fees is directly correlated with increased inequality of access. Quirke and Davies (2002) found that the representation of students from low-SES backgrounds in undergraduate degrees fell as tuition fees increased, and that "[s]tudents from low social class backgrounds were substantially more likely than their higher-SES counterparts to worry about paying for school" (p. 97). In a study examining the impact of increasing fees in professional programs (dentistry, medicine, and law) on enrolment by socio-economic background, there was a statistically significant increase in the proportion of students from upper-SES backgrounds pursuing professional degrees after the massive fee increases that occurred in Ontario during the late 1990s (Frenette, 2008). As a comparison group, the researcher looked at students pursuing professional programs in Quebec and British Columbia, where fees for professional programs remained stable; in these provinces, there was no shift in student access by SES. Increasing tuition fees in Canada is also correlated with students taking on more paid employment during the school term, which can have a negative impact on school performance (and thus ultimately impact future opportunities) (Neill, 2015).

Federal cuts to transfer payments in the 1990s also had a detrimental impact on social assistance programs across the country. While these social assistance policies have shifted over different time frames in different provinces and territories, the overall impact has been a net decline in social assistance rates in Canada. In a large-scale comparative study of social assistance rates between 1990 and 2009 across the EU and select OECD countries, Wang and Van Vliet (2016) found that Canada's "real annual minimum income benefit levels" (p. 341) *decreased* by US$2389 over this nineteen-year period. The US rates also decreased, although not quite as drastically (by US$2126), whereas the other three study countries saw a modest increase in their social assistance rates over time due to the fact that they had been indexed to price levels (AU by US$4643; NZ by US$1321; and the UK by US$3394).

Every province and territory has its own social assistance programs and policies, which vary in the amounts provided and the requirements attached to those

---

2 As calculated on the Bank of Canada inflation calculator, https://www.bankofcanada.ca/rates/related/inflation-calculator/.

provisions. Despite this variety, every program shares one important trait: *all* of them generate an annual income that is far below the poverty threshold established by the federal government (Laidley & Aldridge, 2020). The highest welfare provision for a single adult considered employable is available in Prince Edward Island; in the largest city in that province, Charlottetown, this represents only 51 per cent of what is required to live at or above the poverty threshold, as established through the Market Basket Measure[3] (ibid.). The lowest welfare provision for the same category is in Nova Scotia; in the city of Halifax, this represents only 32 per cent of the amount needed to live at or above the poverty threshold (ibid.).[4]

Most of the young activists and all of the homeless youth with whom I spoke in Canada live in Ontario. As mentioned previously, Ontario is the most populous province in the country, with more than 38 per cent of the entire Canadian population living there as of 2016 (out of thirteen provinces and territories). Ontario's social assistance rates were radically transformed under the Mike Harris Conservatives in 1995, when welfare was linked to seeking employment or participating in "workfare" programs, and draconian new surveillance policies focused on catching "welfare fraud" were introduced (Little & Marks, 2006). Rates were cut by 21.6 per cent (Oliphant & Slosser, 2003) and have remained more or less constant in the intervening twenty-five years – that is, they have *not* been indexed to inflation, and thus have covered less and less of monthly expenses for recipients as the years have passed. The changes introduced by the Harris Conservatives strongly resemble those brought in by Reagan and then Clinton in the United States; as argued by Little and Marks (2006, p. 20), these changes shifted the discourse around poverty, "to condemn the poor as lazy, dependent, and unworthy and promote the belief that work will transform the poor into moral citizens who are independent and industrious."

There are two main types of social assistance available in Ontario: Ontario Works (or OW), which is the "welfare" form of assistance meant to temporarily support people who do not have access to employment insurance (a benefit that is indexed to an individual's previous contributions through their work) and otherwise are not receiving any kind of income; and the Ontario Disability Support Program (or ODSP), which is for people who can provide documented evidence of a debilitating disability and who are not receiving other forms of employer-related benefits

---

3 "The Market Basket Measure (MBM) is based on the cost of a specific basket of goods and services representing a modest, basic standard of living. It includes the costs of food, clothing and footwear, transportation, shelter and other expenses for a reference family. These costs are compared to disposable income of families to determine whether or not they fall below the poverty line" (Statistics Canada 2017).
4 As of 2022, Quebec had surpassed Prince Edward Island as having the highest social assistance rates, and had also brought its levels up above the poverty line (although barely) (Laidley and Tabbara, 2023).

such as worker's compensation or long-term disability insurance payments. As of this writing, Ontario Works' social assistance rates for a single adult are CA$733/month, of which CA$390 is allocated to "shelter" costs. For a single parent with one dependent, they are CA$1002/month with CA$642 of that allocated to "shelter" (Zon & Granofsky, 2019). ODSP rates are slightly higher. The majority of welfare recipients are female, in large part due to the fact that 93 per cent of the lone parents receiving welfare are mothers. Additionally, welfare recipients skew towards the young, where "[n]early half the recipients of OW are under the age of 34, and the majority of beneficiaries are children and young adults" (ibid., para. 17).

The "shelter" allocation in the Ontario Works' monthly payment means that amount can only be used towards shelter costs, such as rent, which might be supplemented by a rent-geared-to-income (RGI) spot in public housing or by receiving a government rent supplement that can be used in the private market. As noted above, deeply affordable housing is in very short supply in Canada; without an RGI unit or a rent supplement, an individual on welfare cannot afford rent in *any* Ontario city, where rents average CA$1347/month (Canada Mortgage and Housing Corporation, 2020). As a very large province with a wide diversity in urban size and density, these numbers can vary drastically: in the city in which I live, Ottawa, also the capital of Canada, average rents are CA$1379, with a 3.4 per cent vacancy rate. The community with the least expensive rent in Ontario is about 100 kilometres south of Ottawa, but even at CA$620/month (and an extremely low vacancy rate of 0.6 per cent), it remains far above the welfare shelter rate for a single adult. The Greater Toronto Area, where the majority of people in Ontario live, has average rents ranging from $1100 to $1500 per month.

Conclusions

One of my favourite music bands during my undergraduate years was The Rheostatics, an esoteric and multitalented Canadian group who played small venues across Southern Ontario during the 1990s, including in Hamilton, where I was pursuing my degree. I started this chapter with a lyric from one of their songs; that song has been an earworm for me as I have been writing. It is, indeed, a bad time to be poor, when young and poor go hand in hand. As I hope to have conveyed through the chapter, this combination – of young and poor – *is not inevitable*. Poverty has been entrenched and expanded through political decisions made by governments across several decades, and in imitation of one another's neoliberal ideologies, until it has become the doxa, or common sense, of each of these so-called liberal democratic countries. Both the expansion of wealth inequality and the growing impoverishment of children and young people are reversible. If every country documented here re-prioritized the building of non-market, deeply affordable housing, levelled tuition, and provided reasonable rates for their social assistance benefits, these trends could be reversed within one generation or less. As these trends are reversed, so too would democratic participation grow, *if* young people are provided with meaningful, critical, and engaging education about what democracy means – beyond walking into a polling station every few years. As we shall see in the chapters to come, democratic participation is a skill that is learned. Currently, it is learned primarily via familial socialization or postsecondary education, which largely limits it to the affluent classes. It does not have to be this way. Indeed, to be truly democratic, it *must not* be this way.

2 Democratic Dispositions in the Twenty-First Century

The need of reason is not inspired by the quest for truth but by the quest for meaning. And truth and meaning are not the same.

– Hannah Arendt (1971, p. 15)

The previous chapter traced the startling similarities in the growth of inequality across five liberal democracies, coinciding with their respective adoption of neoliberal policies and practices. There are many moral and ethical problems associated with this rapid growth of inequality, including questions of fairness and equality of opportunity. My focus here is somewhat different. What I seek to demonstrate are the social and cultural effects of inequality on the capacity of individuals to engage with democracy. In his enormous study of the growth of economic inequality across advanced Western nations in the twenty-first century, Thomas Piketty (2017) cautions that capitalism's "powerful forces of divergence ... are potentially threatening to democratic societies and to the values of social justice on which they are based" (p. 746). Saskia Sassen (2014) describes the rapid growth of inequality since the 1980s as setting the conditions for the expulsion of the poor "from the social contract at the centre of liberal democracy" (p. 29). Wendy Brown (2011, p. 20) points out that "what is too rarely considered is the effect of ... extreme and growing inequality on the principles and practices of democracy." Each of these influential thinkers is pointing to the same problem: inequality damages democracy. What they do not offer is an empirically based socio-cultural analysis that helps to explain *how* inequality damages democracy. This is the goal of the remainder of the book.

My first claim ought to be non-controversial: individuals *learn* how to be democratic, including how to participate in a democracy. Indeed, this is the basis on which multiple civics courses directed at primary and secondary students across all five countries have been developed (to what extent they actually serve this function shall be addressed in chapter six). However, I wish to nuance this claim with the help of the theorizing of both Hannah Arendt and Pierre Bourdieu. Although meaningful participation in liberal democracies is certainly a skill that can be taught, it is important to remember that *liberal democracy* is not equivalent to *democracy*. As outlined in the Introduction to the book, both Arendt and Bourdieu understand democratic participation as something that is, in theory, available to everyone. Liberal democracies narrow this participation to those above the age of eighteen, who have also been classified by the state as citizens.[1] Aside from these criteria, the major difference between liberal democracy's concept of public participation and those of Arendt and Bourdieu hinges on the role of the individual. Under contemporary liberal democracies, and even more so under neoliberalism, it is not only that the *individual* is the unit of participation, but also that this is an individual of a very specific kind: the rational, reasonable, responsible, and state-recognized member of the polity (i.e., a citizen), who comes to their own thoroughly considered decision and enters into a voting booth by themselves to individually select their chosen candidate.

For Hannah Arendt, participating in a democratic public sphere is fundamentally opposed to individualism. The only manner in which one may participate in the public is *through* one's relations with others, the web of relations that connects us to one another. If this is not happening, then the individual is not actually engaging with the public sphere, or, put differently, participating in a democracy. The individual, without interactions with others, is reduced to the mere social aspects of being human, or what Agamben (1998) terms "bare life." It is through one's participation and interaction with others in the public realm that Arendt sees us each as gaining our full humanity. This is because *"we are of the world and not merely in it"* (Arendt, 1971, p. 22; emphasis hers) – that is, we are born into a world that pre-exists us and shapes us, and which we perceive while being perceived by others. Although Arendt deeply values a quality of individuals that she identifies as *thinking* – a quality she famously identified Eichmann as missing in her analysis of his trial in Jerusalem (Arendt, 1963) – this is not the same as the rational individual of the (neo)liberal democratic state. The life of the mind, as described by Arendt, is marked by its capacity to "withdraw from the world," but, unlike within Cartesian philosophical traditions that see this as the means by which an individual can make "objective" (read: rational) decisions, she recognizes that the mind may never leave the world nor transcend it (Arendt, 1971, p. 45). Rather than "thinking" being an attempt to ascertain truth, Arendt understands this important human faculty as being the search for *meaning*. "To expect truth to come from thinking signifies that we mistake the need to think with the urge to know. Thinking can and must be employed in the attempt to know, but in the exercise of this function it is never itself; it is

---

1 Of course, the boundaries around who could participate in liberal democracies were much narrower when the system was first conceived, limited only to white male landowners.

Democratic Dispositions in the Twenty-First Century   55

but the handmaiden of an altogether different enterprise" (Arendt, 1971, p. 61). In other words, the thinking self is not at all related to the rational, reasonable, and responsible individual of the (neo)liberal democratic state who fills the pages of civics curricula.

Bourdieu, like Arendt, sees public participation as inherently an interactional dynamic, whether the people in question recognize it themselves or not. He also agrees with Arendt that all humans carry the potential to participate democratically. However, he would not agree that everyone thus simply has the *capacity* to engage with democracy, certainly not within our current systems, riddled with hierarchies and struggles for power. Bourdieu's view is tempered by his many years of empirical work, through which he continuously explored the dynamics of dominance and symbolic power in the everyday lives of people. As Loïc Wacquant notes, "In the end, it is an empirical matter, not a conceptual one, whether resistance manages to overturn existing patterns of domination or not. Bourdieu himself has often expressed surprise, even astonishment, at the degree to which structures of class inequality remain impervious to the individual agency of [people].... The rigid determinisms he highlights are for him observable facts that he has to report, no matter how much he may dislike them" (Bourdieu & Wacquant, 1992, p. 80, footnote 24). From this flows Bourdieu's major critique of phenomenology – the tradition within which Arendt was educated and where her work is generally categorized. According to Bourdieu, while a phenomenological view rightly identifies that we are all born into a world that is not of our making, and thus are *of the world* in ways that we cannot always discern, phenomenology gives insufficient attention to the power dynamics that shape said world and their differential effects on people born into them (see Kennelly, 2017, for further discussion of Bourdieu's critique of phenomenology).

Bourdieu states that "[T]here is no denying that there exist dispositions to resist; and one of the tasks of sociology is precisely to examine under what conditions these dispositions are socially constituted, effectively triggered, and rendered politically efficient" (Bourdieu & Wacquant, 1992, p. 81). In what follows, I begin by defining what I am calling a *democratic disposition*, which Bourdieu might see as a "disposition to resist" that has been "rendered politically efficient." I approach this through the words and experiences of young activists and homeless young people, comparatively building a picture of the key views regarding political life and democracy that distinguish between an individual who has developed a democratic disposition and one who has not. I then situate these views within the complex biographies of four individuals from the study, seeking to ethnographically describe how a "democratic disposition" can emerge and be nurtured in some circumstances, and how it can be suppressed and neglected in others. In the chapters to come, I dive more deeply into the biographical conditions that lend themselves to generating a democratic disposition (chapter three), the withering effect of state failures on the capacity of individuals to effectively participate in democracy (chapter four), the manner in which democratic dispositions can easily be transposed into more formal modes of participation under liberal democracies (chapter five), and the role of neoliberal doxa, via school-based civics curricula and other means, in generating specific limited ideals about the duties and place of the citizen in liberal democracies (chapter six).

Defining Democratic Dispositions

As always when speaking of dispositions from within a Bourdieusian framework, it is important to emphasize that these are *not innate traits*. Rather, these are social traits developed through social interactions, rooted in conditions that are themselves shaped by dominance and subordination within the field of power. Bourdieu argues that any of the "possibilities that we tend to think of as (potentially) universal ... remain the privilege of only a few because these ... potentialities find their full realization only under definite social and economic conditions; and because, inversely, there are economic and social conditions under which they are atrophied, annulled" (1998, p. 136). While everyone has the human *potentiality* to develop a democratic disposition, not everyone has access to the social and economic conditions under which such a disposition can flourish.

There is an act of mystification at play in the manner in which liberal democracy is represented by dominant forces, primarily through schooling but also through mainstream media. This is encapsulated by the myth of the "one person-one vote" vision for democracy, which wrongly claims that each individual citizen, with their individual vote, can and does contribute equally to a democratic outcome. This is incorrect on many levels, not least of which, as Bourdieu points out, because voting is not in fact an individual act but emerges from a social context that shapes the views of those individuals who enter the polling station. Bourdieu sees voting and its glorification of the individual as inherently "prejudicial to subordinate groups" because it "forces them to enter into the political game serially, in mechanical isolation, against a social order that is already constituted to their detriment" (Wacquant, 2005). But it goes even deeper than this. To actually create meaningful change under liberal democracy, it is rarely enough to merely show up at the polling station. Unless you are fortunate enough to live in a riding where your views are shared by the majority of those around you, voting as an individual can make no difference whatsoever, or at least it will feel that way to those who have shown up to vote and seen their vote "wasted" because their needs or priorities are rendered irrelevant when their favoured candidate or party does not win. This is part of what can become so demobilizing about the liberal model of individuals voting.

To meaningfully participate under current liberal democratic systems is the opposite of "one person-one vote"; as demonstrated by the stories of young activists across all five countries, to be democratically engaged means to collaborate with others to generate social change either through pressure from the outside (often via activist strategies such as demonstrations or other forms of organizing) and/or to create pressure from the inside (through canvassing, supporting specific electoral candidates, or participating on committees or as elected officials themselves). These two tactics are not mutually exclusive, and the skills acquired through one are directly applicable to the other – a confluence that Bourdieu might call homological, and which I will explore in more detail in chapter five.

A democratic disposition, or habitus, emerges from within a specific political field, with its own *illusio* – or rules of the game – that cannot help but be strongly influenced by liberal and neoliberal doxa when taking shape within contemporary liberal democracies. Every social field, including the political field, requires of those entering it to have some sort of relationship to that field's illusio. Whether an individual is able to play the game skilfully or not, their participation in that field – or indeed their apprehension of the logic of the field that results in them conceding that they *cannot* effectively participate within it – is granting recognition to the stakes of the field. Contesting the field, likewise, is to acknowledge its logic: "Wanting to undertake a revolution in a field is to accord the essential of what the field tacitly demands, namely ... that the game played is sufficiently important for one to want to undertake a revolution in it" (Bourdieu, 1998, p. 78). To enter into the political field of activist contestation of the state is, at some level, to concede to the state's logic: how would it be possible not to? Every participant in this project (including this book's author) has been swimming in the soup of liberal and neoliberal logic since childhood, with the exception of two participants who moved to New Zealand and Canada, respectively, as young adults after early political socialization in authoritarian countries.[2] On the other hand, young people who had experienced homelessness, broadly speaking, were not even aware of this alternate political field, nor its illusio. Their sense of political action and its efficacy

---

2 Ironically, their perception of the liberal democracies to which they had moved, while critical due to their activist engagements and experiences with racism, were in some ways even more powerfully tinged by the global myth of liberal democratic freedoms, such as the right to protest. Despite this right being steadily eroded in each of the liberal democracies under study – particularly under the constraints imposed by the COVID-19 pandemic – the contrast between absolute authoritarian control and the severe penalties that resulted for expressing opposition to the ruling party in their countries of birth, with the opportunity to gather in public to express (futile and generally ignored) opposition to public rule in their adopted countries, was remarkable enough to be something on which they both commented. Likewise, children of immigrants who had fled such repressive regimes would also comment on this contrast.

emerged as a mix of reiteration of liberal democratic doxa (e.g., their luck to be born into a "free" country and the responsibility to vote), and frustration about how irrelevant, illogical, or corrupt formal political systems were.

What I am calling a democratic disposition, then, is much more than a proclivity to vote. A democratic disposition is the set of skills, attitudes, beliefs, and experiences that enable some people to realize their capacity to effect meaningful change under liberal democratic structures. These are complex skills that are *learned*, both passively through exposure via familial and/or community norms and actively through engagement in the practices themselves. Under current structures of extreme and growing inequality, such exposures and engagements are increasingly class stratified. In other words, democratic dispositions are not equally distributed across social classes. *This is not inevitable.* Rather, it is a consequence of a wide combination of factors, including the mystification embedded in the "one person-one vote" version of liberal democracy, the growing inequality of access to accurate citizenship education across both secondary and postsecondary schooling, and the increasing desperation of the poor and lower-middle classes under neoliberal policies that have reduced families' housing security, limited young people's access to higher education, and undermined their mental and physical wellness.

To Be a Political Person

It is instructive to turn to the definitions of being a "political person" offered by young activists, which, when combined with their views on democracy, provide a reasonable outline of what it means to have developed a democratic disposition, or habitus, in twenty-first-century liberal democratic Anglo-American states. To be political, according to young activists, encompasses one or more of the following practices and beliefs: (1) being both informed and active on an issue or issues; (2) recognizing how subordinate identities have been politicized and what it means to live in the world as the bearer of those politicized identities (e.g., as Cadence describes, to be female, queer, racialized, and living with a disability; or as Dylan states, "always paying attention to power"); and/or (3) being aware of and willing to act in order to influence formal political structures. None of the young activists identified "being political" exclusively with formal politics, although most included formal politics within a wider definition:

> I think for me, it means showing awareness and acknowledgement and showing some form of action that you could do to be able to be part of a political system that creates change (Alejandro, United States, age twenty).
>
> I think I am [a political person] just because that's what my interest is. Like I mentioned earlier, my existence, every part of my identity is politicized because I'm Black and I'm also queer and I'm also a woman and then I also have a disability.

So every part of me is being politicized. I really lucked out there with all those. I wish I had a bingo card, actually [laughs]. That's pretty fun. So I think I'm always going to be political just because I have to be. But outside of my identity politics, just politics in general is interesting to me. So I think even if I didn't carry all this with me, I'd still be interested in politics (Cadence, United States, age nineteen).

I think it's about viewing society not as a group of individuals but as a society, as a community, and decisions are made that impact the collective whether it's done by the collective or not. And I think there is extreme importance at every level to ensure as many individuals as possible if they want to have the ability to have equal say, have equal weight within the system while at the same time not infringing on what are basic rights (Darryl, Canada, age twenty-nine).

It means engaging my life with politics. And that means very explicitly engaging with politics and building political movements and organizing politically in my workplace, my student life, community group, but it also means dealing with my life politically, that my life is part of structures and systems.... Whether it's understanding my relationship and understanding gender roles and sexism inside relationships and working them out or whether it's building my union. I see them as political, both of them, hand in hand (Brendan, Australia, age twenty-seven).

Do I feel like I'm a political person? Yeah. I'm involved politically. I think there is something called being politically vocal. I guess I'm vocal when it comes to politics I'd say.... Ugh, okay, before I even answer that, my skin colour is politics. Like, my race, my gender is politics. My religion can also be politics. I think we are all political people. We are all political people, it's just a matter of understanding where you lie on the political spectrum (Gregory, Canada, age nineteen).

Politics affects every single element of our lives, so I would say just by existing in the system we are all political.... I think the word politics can sometimes be too closely attached to the whole party structure and system and party politics.... And I feel like, yeah, we need to try to decouple that a little bit because it's dangerous. I think that there's this kind of misconception where being a political person is kind of seen as being a negative thing sometimes (Leila, New Zealand, age nineteen).

Several activists identified the impossibility of political neutrality, captured succinctly by Sanaya (Canada, age twenty-eight): "I think even if someone is neutral, they are taking a political stance. They are taking a stance to support the status quo." Sandra (Canada, age nineteen) feels that, "Even a phrase like, 'Oh, I'm not political' does come down to privilege. Like, I don't think I've ever met a Palestinian person who says 'I'm not political' because their entire existence is politicized." Michael (New Zealand, age eighteen), who was running for office in the New Zealand federal election at the time of our interview, told me he has a "usual speech" on the topic of being political: "There is a usual speech I do about how people that drink water, who like fresh air, by opposing action on climate change, by some political parties opposing action on climate change, it means everyone is political, not just the downtrodden. Every single person in the world, their human rights are being threatened by politics, by some politicians. So, yeah, everything is political."

By contrast, homeless youth across all five countries almost exclusively associated "being political" entirely with formal electoral politics, and rarely with their everyday lives. The exception to this view among youth who had experienced homelessness were those who had received some sort of direct organizing/activist instruction (a point I explore in more detail in chapter four), or those few who had access to higher education. To my question "how would you describe what it means to be political?" I received responses such as the following:

> Like all into the political parties and like you know everything. And I feel like just knowledge in that area – politics, I do not have that much knowledge in politics, like Australian politics, right now (Saanvi, Australia, age eighteen).
>
> Political person is like to be government, the country. Yeah. That is what it means to me. I didn't see myself as that. I don't see myself acting that way (Daraja, United Kingdom, age thirty).
>
> Someone who votes. Um, someone who [pauses] keeps up with them, I guess. Someone who, like, keeps tabs on the news. That's all I can think of (Shane, New Zealand, age seventeen).
>
> The reason I don't feel like I'm a political person is because I feel like I don't have enough knowledge, like academic knowledge [to understand politics] (Tiffany, United Kingdom, age twenty-three).

While some young people who had experienced homelessness felt themselves to be political people, it was almost always in relation to their knowledge of formal politics and how up-to-date they were on current news regarding formal political parties and policies. On the other hand, this view also meant that many disavowed an identity as a "political person," turned off by formal political systems that seemed incoherent, corrupt, and/or completely alien to their understanding of the world. For instance, Dominic (age eighteen) told me he once had an interest in Canadian politics, but has become disheartened and disillusioned by what he perceives to be a corrupt political system working for the benefit of the rich:

> Like, I used to really like politics and used to really want to learn all about it. But lately I've just not been able to focus on it that much. Every time in the past, politicians say they're going to do something to get votes, but then once they're actually in power they don't ever make those changes. They only do like a couple and then they focus on what, to make money I guess. And there's a lot of corruption. Even in Canada, I heard that Justin Trudeau donated like hundreds of millions of dollars to a government, a company that he, um, doesn't own but he's like related to, so he's

making money off it. And I know that other countries do that, like America does that and so I feel like a lot of it, most of it, is deception between politicians and corruption, they make changes for big companies so that they make a profit off of it. They don't actually make change for the good of the country (Dominic, Canada, age eighteen).

The contrast in views of what it means to "be political" between young activists and young people who have experienced homelessness is telling. Young activists are deeply invested in a view of politics as all-encompassing and extending far past the boundary of formal politics within liberal democratic systems. Indeed, this value is so deeply held that those who claim themselves to be "not political" are viewed with suspicion and distrust. Yet many of the homeless young people I interviewed described themselves as exactly that: not political. This cannot be attributed to privilege, as Sandra suggests, nor to supporting the status quo, as described by Sanaya. Rather, this reflects very different understandings of the term.

The significance of the term signals that we might understand this self-identity as "political" to be a marker of distinction, following Bourdieu (1984), separating out those who have acquired a democratic disposition from those who have not. As with many markers of distinction, this one is class-bound in ways that are not apparent without comparative analyses. As shall be shown in the chapters to come, to acquire a democratic disposition under current conditions of inequality is to inhabit a field that is middle class. The different meanings given to the term "political" reflects the habituation of language use acquired through exposure to a middle-class field of activism. Bourdieu describes this as part of a "linguistic sense of place," which "governs the degree of constraint which a given field will bring to bear on the production of discourse, imposing silence or a hyper-controlled language on some people while allowing others the liberties of a language that is securely established" (Bourdieu, 1991, p. 82). The "securely established" language of "being political" marks one as "in the know" within activist circles and is part of a wider display of having acquired a democratic disposition, one that can fairly easily be transposed into more formal political fields under liberal democracies (to be illustrated in chapter five).

By listening to Maggie's experience with the term, we can see how changing ideas about what it means to "be political" signal the transformation of habitus as one acquires a democratic disposition. As shall be described in more detail in chapter four, Maggie came to activism via postsecondary schooling and then through engagement with other young Gypsy/Roma/Travellers who described themselves as activists. Coming from an impoverished history marked by systemic failures against herself and her community, she claimed the term "activist" to describe herself only recently. Maggie articulates her transition from one view of what it means to "be political" to the other when I ask her whether she considers herself to be a political person:

Yes. I think if this was a year ago, I would have said no because I would have associated being political with politics. But sometimes your existence in itself is a political act. Um, in merely existing, that's a political beast, but also then, like in existing and speaking as a Traveller woman and as a gay Traveller woman. [And] sometimes even silence is a political act. All of those things, that like, whether we realize it or not. Like, sometimes it's a privilege to remain silent. That in, silence is a political act. So, for example, I spoke out about the Black Lives Matter campaign [as a white woman]. I did that because, sometimes remaining silent is to align yourself with the oppressor. And that is like, everything is political.

Maggie's account captures here her original view of "being political" as associated only with formal politics, just as was described by young people who had experienced the extreme poverty that accompanies homelessness in all five countries. As she moved forward in her activism and found her community of activist supports, her account of "being political" transformed into one that is identical to that described by young activists in all five countries: to be political for Maggie has come to mean everything, including both her identity and her silence.

This Is What Democracy Looks Like

Such an expansive view of what it means to "be political" demands a much more elaborate set of ideas about democracy than that on offer through the doxa (or pervasive common sense) of the (neo)liberal state. For young activists, democracy is a concept they have largely freed from the constraints of liberalism, a feat that would be difficult to achieve without considerable exposure to alternatives that are not typically on offer within public school civics courses. On the other hand, homeless young people, who typically had limited exposure even to the narrow definition of democracy available through secondary school civics, defined democracy almost exclusively through the terms of formal liberal democratic systems, if they had any definition for it at all.

In the table below, I have categorized the responses of participants to my interview question "when I say the word democracy, what comes to mind?" There were four broad ways in which participants answered the question: among young activists, the vast majority provided an alternative definition of democracy (twenty out of twenty-four respondents); the remainder provided a definition that mixed both alternative and formal, liberal democratic definitions. When I asked the same question of youth who had experienced homelessness, they either had no idea or were unsure (seven out of twenty-two), or they offered a formal definition of democracy that was focused solely on the liberal democratic system (eight out of twenty-two). A small minority offered an alternative definition of democracy, although this typically was not

Table 1. Categorizing democracy

Definitions of democracy:	No idea/ unsure	Formal definition of democracy	Alternate definition of democracy	Mix of both formal and alternate definitions of democracy
Young activists	0	0	20	4
Homeless youth	7	8	5	2

as well developed as those of the young activists (five out of twenty-two), or they offered a mix of both (two out of twenty-two).

The alternative forms of democracy that young activists described were similar across all five countries. An ideal form of democracy involves collective decision-making between those actually impacted by issues; the ability to make decisions for oneself or one's community; and/or the freedom to self-govern. Democracy includes everyone, regardless of race, class, gender, sexuality, ability, or age. Here are a sample of responses from young activists when asked to describe democracy:

> A group of people, if they decide on a thing or on a person or whatever it will be, it's going to happen. And a person's race, background, whatever it may be, no part of their identity will allow anyone to count more than someone else (Cadence, United States, age nineteen).
>
> I would say when I think of democracy I think of collective decision-making between individuals that have a shared alignment or goal or something like that (Darryl, Canada, age twenty-nine).
>
> The word fairness, just everybody having a voice and having their voice heard (Julia, United Kingdom, age eighteen).
>
> I feel like it should be equal participation and representation by the complete population (Mahala, New Zealand, age twenty-five).
>
> The first top thing I think about is freedom, equal rights, everyone is seen as equal, there shouldn't be room for discrimination or anything similar, and just happiness as well. They're kind of the main three things (Rima, Australia, age eighteen).

Young activists generally had a very sophisticated take on democracy and its possibilities and limits, as well as many insights into the intricacies of how formal politics were playing out in their respective countries. Representative democracy, the form of liberalism that is prominent in each country, was rarely seen as meaningfully democratic, although some felt it was possible to reach democratic ends from within that system if done carefully and with attention to power. Young activists from New Zealand tended to think of their own country, with its ranked ballot system (a form of proportional representation called MMP, or mixed-member proportional), to be more democratic than first-past-the-post systems. On the other hand, young people from Australia, with a similar ranked ballot system and mandatory voting, were split on whether this resulted in truly democratic decisions. This difference could be due to the differences in political leadership at the time of the interviews; in New Zealand, Labour Party leader Jacinda Ardern was in power, with progressive left politics that resonated with many of the young activists with whom I spoke. Australia, on the other hand, was led by the right-wing Liberal Party, whose leader, Scott Morrison, is an evangelical Christian and a self-professed admirer of then US President Donald Trump. Below are some examples of activists contrasting their vision for democracy with what they see within the formal liberal democratic systems in their countries:

> People have continuously contested the more conservative nature of democracy in the United States and then thinking about democracy as – I mean I definitely agree with a government that is ruled by the needs of the people and so in that way I feel like socialism and democracy have a much stronger connection than capitalism and democracy. My dad always made a joke that stuck with me, "In the Soviet Union communism defeated democracy, in the United States capitalism did." I mean that was the kind of corny dad joke, but I think there's sort of something about that, that stuck with me about how the idea that capitalism and democracy are natural [allies], it's just not, it doesn't make sense (Dylan, United States, age twenty-one).
>
> What I would consider the central tenet of democracy's concept is self-governance. And I don't think that we have that, probably, anywhere in the world. But definitely, I can't speak on behalf of everyone in the world, but we're definitely not governing ourselves here in Australia. And I think the illusion of choice is something that is a related concept. We're given a choice between two parties that I don't like, either of them. And, yeah, I guess, in terms of what is the lie, I think the lie that we are actually in control of our world, of our environment, of our lives, of our personhood, I think that's the lie. Just because we go and vote in a federal election once every three years, that's not enough for me. So, that is not enough direct control over my life (Joanna, Australia, age twenty-six).
>
> I think it [democracy] sounds lovely in theory. [laughter] I think it's a lovely idea. I think that, like it's the dad joke that I often make to my friends which is, you know, like "Liberal democracy, which is never really liberal or democratic." And I think that's true. But I also think the idea of democracy to me in and of itself is a really powerful one and many of my objections to the world happen when people don't live up to their standard ideals and I would think that democracy is one of those that really does – like, to me, democracy should mean that the people col-

lectively have control over what happens to them and their communities. That's what it should mean. And the fact that it has not been that and that it has in many ways been reduced to every four years you check a box and you hope the person that you checked that box for maybe doesn't completely fuck you over is not what it ought to be (Angie, Canada, age twenty-four).

For young activists, democracy is an ideal they reach for, and it is an ideal they do not generally see reflected within current formal political systems. Their critiques of the limits of liberal democracy and its individualized approach to participation is an important aspect of their commitment to change. Every young activist I spoke with values democracy; none of them believes that democracy is happening to its full potential within the country in which they live. If they did not have an alternative view of democracy, it would likely be difficult for them to mobilize against the system as it is. Their critique has coherence; unfortunately, it is a critique they have learned either from parents, via activist organizing and/or exposure to critical education about democracy in postsecondary schooling. In other words, this is NOT a critique they could typically learn through the widely available public education system, nor through publicly accessible mass media.

The lack of widely available critical education about the limits of liberal democracy generates perverse consequences for those who are being most failed by the current system. Despite repeated experiences with Australian racism and systemic failures that kept him homeless and unable to attend school for years, Armin (age twenty-two) sees Australia as a democratic country. True to the messages he has absorbed about what it means to be a valuable citizen in a (neo)liberal democracy, Armin's aspiration is to finish secondary schooling so that he can study engineering at university, not so much to have a career as to be able to escape the stigma he has carried since arriving in Australia from Iran at the age of twelve: "my main goal is to be educated. Because when I'm an educated person, then that's my label. Not that I'm brown, not that I'm you know, all those negative [labels]." Armin's only recourse to combat the racism and Islamophobia he has faced is an individualized one: to make himself into the respectable, professional, educated consumer-citizen who can no longer be mocked for his race or religion. Monica (age sixteen) has keen insights into the effects of class inequality in New Zealand and a strong analysis of the failures of the school system and policing in her small town; yet despite living on state benefits herself, she reiterates the neoliberal line about welfare fraud as an issue of concern and mimics the conversative media's view that immigrants are taking all of the available jobs. Dominic (age eighteen) responded "yeah" when I asked whether he thinks Canada is a democratic country, despite his lived experience of being born to an Inuit mother and watching the suffering of his mother's community due to their lack of basic infrastructure such as water and schools. When I asked him what makes him think that Canada is democratic, he responded: "Um, like you get, like, rights. You have like freedom of speech. You have um freedom of religion. You like get to vote for the people who you want, like, what changes you want in the future. And, yeah. Like, you have a lot of rights I guess."

When homeless youth had a definition for the word democracy – which was not the case for more than a third of respondents – they typically also thought of their own countries as democratic. Dominic's description above, of why he thought Canada was democratic despite the state failures he had experienced first-hand, is replete with the virtues of liberalism: freedom from state interference (for speech and religion), the opportunity to vote, and the protection of individual rights. I labelled this a "formal" definition of democracy, and it was echoed by several of the young people who had experienced homelessness, sometimes by drawing comparisons to other countries they believed to be undemocratic:

> I feel like it is. Um, because I don't, like, because I feel like in what's it, in China it's a definitely different kind of situation going on there? Like, I've heard many things but like honestly I can't really pinpoint what. I feel like, it's just, it's a very different situation over there. I would say it's definitely more strict. And there's not, people don't really, not that they don't have a voice – I don't want to speak because I don't really [know], what it's really like to be there – But people don't really have too much of a voice there. Whereas here we have, we definitely have a voice, we definitely like, we vote and we get to see, we get to hear everyone's kind of like point of view or like, what they have to say. And we, obviously, we vote to see like, for who represents our views, which is, I feel like it's really good (Caitlin, Canada, age nineteen).
>
> I feel like we're very, like, free. Like, we make our own decisions. I don't know. It's kind of, I don't really know much about it, like, all I know is I feel like our system is extremely fair and yeah (Rachel, Australia, age eighteen).
>
> So the system of governments. It's, um, it generally involves voting. Every person casts one vote and that determines how the state is run. It's popular in most affluent, Western countries.... I think I do tend to think of it in quite formalized ways. I generally broadly think democracy's a good thing. I worry that it's not doing too well internationally (Elizabeth, United Kingdom, age twenty-two).
>
> Like, where it's everyone's vote, like everyone's country (Shane, New Zealand, age seventeen).

When young people experience being catastrophically failed by the state – in public education, in meeting their basic human right to housing, in protecting them from systemic racism, etc. – and yet absorb the state's definition of democracy, agreeing with the liberal state that it is, in fact, democratic, particularly in comparison to all of those *other* undemocratic countries, they are experiencing symbolic violence. As Bourdieu (2000, p. 174) points out, "The primordial political belief is a particular viewpoint, that of the dominant, which presents and imposes itself as a universal viewpoint." The view of the dominant is absorbed by us all, becoming part of our acquired dispositions (or habitus); it can only be shaken loose through "a thoroughgoing process of countertraining [to] durably transform habitus" (Bourdieu, 2000, p. 172). When the view of the dominant, such as the liberal definition of democracy, is absorbed by the dominated, they are left with little recourse but to accept their own domination as inevitable, and unchangeable. If homeless young people are living within democratic countries, and democracy means the protection of their freedoms and rights (to vote, at least), then their failings must be their own. This cultural messaging is even more powerful under neoliberalism, with its undiluted emphasis on individual responsibilities *to* the state, without expectation of protections *from* the state.

The Synthesis and Obstruction of Democratic Dispositions

In order to illustrate the distinct pathways that shape the acquisition of a democratic disposition by young activists and the barriers faced by young homeless people in developing a similar capacity to participate meaningfully under liberalism and neoliberalism, I turn here to a more in-depth comparison of four young people who participated in this research. Armin and Khalil are racialized young men living in Australia and the United Kingdom respectively, who have both experienced homelessness intermittently over the previous five to seven years. Their biographies are shaped by the inequalities wrought by neoliberal policies described in the previous chapter. Both Armin's and Khalil's homelessness had been severely exacerbated by the lack of affordable housing options in Australia and the United Kingdom; for Khalil, the casualization of labour had impacted both his own biography and that of his father, who was also struggling to stay securely housed. Noor (Australia) and Matt (United Kingdom), by contrast, are young activists involved in the climate change movement in their respective countries who have benefited from being born to affluent families where they have been largely shielded from the excesses of neoliberal cuts to public housing, schooling, and welfare benefits. Race intersects with class in their stories in ways that will become clearer below, where each young person's vulnerability to the added burden of racism in their respective white-dominant countries is mediated by both their class position and their racialization.

In Australia, Armin (age twenty-two) told me he did not feel voting was important, despite it being compulsory, because "I'm a nobody." Armin's experience of continuous and unrelenting racism in Australia had taught him that, "as a minority, I don't matter." Armin had migrated to Melbourne from Iran as a young teenager, sponsored by his father who had been in Australia for many years. Family conflict had prevented him from settling with his father, and he had essentially been homeless since his arrival in Australia until about six months before our interview, when he had finally attained stable housing. He was living on government benefits in the private market with a government rent supplement and was unemployed but hoping to get back into the education system when we spoke. During his seven years in Australia, he had learned that his identity as a Muslim was not one he could be open about, lest he be labelled a "terrorist." He was often mistaken for South Asian (from India) by white Australians and taunted with the name "curry," meant to be a diminutive insult about Indian cuisine. His experience of Australian culture was of one deeply divided by race:

> I don't want to get too deep, but I believe there's tremendous hatred. Because Australia always brags about "multiculturalism" and all that. But, in my belief, I don't think people give a damn about that. I think you know, they say America is divided, blah, blah. I think Australia is very divided. Because, I mean, correct me if I'm wrong, but the idea of multiculturalism would be to be mixed, right? To be like, you know, you walk up to a place unannounced and you see, you know, two Blacks, three Asians, ten whites. Whereas what you see, all the whites are together, like freaking apartheid.

Despite his experiences of racism, Armin told me he had not attended the recent Black Lives Matter protests because he believes in "action" like legislation, rather than what he saw as largely symbolic posturing through rallies or demonstrations. Taken in combination, this means that Armin feels himself to be incapable of effecting change either through formal politics (i.e., voting) or through informal or activist politics.

In the United Kingdom, Khalil (age twenty-three) expressed similar cynicism about the possibilities for change, noting that he was naïve when he first voted at age eighteen, thinking it would make a difference. "I now have literally zero hope for politics," he told me. Khalil was also a migrant, moving to London from Algeria with his parents when he was a young child. His mother stayed at home with him while his father worked a series of working-class jobs (factory worker, garbage collector ["bin man"], concierge). Khalil was schooled in "the lowest of the low" of state schools in East London, "that's how it was perceived, should I say. Not how it felt from the inside, but how it was seen from other people." The school ranked low in the league tables, which are based on standardized exams in the United Kingdom, and it did not have a good track record for sending students to postsecondary. But, for Khalil, it was a place of belonging and support: "the most amazing thing is I never realized that I was a minority until I left that school and that area." In an effort to improve their results of moving students into postsecondary, the school developed a sixth form program that provided intensive one-on-one mentorship for its brightest students, to get them into university. With their support, Khalil successfully applied for and was accepted to Leeds University and became a celebrated hero in his local community for being one of only five students to get into the "Russell Group" universities, which Khalil described to me as being the "Ivy League, the top twenty universities in the UK." When I looked into this category, I discovered that these are the top *publicly funded* universities in the United Kingdom, leaving out privately funded and extremely prestigious institutions such as Oxford and Cambridge. It was upon attending university that Khalil first experienced his racialization in a white-dominant society:

> So until I went to a highly respected institution where the majority are English, white, middle class – completely different to where I had grown up. So, like, that's where for me, even as an Algerian, like, obviously I'm not Black, but growing up in a very Black community, I didn't see myself as different to Black people. Do you get it? But then going to university, I felt even the Black community didn't receive me as well as my own people received me, because it's like you're not white but you're not Black as well. Do you get it? Whereas where I grew up I was just me and it didn't matter what race I was.

He also quickly learned that the success for which he was celebrated at home was viewed very differently by the white, middle-class students with whom he attended classes: "So I was like one of five [to go to Russell Group universities] so then it's like, oh my God, it's great. Like, he did amazing. You're going to go super high, far away, etcetera. But then you get to Leeds and you realize that half of them chose it like a second option, instead of Cambridge. Do you get it? And it's like, it's not as prestigious as you may have thought." Khalil began to experience homelessness the same year he began university. After his parents separated, he lived in what he described as "a private association, so council house," dwelling. I assume this means he was living either in a council housing or housing association unit, both of which are funded by the UK government and meant to be affordable for those in greatest housing need. Living in Stratford after the London Olympics of 2012 meant that his neighbourhood had experienced rapid gentrification (see Kennelly, 2016) and his (presumably public) landlord was raising rents. This housing pressure motivated his mother to move to France with her new partner, leaving Khalil to fend for himself when he came home from uni for holidays and the summer. He was able to pay for university through a combination of loans, bursaries, and part-time jobs, and he would couch surf with friends or cousins in the summer months. He was not getting along with his father at this point, who was under-housed himself at any rate and could not offer a very comfortable place for Khalil to live. He decided to start his master's degree in part as a response to his likely homelessness upon returning to London; as he would be able to access further loan funds for the master's degree at Leeds, this was a better option than returning to an over-priced city with few job options even for a young person with a university degree. He completed his master's degree with a dissertation on liberalism and the emergence of liberal democracy – which yielded a lively side chat between us halfway through the interview about books we had both read and enjoyed. When he returned from the master's program, he reconciled with his father and slept on his father's couch for a few months until he was able to secure a job and save enough money for he and his father to rent a flat together. This was where he was living at the time of our interview. Prior to the COVID-19 pandemic, he had been working in the stock room and doing sales for a high-end clothing store. His efforts to find work that match his high level of education had so far come to naught.

Like Armin, Khalil sees protests or demonstrations as ineffective, particularly if they are peaceful protests: "I'm much more Malcom (X) than Martin (Luther King)," he told me with a chuckle. Despite his strong and abiding interest in politics, fostered through both of his university degrees, and an ongoing podcast where he explores a variety of issues, Khalil does not consider himself an activist because activists "are fighting for change…. It's not like sharing of posts on Twitter and thinking you're doing something." In other words, like Armin, Khalil saw no space for himself as an agent of change under liberal democracy, either through formal or activist politics, nor did he hold out much hope for change through either means.

Now compare and contrast Armin's experience with that of Noor (age nineteen), another ethnic minority young person from Australia; and Khalil's experience with Matt's (age nineteen), another student reading (studying) politics in the United Kingdom. It was Noor who alerted me to the phenomenon of the "democracy sausage," a tradition in Australia of having barbecued sausages available for Australian voters to eat as they leave the polling booth. As she told me, "election days tend to be kind of a huge celebration. Like, food and 'I've voted!' and you know, stuff like that." Noor grew up in what she described as an "affluent suburb" of Melbourne to highly educated, upper-middle-class parents who had immigrated from Bangladesh. Like the majority of young activists I spoke with, Noor's family were politically aware and often engaged in issues of importance to them, particularly her father, who brought Noor with him as a child to the voting booth (to get a democracy sausage) and rallies. In contrast to Armin, Noor saw both voting (formal politics) and activism as essential to creating social change. When I asked her whether she felt it was important to vote, she answered with five successive "Yeses": "Oh, yes. Oh, yes. Yes, yes, yes. Absolutely!" followed by laughter. She then went on to say: "If I'm so passionate about issues, I think to create change, part of that is voting people in who will create that change. You know, we can do so much through protests and advocacy but ultimately people who make the decisions are the ones who are in parliament. So, voting is a key way of doing that." When I spoke with her, Noor was completing her first year at Monash University, studying remotely courtesy of the COVID-19 pandemic. She had graduated from an elite private girls' school, for which she had earned a scholarship to attend: "that scholarship really helped my parents put me through because they wouldn't have really been able to afford the fees otherwise." The school provided multiple opportunities and was very supportive of her activism, despite being quite conservative in its orientation, according to Noor. Although she described the school as very diverse, when pressed she told me there were only "three brown girls including me, and one Black girl" out of forty-four students in her year. As a private school, the students tended to come from affluent families, and there were a number of international students. Noor felt the school could have done a better job at addressing mental health for their students, but she did not believe that racism was an issue: "there wasn't really so much racism that I saw because it was really inclusive." Noor's activism emerged directly from her leadership experiences in the school, with opportunities like debating and public speaking. In grade twelve, she was elected the "environment captain," and through the school she participated in fundraising for an organization called One Girl that supports girls' education in Africa. In an effort to be "the best environment captain," she joined the Australian Youth Climate Coalition (AYCC), which launched her into community activism:

> [The AYCC are] all about activism, advocacy, but most importantly, like education. Like, informing young people about climate change. So I kind of went to one workshop and I was like, "oh, this is really interesting. I'm learning about coal and the Adani Coal Mine and I never really understood it properly." Like, in school you just kind of skim over it – like, we don't go in depth. And from there, things started changing. I started getting involved with like, the school strikes, which were happening November, what was it? 2018. And then throughout year twelve I was helping organize, doing meeting stuff for School Strike, and that kind of exploded with a lot of different opportunities for activism, so. Yeah. And I ended up looking at things like climate leaders, so setting that up with some other Australian young people, about trying to get people elected into parliament who were going to advocate for climate action.

Their efforts at getting a pro-environment candidate elected to parliament worked: "We got one candidate in. Her name's Zali Steggall. She overthrew an ex-prime minister. No one really liked him, so, yeah. So that was really good. It was really satisfying to get her elected into federal parliament. We were really proud."

Armin and Noor are both young ethnic minorities from immigrant families living in and around Melbourne, Australia. After that, the similarities abruptly end, due to their extremely different classed experiences of their community and country. Where Noor was largely shielded from overt racism within her affluent suburb and elite private school, Armin faced it head on as a young homeless man. Of course, the whiteness of Noor's school and the kinds of things taught in the classroom are all part of larger structures of systemic racism, and she had some awareness of this, which came out when we discussed whether there were Indigenous students at her school: "No. I don't think we had a single Indigenous student at our school, which is such a shame because you know, in Australia we have a lot of issues around, you know, Indigenous reconciliation, and at my school I really tried to advocate more for it, but like, we didn't have a single Indigenous student, which was really shocking to say, actually." However, unlike Armin, Noor did not walk the streets with taunts of "curry" echoing in her ears, nor did she see Australia as a country divided by race, comparable to South Africa under apartheid, as Armin described it. Instead, she learned how to take on leadership roles through school, which then led her directly into community organizing. From there, with the skills developed and support provided by the AYCC, she was able to participate in a campaign that elected a progressive and pro-climate member of parliament. With these experiences under her belt, it is not at all surprising that Noor sees social change as possible, and herself as someone who can actively participate in making it happen, both through activism and through formal politics.

In the United Kingdom, Matt (age nineteen), like Noor in Australia, came from an educated and politically progressive family, grew up in a high-income suburban neighbourhood, and attended a private secondary school. As a white British man descended from several generations of white British ancestors, living in a white-dominant society, Matt could take his racialization for granted, unlike Armin, Khalil, or Noor. By this I mean that he did not have to contend with his race as a personal issue negatively affected by individual and structural racism; Matt did, however, have a critical awareness of race and racism, which he tried to bring to his organizing. Like his UK counterpart, Khalil, Matt was studying politics in university and had a well-developed critique of liberalism and neoliberalism. There the similarities end, however. As between Noor and Armin, the extreme differences in class background permeate all aspects of Khalil's and Matt's experiences. This meant that despite a shared interest in politics, and despite the fact that Matt was only in second-year university while Khalil had already completed a master's degree, it was Matt who had the more detailed understanding of the possibilities for social change through formal and informal politics.

Although they grew up in the same country, Matt's experience of secondary school could not have been more different from that of Khalil. Where Khalil attended a state school with limited success at moving its students into postsecondary, "as in the first person to ever reach Oxford or Cambridge from my school happened a year after I left," Matt attended an exclusive private school, where one of the tactics they use to attract families is, "how many people they send to Oxford and Cambridge every year." For this reason, Matt experienced his transition to study at Oxford University as "like a natural thing, like if you get good GCSE exam results, like your year eleven exams, you're kind of nudged, do you want to apply to this?" Matt described his secondary school as "pretty liberal" politically, but with a distinctly upper-class sensibility: "I'd say pretty liberal in the kind of American sense of like social-liberal. But they're a private school, right? And they argue against taxing private schools and they wield the arguments about private schools helping the state schools, having positive spill-over effects or whatever. So, yeah. So it was sort of like, a weirdly neoliberal education I guess at the secondary school." What Matt named their "veneer of liberalism" meant that, "when the Black Lives Matter thing happened recently, they put out a statement about like Black lives matter, obviously, like, avoiding the irony that they have like one or two Black students every year." By contrast, Khalil described his school as, "the most diverse in the community," where "there'd be four white people in the class. Only two of them are English. The other two are Eastern European or something." Where Khalil described his school as inclusive and welcoming, Matt said his was "not a school that actually really care about inclusion and they're not ones making great social waves, they're still this kind of exam-factory focus. No matter how much they talk about diversity."

Matt's critique of his school was sincere but also seemed a tad defensive, as if he was accustomed to concealing or explaining his privilege to an audience that knows such privilege is largely unearned. If UK activist cultures are in any way similar to Canadian ones – and after speaking with five young activists there, I strongly suspect that they are – then there is likely a version of what I named "performing grunge" in my 2011 book on Canadian youth activist subcultures. This refers to a form of subcultural performance demanded of young activists within certain milieus whereby one's middle classness must be obscured or elided in favour of a more working-class comportment (Kennelly, 2011a). This happens for an array of reasons and tends to unfortunately mystify the fact that many of these activist spaces are, in fact, middle class (and often white). In my view, Matt's defensiveness – and the broader performance used to accrue subcultural capital that I would argue is associated with certain forms of activism across all five of these liberal democracies – is not only unnecessary but also harmful to progressive social change. Rather, what scholars, activists, and others interested in democracy need to deeply understand is that neither Matt nor Khalil chose their social settings or circumstances of birth. These accidents of demography have shaped their life chances and access to democracy in ways that are structural and can only be changed through structural means.

As a case in point, and as also happened for Noor, it was an opportunity at his private secondary school that led Matt into activism, although he otherwise did not attribute his politicization to schooling. Asked to complete a "political compass" questionnaire for a politics class that assessed where you stand politically, Matt "came out like bottom left on that. So I joined the party that was nearest on that, which is the XX Party."[3] As a small party, the XXs held open conferences for any members to attend; it was at Matt's first conference that he met "young activists there and they invited me to the door-knocking event in a couple of weeks' time for the local elections that were coming up. I went to that and then I went to another after that and then kind of got involved from there." The "door-knocking event" involved pamphleting for the XXs door to door prior to the election, to inform voters of their position on the issues. From there, Matt became more involved in efforts to engage young people in the party, eventually becoming chair of the national youth wing of the XXs. The youth wing of the UK XXs have been active in a range of social justice issues, beyond the limits of their party's platform. At the time of our interview, this included organizing to protest the Education Minister's decision to create a "bell curve" based on teachers' predictions of student grades, to replace the national exam results that would normally have happened outside of the COVID-19 pandemic. These exam results are a major determining factor for university entrance, and the creation of what many saw to be an arbitrary bell curve was likely to disproportionately affect low-income and otherwise disadvantaged students: "All these working-class students who like had a bright future but now won't get to meet it because of the system. And, it's a similar thing and you can feel the outrage building. So just trying to bring that together and focus our anger in a way that will have an effect and hopefully get the government to do a U-turn on it" (Matt). Although Matt was more sceptical than Noor of the possibilities for democratic change through conventional, formal politics, he had direct experience of how to work within that system to try for change (through his work with the XX Party) as well as opportunities to organize from outside of the constraints of formal politics in order to put pressure on politicians to make progressive change. Unlike Khalil or Armin, both Matt and Noor had received direct training in how to circumvent the limits of liberal democracies in order to participate in other kinds of organizing efforts that they saw as avenues towards making their respective governments respond meaningfully to their concerns. Armin saw no place for himself in the liberal democratic state whatsoever, thanks in large part to the impacts of Australian racism on his sense of belonging there. Khalil had a sophisticated knowledge of the limits and problems of liberal democracy, courtesy of his university degrees, but had not encountered opportunities or networks that would give him the tools to make those systems work towards the ends in which he believed. As I will return to in chapter six, this is *despite*

---

3   I have obscured the name of the political party to maintain Matt's confidentiality.

the fact that he became very actively involved in the UK government's National Citizen Service, "a short-term state-funded voluntary youth scheme motivated by wider policy objectives and ... at the centre of a push by the UK government to foster" active citizenship (Mills & Waite, 2017, p. 67).

Conclusions

What can the stories of Armin, Noor, Khalil, and Matt tell us about the development of a democratic disposition? As I hope will be clear by the end of the book, what Bourdieu calls the "disposition to resist" – which I include as part of a democratic disposition – is bound up with structural opportunities and constraints that are inextricably linked to decades of policy-based retrenchment of the social state and higher-education systems. Khalil, Armin, Noor, and Matt are all embedded in what Arendt calls the *web of relations*, using their reflexive and deeply human capacity to *think* in order to find meaning in a world that preexists them. However, they can only make meaning from the knowledge they have acquired of the world, which is circumscribed by their respective social status and position in the field of power. Forty years of neoliberalism has widened the gap between dominant and subordinate fields, simultaneously widening the gap between those who can attain a democratic disposition and those who cannot. These differences in dispositional acquisition do not emerge through one experience alone: they are acquired through a multitude of experiences, kaleidoscoping forwards and backwards to shape the possibilities available to the individual subject. With his complex academic understanding of liberalism and his abiding interest in politics, Khalil might have become an activist, had he encountered a community of people who identified as activists and drew him into that world. But too many other things in his lifeworld obstructed that possibility, including his paid experiences with the National Citizen Service, which ironically is meant to generate active citizens in the United Kingdom. For both Matt and Noor, there were so many pathways into activism available to them that it would have been surprising had they *not* become activists.

To describe a disposition and its acquisition is an uncertain enterprise. Through careful parsing of the language-in-use by forty-six young people describing politics and democracy across five liberal democratic countries, I was able to discern at least one of the distinctive patterns of repetition that marked one's position within the political field. The *illusio* – or rules of the game – within this field includes the belief that *everything* is political, including one's identity, actions, and even one's silence. All of the activists knew the language of this field, absorbing it as part of the acquisition of habitus that allows them to traverse this political field. Young people who had experienced homelessness, on the other hand, were almost all unaware of the existence of this field and its *illusio*. Without alternate educational opportunities – available to activists through family of origin, mentors, or higher education, as will be described in more detail in the next chapter – the only language of politics available to young people who had experienced homelessness was the barren discourse of formal structures under liberal democracy. This means, effectively, that young homeless people are barred from the political field, the one in which actual politics happens and change can be made. Instead, they are left with a futile sense of dispossession from political change, seeing the system as corrupt, meaningless, or too opaque to be understood. This, in turn, drastically undermines the possibilities for a democratic society to exist, as one which meaningfully responds to the needs of all members, most particularly those who have been most disadvantaged by the current system.

3 Democratic Biographies: Pathways towards a Democratic Disposition

There is no genuine democracy without genuine opposing critical powers.
– Pierre Bourdieu (1999, p. 8)

What are the biographical conditions that shape democratic dispositions among young people? As I am using it, a democratic disposition refers to the capacities of young people to engage with the complex systems of liberal democracies in a sophisticated manner, with detailed knowledge about how to leverage impacts and create change. This is not unique to young people involved in left-wing social movements, but these are young people who universally carry this capacity, to varying degrees. In other words, these are young people who know more about the political system than how to vote; they know how to disrupt, protest, engage, change, and reshape political systems from both the outside and the inside. None of them learned these skills through formal public schooling.

There are three overlapping origin stories for young people coming into activism and identifying themselves as "political" in the manner described in chapter two. These origins cross national lines, and are shaped by class, race/ethnicity, sexuality, Indigeneity, and gender in complex ways. It matters less what liberal democracy a young person comes from than their social origins within that country to understand their biographical path towards political engagement. Class background and access to higher education are among the most important factors that facilitate young people's involvement in politics, when combined with coming from a political family. However, young people from relatively poor or working-class families could develop a democratic disposition without the class privilege if they came from highly politicized families themselves (generally in trade union or civil rights movements), or if they encountered mentors or movements which helped them into political organizing, sometimes directly, sometimes indirectly.

The first origin story for young people's politicization is the most common: they develop a democratic disposition through their families. This is typically complemented by immersion in political communities either shaped by their parents' extended networks, the places they lived, or developed on their own but with the encouragement of parents. Of note is that this manner of becoming politicized is clustered most clearly among middle- and upper-middle-class activists.

The second origin story is fairly equally shared between middle-class and working-class activists, with important distinctions explored further below: this is to come to activism through exposure in university to political movements, sometimes combined with politicizing courses that foster their interest in engaging in activism. Noteworthy is that every activist I interviewed, across all five countries, had a degree-granting university trajectory (either completed, in their near future, or in progress), rather than a diploma-granting college, completing only secondary school, or being an early school leaver. Pathways into university are distinguished by class background in typical ways: middle-class young people are expected to attend university and are matter of fact about their participation, whereas those from working-class or working-poor histories are typically the first in their family to attain a university education.

The third origin story complements, rather than contrasts with, the other two: a small minority of young activists come to their political engagement through adult mentors outside of their families. This was true for three out of eight working-class activists, but only one out of sixteen middle-class activists. The opportunities opened up by mentorship are often helpful in getting working-class or working-poor young people into university, where their politicization continues through engagement in student activism or other youth-led political work.

As was true in my Canadian research, documented in *Citizen Youth* (Kennelly, 2011a), the overwhelming majority of young activists I interviewed come from middle- or upper-middle-class backgrounds, despite sampling across a wide range of social movements in all five study countries. Of twenty-four activist participants, sixteen of them (or 67 per cent) grew up in middle- or upper-middle-class circumstances, signalled by parental homeownership, mid-ranking or professional parental occupations, and parental university education. This class story is striated by important distinctions, particularly the impacts of migration and the accompanying deskilling that occurs for families moving from the Global South to any of these Western liberal democratic countries. Nonetheless, even in families that experienced deskilling – or, more accurately, the non-recognition of their previous university credentials – after some time in their country of choice they were able to regain a comfortable foothold in the middle classes. Notable is that the migrant families of young activists were all economic-class migrants, who had moved to Canada, the United States, Australia, the United Kingdom, or New Zealand on either work visas or to pursue graduate degrees. The only exception to this among the young activists was

Alejandro, whose family moved as unskilled and undocumented labourers to the United States from Mexico.

The middle- and upper-middle-class activists are much more likely than the working-class or working-poor activists to have come to their activism through direct familial politicization – that is, attending their first protests with a parent and/or sibling, or being exposed to the mechanics of political organizing by witnessing it first-hand through family members. Of the sixteen from this class category, half of them (eight) reported that they had been politicized through family. Of the eight young activists who grew up in working-class or working-poor circumstances, only one had received direct politicization through her family, who were active trade unionists; the other seven came from politically left-leaning or non-political families who supported their activism but were not themselves politically engaged outside of voting. These seven came to activism through direct mentorship by other engaged adults (outside of their families) or were politicized through experiences in higher education, generally a mix of taking classes that educated them on political issues combined with the opportunity to engage in student or youth-led activism on campus. Of those politicized through access to student activism, two had not yet attended university at the time of our interview, but had been drawn into activism through the Student Strikes for Climate movement – Julia, who came from a working-class background in the United Kingdom, and Kanoa, who came from a middle-class background in New Zealand.[1] Both intended to go on to university in future, although for Kanoa it depended on whether she won her bid for a federal seat with a progressive political party in the upcoming New Zealand elections. Pathways into activism of the other eight middle- and upper-middle-class activists, who had not been directly politicized through activist families, were similarly linked to mentorship and/or higher education.

The clustering of middle-class activism around familial socialization and that of working-class activism around higher education and mentorship is indicative of the important role played by wealth inequality in liberal democracies. Higher education is becoming less accessible to the poor and working classes in every country in this study, which means that pathways to democratic engagement, such as those represented by activism, are narrowing. At the same time, the transmission of democratic dispositions by families with higher economic and social capital means the reproduction of this habitus among young people from more affluent backgrounds, rather than an even distribution of such resources across the entire population. Middle-class young people are also quite likely to have

---

1 Both Michael and Leila, also from New Zealand, had not yet attended university and were involved in the Student Strikes for Climate, but both came from politically active families which I categorized as their pathways into activism.

80 Burnt by Democracy

Table 2. Democratic biographies of activists broken down by class origins

	Politicized through families	Politicized through higher education and/or student activism	Politicized by other adult mentors	Total
Middle or upper-middle class	8 (50%)	7 (44%)	1 (6%)	16
Working class or working poor	1 (12%)	4 (50%)	3 (38%)	8
				24

come to activism through higher education or student activism, but one distinction between class backgrounds in this trajectory is that middle-class young people are much more likely to have experienced a politicizing opportunity prior to attending higher education, which then directs them into their course of study and also has them seeking out activist communities upon starting university. Among the working-class activists, this was also true of the three who had been politicized through adult mentors (Alejandro [US], Gregory [CA], and Karen [NZ]), each of whom directed these awakened political interests into their choice of pathways through higher education. But of the four working-class youth who were politicized most directly through higher education, for two of them it was almost accidental, a stumbling upon the right combination of timing and individuals that led them down that political path. This is significant, as it signals the degree to which structural and dispositional alignment between habitus and democratic field shapes middle-class trajectories into higher education and activist pathways; whereas working-class activists are more likely to find their way by chance, and then need to work towards aligning their habitus with that of the (largely middle-class) activist networks they encounter in higher education.

Rochelle's story provides an illustration of this process. Raised in a working-class Irish Catholic family in Glasgow, Scotland, Rochelle was the second in her family to go to university, attending only slightly after her mother decided to get her credentials to become a nurse after many years working as a cleaner. Tuition is free in Scotland for Scottish residents, which provided both Rochelle and her mum with a pathway into higher education, despite coming from a poor family without prior experience attending postsecondary institutions. As she entered university, the rest of the United Kingdom was embroiled in the largest student strike against tuition hikes that the region had ever seen. While Rochelle had an existing interest in social justice, based on her family knowledge of the oppression of Irish Catholics, she had not yet been directly involved in any kind of political action, activist or otherwise. In her first year at university, she joined protests against tuition increases, taking free buses to London that had been organized by the student strikers, and later participated in an occupation of a university building. She left university after that first year, ultimately ending up with a "patchwork kind of education," and eventually moved to London as a young adult to pursue her interest in the music industry. While in London, she joined up with other activists who were protesting housing evictions and later became one of the core organizers for a campaign begun by a group of young mothers who had been evicted from their supportive housing in East London as a direct result of government funding cuts. Rochelle described the democratic process they had developed through their collective organizing:

> I think that any organization has to have people who are pushing things forward and that have more time maybe to give, or things like that. I think that normally exists, but it has to be very transparent to the wider periphery of an organization. And what I mean by that is like certain people, if they want to become more committed to a campaign, can be on an organizing committee or structure [and] the people that are on that have to be elected by a wider periphery and everyone has to know that those certain people are able to take some decisions on behalf of the campaign. But for that to function properly, there needs to be a lot of time and space given to the wider periphery of everybody, to feed into what the campaign is doing. And you can only do that by having really regular meetings, like they can be campaign meetings and those meetings need to be very open about what the campaign is doing and about who's on the kind of more central core and allow people to feel like they are part of a campaign, even if they're on the wider periphery.

Rochelle is here describing a very intentional democratic structure and process for ensuring that there is a broad space for inclusion of diverse views, as well as a sense of accountability for those who are doing the core organizing, and ownership for those who are on the periphery of the campaign. She contrasts this mode of organizing with the student activism that she had first encountered in university:

> I've learned to kind of work in a different way because I think that [the student organizing] wasn't democratic. So one of the first points of that was that things were sort of hidden. I think maybe it's because people, they just think, "Oh, there's you know, these people here, and we know what we're talking about, we've been really involved and so we just want to push things forward" and that's all well and good. But if you're not clear about whose taking decisions and making decisions, you lose a huge important part of campaigning and it can fall apart. And so that, I think that's what I saw in some of the student bodies, that that wasn't working and that maybe they lost sight of why it's important to push democracy in a campaign, because then it makes things inclusive. And that's really important in the long run.

Her description of these two types of organizing makes a distinction between them based on being inclusive, or not; whereas the type of organizing with which she is currently involved is designed to be as democratic and inclusive as possible, her first exposure to activism at university had "lost sight" of the importance of being democratic, and thus inclusive. Beneath this description is a class story, one that I have heard described in many ways over the years I have been speaking to young activists. In my 2007–8 ethnographic fieldwork with young Canadian activists, Vincent told me: "I find if it's too friendly then there's less attention paid to internal processes and dynamics" (Kennelly, 2011a, p. 128), and Angelina explained that all of the activists are "usually all friends with each other" (ibid., p. 127). Friendship groups without democratic processes in place are likely to contain people with shared habitus; if these are friendship groups originating in university, then that habitus is likely to be a middle-class one. Thus, while Rochelle gained important organizing knowledge and networks through her time with the student activists, she ultimately left that group in order to seek out organizing opportunities that were "transparent" and "inclusive," creating grassroots democratic spaces where people from across class backgrounds could be meaningfully engaged.

Classed Origins of Democratic Dispositions

In this section, I illustrate the three origin stories I outlined above – (1) coming from a political family, (2) being politicized at university, and (3) being mentored into activism by politically knowledgeable adults outside of the family – through the stories shared with me by young activists across the five study countries. As with any attempt to categorize the complex lives of individuals, there are ways in which each person's story bleeds past the edges of a specific category, or blends one, two, or three of the categories into their biography. My intention here is not to provide firm and incontrovertible boxes within which any activist from a liberal democracy might fit; rather, I seek to draw upon their complex stories to provide what Bourdieu has called "the particularity of an empirical reality, historically located and dated, but with the objective of constructing it as a 'special case of what is possible,'... that is, as an exemplary case in a finite world of possible configurations" (Bourdieu 1998, 3; see also Kennelly 2020). In other words, I seek to demonstrate the broad patterns of biographical similarity across diverse liberal democracies for the sake of demonstrating that *biography matters*, and it can be understood sociologically through imperfect but useful categories such as class, race, and gender. This is particularly important when seeking to demystify the liberal democratic story that posits everyone as equal and thus equally able to contribute to the polis, and instead replace it with a story that agrees that everyone is equal but recognizes that everyone most decidedly does *not* have equal access to democratic engagement. The consequence of this unevenness is that we do not, and indeed *cannot*, live in a democratic society – at least not if we believe (as most people do) that democracy means attending to the views and needs of the entire population, rather than an elite subset of it.

Origin Story 1: Coming from a Political Family

Dylan's biography fits squarely into the first category. As a twenty-one-year-old, white, cis-gender, male participant from the United States, Dylan's life experiences could not help but produce a politically engaged and knowledgeable activist. "I guess I have been involved in activism really for as long as I can remember, primarily because, just, I grew up in it ... I remember when I was in elementary school, just like going off on my own, walking to town for anti-death penalty protests." Both of his parents and all four of his grandparents are vocal activists in a range of movements, including civil rights, women's, anti-apartheid, labour, and anti-war movements. Dylan grew up in a small community in the north-eastern United States, with five universities in proximity to his town. He identified this as the likely reason for the prominent protest culture in his community, and also the opportunities this opened up to him, "like when I was in high school I would skip class and go and hear people like Angela Davis [Black feminist and prison abolition activist and academic] speak." Dylan's friends were similarly steeped in politics, also with politically engaged families where "politics was just what you talked about around the dinner table."

Dylan identified himself as from an upper-middle-class family, and he grew up in a stable family home with both parents present, and grandparents active in his life. When we met, he was in his final year of an undergraduate degree at a progressive university in New York City, where he was studying the history of student, Black, and women's social movements. He had applied for a PhD and was poised to begin in the fall of 2020, should the COVID-19 pandemic permit. His entrance into university had precipitated an even deeper engagement with social movements, and at the time of our interview he was actively involved in prison abolition, immigrant justice, and a free tuition campaign, among other issues.

On the other side of the world, in New Zealand, Michael (age eighteen) had been politicized through a similar biography, despite being a mixed-race child of a Māori father and Pakeha (white) mother. Michael's Māori identity had played an important role in his political interests, but his acquisition of an activist disposition seems to have come primarily through his mother, who joined the interview periodically to ask questions and fill in details. The quality of their relationship was clear through the interview, with much mutual respect and affection. As Michael jokingly told me, "Basically, my first experience with activism was because mum couldn't afford a babysitter" or in other words, he was brought along to political meetings from a young age. Although his mother had been raised by politically conservative parents, she had begun to engage politically as a young adult and conceded that she might have been a model for Michael's activism. His father had grown up in poverty with eight siblings in a Māori household; he was the first from his family to attain a secondary school certificate, and then the first to attend university. Michael described his father as not engaged in activist politics, to which his mother broke in and said, "Just in his life, he lives it more because he grew up affected. So he's born with it because he's always been impacted by the disadvantages." Michael reported that his father is now more actively involved, for instance, having participated in the Black Lives Matter protest the week before. "So it's kind of been a bit of the kids dragging the parents," he told me, at least in the case of his father.

Michael's father had overcome intergenerational poverty through his university training as an accountant; by 2020, he was a partner at a New Zealand–based office of one of the largest accounting firms in the world. Michael's mother has a PhD and had become the director of a health centre in the city in which they lived. Both Michael and his older brother attended an extremely progressive public school with a democratic structure of student-led decision-making and flexibility for students to come and go as they pleased and learn in a style that suited them. It also was unique in covering Māori history as part of the curriculum. The family lived in a comfortable detached home not far from the city centre. Michael, who was eighteen at the time of our interview, had just completed high school and was running for office with a progressive federal political party. He had already been a "Youth MP," an opportunity that was opened up to him through a supportive teacher at his progressive school. He had an incredibly sophisticated and detailed understanding of New Zealand's political system and its strengths and flaws. When I asked where he had learned about democracy and all of his associated knowledge of New Zealand politics, he responded, "From my parents, from outside. And I'm very much involved." In other words, his detailed understanding of democracy and its functioning came from his parents, from his ability to take in information from "the outside" and from his active involvement in political life, which had been facilitated by his engagement at a progressive school near to his home in an affluent part of the city.

Angie (age twenty-four), born and raised in a mid-sized, post-industrial city in Canada, was the only young activist I spoke with who came from a working-class/working-poor background *and* received early politicization through her family. Her city's history and politics have been strongly shaped by its industrialized past, with large factories lining the shores of the nearby body of water. Not surprisingly, it is also a city with a lively history of trade union activism, including a movement begun there in 1872, seeking to standardize shorter working days. This was a major milestone in building the Canadian labour movement

(Rouillard et al., 2006). This is likely part of the reason that this city's trade union movement has been able to better withstand the attacks on unions that characterize neoliberal politics than that of other communities in Canada. This is the legacy into which Angie was born: "Most of my politics is through my mum. Like, my mum's a big trades unionist and my mum's family are all good [name of city] trades unionists. So, I grew up going to union meetings and things. So, politics was never an optional thing I guess, it was just something you did."

Angie attended secondary school in a white-dominant, rural community just outside of the city, where only her whiteness provided her with any form of privilege or invisibility. Identified early on as gifted, she noted that her rural school did not have the resources to support her learning exceptionalities, and so instead she was moved ahead several grades. This resulted in her starting her undergraduate degree at age sixteen, two years younger than her first-year peers. At the time of our interview, she was pursuing a PhD related to urban inequality, health, and LGBTQ2S+ issues, alongside her extensive activist work in the labour movement, tenant organizing, and with the New Democratic Party, the political party in Canada with the strongest ties traditionally to the labour movement. She jokingly stated that her activism began at age six, "I was one of very few six-year-olds who could really sing 'Solidarity Forever' very well."

Angie was acutely aware of how her class history set her apart from other students in her doctoral program. As the first in her family to attend university, and the only individual from her secondary school to go on to graduate training, Angie had to find her own way through the complex bureaucratic quagmire of postsecondary schooling, replete with unspoken and unwritten rules about almost everything. Growing up with a physical disability, she had learned early on from her family that her life path would have to be one that used her mind, since she could not use her body for the type of physical labour that the rest of her family did: "Post-secondary was always an expectation for me because I'm physically disabled, that this is the only thing that I had to use, it seemed I was good at, and that's what I had to do." The emphasis on practicality from both her family and her high school classmates steered her towards engineering, a field which remains sadly notorious in Canada for its sexism, even thirty years after Marc Lepine's misogynistic murder of fourteen female engineering students at Montreal's École Polytechnique shook the country to its core (Dutta 2019). Angie transferred out of engineering after her first year and shifted towards the social sciences for her graduate degrees. There she found more feminist environments but continued to face the class injuries experienced by young people from poor and working-class backgrounds who attend university: "I definitely had a bit of a chip on my shoulder and while I would like to think that's gotten smaller, it hasn't. I was like at a PhD meet and greet thing last year and a girl was talking about how she rode horses and I went, 'oh, did you do 4H?' [a rural youth program that has traditionally focused on agricultural skills]. Because that's the only way people get to do horses. No, she went to boarding school and they had horses there. And I just felt like I should dive into a pit, you know?"

When I asked Angie about who or what had most influenced her activism, she promptly said, "My mum. Like, honestly, that's the core of it." Also important in her developing politics had been a number of older activists in the labour movement who had taken her under their wing: "My former roommate jokes that there are like eighty men named Wayne who all think of me as their surrogate child. [laughter] They're all called Wayne or Rob, you know? Like that kind of guy." This was a direct consequence of her mum bringing her to organizing and union meetings from a young age, resulting in her easy acquisition of an activist habitus. Unlike male, straight, able-bodied, middle-class activists, however, her passions were also fuelled by direct experiences of injustice:

> To me politics fundamentally has to be about, this sounds so childish, but like fairness. And, like, growing up at the sharp end of politics, right? Like being disabled and working class and queer and in a tiny rural town that was completely decimated by various events that occurred at so many levels above us. Right? Like when you see your own neighbourhood and your own community be decimated by international trade deals and whatever and you're like, "this was decided by someone who would never set foot here. And because of someone's decision who has never set foot here, who has never worked a day in their lives, whose life has been just so easy, my Dad doesn't have a job now." And, that connection's always been clear to me and it's always just been so, it makes me very angry I guess. And I try to channel that anger into doing something with it.

As we will see with particular clarity in the next chapter, being impacted by injustices alone does not lead one into political action in liberal democracies. Every single young person I spoke with who had experienced homelessness had direct and often excruciating experiences of injustice. Unless they had received some sort of mentorship or support to take political action, they either turned those experiences inwards and believed themselves to blame, and/or their futile rage and feelings of powerlessness fuelled their sense that influencing the political structures around them was out of their reach.

Although Angie was the only young activist from a working-class history to be politicized directly through her family, she was not the only young activist to be fuelled at least in part by experiences of injustice. For Cadence (age nineteen), growing up Black, queer, female, and with a disability gave her plenty of avenues through which to experience injustice. But it was her family's long history with the American civil rights movement, Black student politics, and community organizing that provided her with the knowledge and skills to become an activist in response to these injustices:

[My mum has] definitely always been a strong, strong feminist just because she was the typical working woman of the '90s and like, "I have a job and I also have a family and I've got children" and stuff like that, especially only having daughters. My politics in women and women's rights has definitely been shaped by my mum. But my politics in terms of Black politics has super been shaped by my dad. So I'm the executive vice president of our Black Student Union. And my dad was also in leadership at his Black Student Union in college. So I kind of copied him a little bit. So there's that and then just going to a Black church and then also going to a pretty Black school. My upbringing was selectively homogenous. I still interacted with a lot of different cultures and a lot of different people. But when it came to community, it was definitely, definitely centred on Blackness and Black people. So both of my parents are registered Democrats. So that's always been a thing for me. Obama was a big deal. We still have the signs in our house. And my grandmother is actually really big on food insecurity and also homelessness within the Black community. So that was her job. I don't remember what her job was exactly before she retired but she did something relating to social work and food insecurity and health education. Which is also what my sister does now. So we keep a lot of our professions in the family.

I classified Cadence as "middle class" because her family owns their own home and both of her parents as well as her grandparents are university educated. But as was true for all three Black activist participants in the United States, Cadence's class background is powerfully mediated by her racialization and the racism she and her family and community face. For instance, although all three Black American activist participants had grown up in family homes that were owned by their parents, two of the three lived in majority Black and lower-SES communities that were not as well serviced in terms of maintenance and infrastructure, and all three were eligible for needs-based scholarships and bursaries for university. Given the staggering cost of higher education in the United States, this is not that surprising. On the other hand, it may be that the United States' historical emphasis on supporting home ownership over and above building or maintaining affordable public and rental housing positively benefited their university-educated and upwardly mobile families, allowing them to own their home despite racism and the high cost of living (see chapter one).

The majority of racialized activists in this study were migrants or children of migrants, the only exception to this being Indigenous participants and two of the three Black American participants (the other Black American participant and one Black Canadian participant were both the children of recent migrants from African countries). Anti-migrant employment laws and racist hiring practices mean that migration histories for racialized participants also influenced their class trajectories. As demonstrated in the previous chapter with the stories of Armin and Khalil, both racialization and migration histories can contribute significantly to the conditions that lead to impoverishment and homelessness. The activists with migration histories in this study, as noted above, were buffered somewhat from extreme impoverishment as economic-class migrants who typically came from relatively affluent origins in their home countries. Similarly to activists who had been in the study countries for multiple generations, activists with migration histories often came from politically active and engaged families, who helped them develop their skills, interests, and knowledge. Noor's story in the previous chapter provides one example of this. Mahala (age twenty-five, New Zealand) provides another.

Mahala was born in the United Arab Emirates a few months before her entire family emigrated to New Zealand, courtesy of an economic-class visa granted because of her father's profession as a medical doctor. Ironically, but not uncommonly, her father was not permitted to practice medicine in New Zealand and instead ended up moving his family back and forth between the UAE and New Zealand throughout Mahala's childhood. Mahala was thus educated fairly evenly in both New Zealand and the UAE during her elementary and secondary schooling. She decided to attend university and settle in New Zealand ultimately because of the political freedom she experienced there, which she compared positively to the repression of political activism and free speech in the UAE. Nonetheless, she was acutely aware of the limits to such freedoms in a racist and colonized nation, where her hijab marks her as an outsider no matter how long she has lived in New Zealand. Now a human rights lawyer, Mahala's current activism circulates around anti-racist organizing and decolonization, with much of her work happening in solidarity with Māori and Pacifika peoples. But her very first protest, like that of the majority of young activists, was one she attended at the behest of her mother, at age thirteen. Despite protests being banned in the United Arab Emirates, a rally for Palestine had been approved and was taking place in Abu Dhabi, the federal capital city: "I went with my mum and I think it was one or two of my sisters. [M]y mum was like, 'There's a protest. Do you guys want to go?' Because mum has been really, really active. Mum is quite an activist." Mahala describes that protest as very influential, because "that was the time where you can go out there, you can protest, you can stand up for what you believe in. That was a big pivotal time in my life. Because as a young person, it allowed me to go, 'It's okay to actually speak up.' And then right after, they banned it again, unfortunately. After that, it was like, 'Well, maybe it's not okay to speak up.'"

Although Mahala's activist organizing could not begin in earnest until she was living in New Zealand, this early experience shaped her sense of what is possible and helped generate a disposition oriented towards the potential for creating democratic social change. This was then nourished through her involvement in politically oriented extra-curricular activities, and university education in the social sciences, followed by human rights and immigration law. As with all of the activists whose biographies begin with politically active parents or families, Mahala then nourished and expanded her capacity and knowledge to more effectively challenge the injustices and inequalities she witnessed and experienced in a racist, colonialist, and class-divided (neo)liberal democracy.

Origin Story 2: Introduced to Activism through Higher Education and/or Student Organizing

The second most frequent pathway towards political activism was via exposure and training through postsecondary schooling and/or student activism, most commonly by connecting with activist cultures on campus but often supplemented by politically engaging courses that helped individuals develop a more sophisticated analysis and understanding of the social injustices they witnessed around them. Whereas eight of the middle-class and one of the working-class activists were politicized directly by their families, as described above, there is a slightly more even split between middle-class and working-class activists within this category: seven of the middle-class and four of the working-class activists described their pathways into activism with explicit reference to the influence of postsecondary schooling and/or student and youth-led activism. An important caveat is needed for this category, however: three of the young people had been introduced to activism *prior* to their postsecondary years by prominent youth-led movements that were active at the time, namely, the Student Strikes for Climate, initiated and inspired by Greta Thunberg in Sweden, and the March for Our Lives movement, initiated by high school students in the United States after a fatal school shooting in Parkdale, Florida. I will discuss these examples in more detail below.

As noted above, there is overlap between these three origin stories. Although the participants I include in this category narrate their politicization as occurring within postsecondary schooling and/or student activism more broadly, they each also describe supportive families with complementary, if not identical, politics. Thus their movement into activism may have already been conditioned by politically liberal or left-leaning parents who may not have brought them to their first protest, but certainly did not stand in their way as they became more involved in activism. I refer to this phenomenon as "dispositional priming," meaning that the acquisition of what I am describing as a "democratic disposition" often originates in a habitus that is already largely aligned with the requirements of the politically active democratic field. It is also the case that some of the people I have included within this category might have fit within the third category – of being mentored into activism by an adult outside of their family – depending on the specific trajectory of their exposure to student activism. The point I am making in this chapter is not tied so much to how many activists fit into which categories, but rather to highlight the degree to which specific class-bound trajectories shape individuals' dispositions towards meaningful political engagement, and, ultimately, what this means for liberal democratic claims about the real potential carried by any citizen to influence politics.

In Australia, Brendan (age twenty-seven) is a white man who describes his introduction to activism as happening at a public lecture he attended at Sydney University, only a few months before he was planning to resume his studies there after some time away to work. Although the talk itself turned out to be underwhelming, he was given a leaflet there about a campaign for refugee rights. He attended their meeting and then became involved, followed by involvement with a socialist group. "I kind of did a tour of the left and met every group I could and read a pamphlet or a book with them and figured out what I thought," he told me. From there, having since begun his studies at Sydney University, he became very involved with a campaign to save the Arts program that was in danger of being cut: "We had a fifty-five-day occupation of the admin building there and some student strikes, so very militant campaign. I learned about union politics through that and joined my union. I'm still a member of the academic union and we had a strike campaign two years ago as well. And I've been very involved with climate organizing for a year and a half now and linking climate organizing with union organizing."

Brendan provides an excellent example of the kind of dispositional priming I discuss above, where an individual's parents might not directly politicize them, but they nonetheless provide some sense of what is possible within activism. Both of Brendan's parents are university professors, and migrated to Australia from the United States when Brendan was four years old. When I asked him about his parents' politics, he said:

> I think my politics are very different to my parents' politics, but I think some of the stories my dad told kind of gave me a spark to be interested in politics and activism. He went to Berkeley in the sixties. He did his undergrad during the free speech movement kind of times. He wasn't really involved. He was much more a hippie in the hills [laughter]. But he would tell stories like he was involved and I kind of found out from other people more that he just wasn't but he was telling his own story. But it made me go, "that's cool, that's impressive, protest is important, protest works, student radicalism is a real thing that's related to the university." It's like, I knew about that before I got to university. So when I met people who were involved with campaigning over things and wanted to do a reading group with me or get me to come to the organizing meeting or whatever, I was like, yeah, definitely. I'll do that if I have the time and I did have the time and did it and then got involved. But there was no, like, "Dad then gave me this book or Dad said X, Y, and Z or Mum said this." Mum likes talking about politics with me but they both have slightly more centrist politics than I do.

In Canada, Darryl (age twenty-nine) also describes politically liberal parents whose politics are not as radical as his own. He situates himself as "solidly middle class," a white man growing up in a family home in a white-dominated suburb of Toronto. Darryl's dispositional priming happened through the alternative program he attended in his final year of secondary school, where the curriculum is voted on by students and there is no principal. There, he was exposed to the potential for direct democracy through the school's organizational structure, plus he benefited from a class called "The Politics of Protest." These influences shaped his interest in attending a university with an engaged activist scene, which he found at Concordia University in Montreal. There, he became somewhat involved in activist circles, but, as he narrated, "I think the real catalyst beyond just me viewing the activism as a sort of side project was the 2012 student strike." He is referencing here the Quebec Student Strike, also known as the Maple Spring, which occurred on the heels of the Arab Spring and received major media attention around the world. This was a province-wide student walkout in protest of government efforts to raise tuition and otherwise create more barriers for poorer students to attend university. The strikers made explicit reference to the neoliberalization of the university, and the need for greater equality. The strike was hugely successful and is part of the reason that Quebec has the second-lowest tuition of any province in Canada, 2.5 times less than tuition in its neighbouring province of Ontario, where I live and work. Quebec is the second most populous province in Canada, second only to Ontario; thus its low tuition fees have an impact on a large proportion of the Canadian population (Statista, 2022). Darryl's intensive activist work during the Quebec student strike led to deeper involvement in the Montreal activist scene, and then into an advocacy-focused career with an environmental NGO.

Edward's parents, like the parents of both Brendan and Darryl, were politically left but not as far left as Edward: "They consider themselves Democrats. They're not as progressive as I am, but [laughs]. They vote for Democrats nonetheless." They had both moved to the United States from Nigeria to attend university. Although his father died when he was fairly young, Edward (age nineteen) and his older brother had benefited from both parents' middle-class occupations and the family home they grew up in. He lived in a relatively small community in the north-eastern United States; when I asked him about the composition he described it as quite diverse, and particularly his secondary school as a diverse place rather than one dominated by whiteness. Of the three Black American activists I interviewed, Edward was the only one not to narrate direct experiences of anti-Black racism, a fact that he recognized as unusual in the United States: "It depends on where I am. So like here, in [the community] where I'm from, I'm treated with respect by everyone in that regards. But I know for a fact that there are certain parts of the country that would look at someone with my skin complexion and would think the other way or would think like oh, he doesn't belong here. We see this all the time."

Edward's pathway towards activism began in secondary school through impassioned conversations about politics with a good friend, which influenced him to shift his chosen major of architecture to political science upon entering university. He and his friend became more involved in activism together, but it was an internship for a state assemblyman that led to Edward being able to attend a Senate meeting in Washington, DC, where he witnessed a large-scale protest happening outside of the Capitol building: "There were thousands of people outside the Capitol in red shirts – I've forgotten exactly what the specific cause was. I think it had something to do with education, or teachers. But to see the way they're able to mobilize to try to get the attention of the people in power, right. That was something that really stood out to us, right? And from there we started to get more and more involved [in activism] to like advance our brand of politics." Edward and his friend started a branch of the Young Democrats at their university after this experience and have continued to build their political skills.

Sanaya (age twenty-eight) is a racialized woman who migrated to Canada with her parents as a child. As is true for almost all of the racialized migrant families, her parents' skills and credentials were not recognized upon first arriving in this white-dominant liberal democracy. They were able to move back into their chosen careers after some re-training, however, which allowed them access to a reasonably comfortable middle-class life after a few years. Like the other young activists in this category, Sanaya's parents were not the ones to introduce her directly to activism, but their politics were aligned with her own, if not quite as radical: "They have been overall very supportive of my activism. I think they initially had some trouble understanding and really making sense of what I do or the risks that I take, but I think they have proven to be much more supportive, which has been really nice."

Sanaya was exposed to activism as she entered her undergraduate degree by the explosion of social movements taking place at the time, including the global Occupy movement and Idle No More, an Indigenous resistance movement in Canada: "I wasn't actively involved in either, but I think just being exposed to them and hearing those discourses definitely shaped my political perspective and I think helped me understand progressive movements a lot better." After this initial exposure, Sanaya's actual entrance into organizing occurred as part of student activism on campus protesting the expansion of various pipelines in North America, including the Kinder-Morgan Transmountain Pipeline and the Northern Gateway Pipeline. From there, she dedicated her career to climate activism, becoming involved in a not-for-profit agency with offices in Canada, further expanding her activist networks and exposure to diverse movements. At the time of our interview, she narrated a long list of movement involvement, such as local Indigenous land defence fights, anti-racism work in the South Asian diaspora, supporting a progressive municipal party, and starting to look at defunding the police in the wake of the Black Lives Matter protests of 2020. When I asked her how she became involved in these movements, she said, "I think just kind of relationships. Meeting folks. I think it's just like you step into things when there's gaps and you know people that you're connected with, [who] kind of inform you or bring you in. I think relationships has been the most critical thing."

The importance of relationships for "bringing people in" to activism was a theme that emerged very strongly in my 2007/8 ethnography with young Canadian activists; from it, I developed a theory of *relational agency* grounded in feminist theorizing and the work of Hannah Arendt (Kennelly, 2009b, 2014). In *Citizen Youth*, I point out that the possibility of developing such relationships depends at least in part on: "[T]he predisposition ... [that] comes from a particular history, one that often includes a set of experiences that make activist work both conceivable and desirable. Neither this disposition nor the set of relationships that permits its development is available to all young people in equal measure" (Kennelly, 2011a, p. 123). Part of my aim with this chapter is to expand upon that earlier insight by describing the "particular history" that "makes activist work both conceivable and desirable," thus generating a particular type of meaningful political engagement. It is clearly not only in Canada where this holds true.

Similarly to Mahala, described in the previous section, who grew up in both New Zealand and the United Arab Emirates, Sandra's pathway into activism was shaped in part by growing up in a repressive regime where dissent was not permitted, in this case in Qatar. The daughter of a university professor and a university administrator, Sandra and her family moved around a fair amount when she was a child, but some of her elementary plus her secondary schooling happened in Qatar. When I met her, she was an international student in Canada, preparing to enter her second year of studies. As she told me, it was the norm for students from her secondary school to apply internationally to university; she had chosen Canada because it "had a better balance between academics and extra-curriculars" than other countries, such as the United Kingdom or France.

Sandra credits social media with her first introduction to social movements, where she was able to follow the emergence of Black Lives Matter in 2014 and where she learned about Palestinian rights, feminism, and other issues. She narrates her transition from social media to activist organizing and the role played by attending university in Canada as follows:

> I was kind of limited in terms of being able to engage in activism on the ground because in Qatar where I lived for eight years you're not really legally allowed to do that. I'm not a citizen there. Even citizens can't do it actually but if you try

they'll just deport you and your entire family which wouldn't have been a good outcome. So it's only when I was able to come here [to Canada] that I've been able to join an organizing group like the Social Justice Center and actually do something rather than just talk about things. It's important to spread awareness I guess [through social media], but it also feels really good to be able to actually organize with people.

When Sandra arrived on her Canadian university campus, she immediately sought out opportunities to become active in social justice issues. By attending a club fair, she discovered a number of relevant campus clubs: "I remember going there and I just kind of screamed. I was just so happy that I found them on campus. I was like 'Ah, oh my god!' ... That was kind of my first point of contact." From there, she began attending weekly meetings of the on-campus Social Justice Centre, where one of the organizers was particularly adept at building relationships and creating a welcoming environment: "Like she tags you specifically as a reminder, oh you know, 'Remember there's a meeting this Friday if you want to come.' So it's what made me keep going to the meetings every Friday and I figured a lot of what they do was in line with what I want to do. So I'd just keep coming and yeah, that's kind of how I got into SJC." Sandra also took a class in her first year that she found particularly inspiring, with a professor who provided readings that were "really critical and focused on structural issues," where she felt she could openly express her views and not be shut down for being, "too leftist, too radical, too whatever."

The contrast between Mahala's and Sandra's experiences in repressive states versus their ability to openly organize in liberal democracies was an important reminder to me of what liberal democracies *do* offer. A few months into the fieldwork for this project, I was confronted with another devastating reminder of the relevance of these differences, when Cihan Erdal, my doctoral student and the research assistant who had been helping me connect with activists for this project, was arbitrarily detained in his home country of Turkey. He had been there for only a few weeks to visit his elderly parents while the COVID-19 pandemic was at an ebb in August of 2020. Cihan's arrest was part of a police sweep of party members from the left-leaning HDP party (in English, People's Democratic Party) by the right-leaning government in power at the time. Cihan had served as a youth member for the party six years prior but had not been involved with the HDP since moving to Canada to pursue his doctoral studies with me in 2017 (see Kennelly, 2022). Cihan is exactly the kind of active and engaged citizen I am profiling in this chapter, the only difference being that the majority of his organizing happened in a country that has made overtures towards democratic norms, such as freedom of expression, but remains vulnerable to autocratic political leadership that can quickly shut down such freedoms.

Freedom to organize, freedom of the press, and freedom of speech are all supposed hallmarks of liberal democratic states and are often the types of freedoms that are being referenced as justifications for, say, the American invasion of Afghanistan and Iraq (with the support of every other country in this study). There are many scholars who rightfully point to the hypocrisy of this position and the embedded imperialist and capitalist interests that are advanced through such invasions. In my view, and in the views of Bourdieu and Arendt (as described in the Introduction), democracy and its freedoms are fragile phenomena that must be fought for and fiercely protected. As so eloquently detailed in Dominico Losurdo's (2014) "counter-history" of the development of liberalism, the initial expansion of liberal democratic systems in eighteenth- and nineteenth-century Britain and the United States were built upon intentional exclusions based on race, class, and gender; they privileged individual ownership and the freedom to profit through capitalist enterprises over and above the equality of *all* human beings. Liberal democracy is *not* the same as *democracy*. Although liberal democratic states have come to protect some of the freedoms that are essential to democracy, they have done so only sporadically and under pressure from social movements and other political groups. Democratic freedoms are always under threat. Importantly, two of the major factors necessary for democracy to function has been almost completely overlooked in every country that is part of this study: wealth equality and access to higher education. Under neoliberalism, disparities of wealth will inevitably grow, and higher education will be increasingly positioned as job training rather than as an essential element to develop an informed and active citizenry.

I hope that the important role played by postsecondary institutions in generating the space of possibilities for young people to become meaningfully engaged in democratic action is becoming clear in this chapter. While the majority of young people who came into activism via exposure to student organizing did so while attending postsecondary institutions, there is a subset of young people who were brought into activism *prior to* attending postsecondary schooling, although still through youth- and student-led activism. There are two recent student-led movements in particular that shaped the trajectories of several participants in this project: the Student Climate Strikes – which occurred in every study country – and the March for Our Lives movement in the United States. In my view, these examples illustrate the power of massive, youth-led organizing for "bringing in" young people who might otherwise not have become directly involved in social movements. Although their manner of organizing focused on young people in secondary schools, rather than postsecondary, the trajectory of those who became involved in such movements tended to be oriented towards postsecondary education – in other words, these movements are still bound by classed dispositions and what this means for *who* feels comfortable becoming involved.

Within my study, there were actually seven young people whose activism was inspired at least in part by these widespread movements. Of these seven, I have categorized two as being initially politicized by their parents (Leila and Michael in New Zealand): in other words, although they got concrete organizing experience through youth-led movements such as the Climate Strikes, they had already been extensively exposed to the logics of activism and political engagement by their families. Matt, whose story I share in the previous chapter, is also one of these seven. As narrated there, he came to the Climate Strikes after being politicized via the national XX Party in the United Kingdom; his activist involvement later intensified as a result of studying Politics at Oxford, surrounded by upper-middle-class peers with related social justice interests and activism. One of the seven I have categorized in the next section, of being brought into activism through a mentor (Karen in New Zealand); however, I could have just as easily placed her in the current category. The other three I have included in this subset of student organizing as their pathway into activism, because the stories they narrated made these movements central, without mention of other forms of mentorship, nor having come from politically active families. Not coincidentally, two grew up working class/working poor, while the third is an Indigenous woman from a lower-middle-class household. Each of them have families who are supportive of their activism, if a bit bewildered by it and sometimes concerned about the risks to which it exposes their children.

Julia (age eighteen) was living with her mother, her brother, and her sister in council housing (public housing) on the fringes of Manchester in the United Kingdom when we spoke. Her family had been living on welfare benefits since her mother lost her job working with autistic children, and her father had been injured in a work-related accident. She typically stayed with her father on weekends, but since the pandemic had begun she had not been able to see him in person. At the time of our interview, she was in her final year of secondary school, awaiting word on whether she would get into her universities of choice, a process that was much less clear than usual due to the COVID-19 pandemic having shut down her school before she could complete her final exams. As she told me, "I'm hoping to be the first person in this little family bubble to complete university and kind of show my little sister, my little brother they can actually go and do it."

Julia provides a beautiful account of how the Student Strikes for Climate not only introduced her to activism but also propelled her into a leadership position. The Student Strikes for Climate began in solidarity with the weekly school strike of then fifteen-year-old Greta Thunberg in her home country of Sweden. After giving a speech at the 2018 UN Climate Change conference, and famously eviscerating world leaders for their lack of climate action with the words, "How dare you," at the 2019 UN Climate Action Summit, Greta Thunberg inspired millions of young people around the world to start organizing and participating in their own regular school strikes. Julia, who describes herself as having always cared about the environment, learned in a secondary school chemistry class about greenhouse gases and climate change. As she told me, "I just assumed that because it was such a big issue that the government was doing things to stop it. I was like fifteen, sixteen at the time. So I was thinking the government's obviously going to be doing stuff about it. It's such a big issue. Why wouldn't they be doing stuff about it?" When the youth strikes for climate started in Manchester in 2019, she was perplexed about the need for it: "I was like, 'Why do we need this? Why are we youth striking?' It came up as an event you might be interested in on Facebook. Like, what's all this about? And then somebody put on that page, 'I need young people to speak about the environment.' I was like, 'Well, I like the environment. I'll research about this.'" As she began her research, she became more and more upset and angry, as she realized the extent of the climate catastrophe and the fact that the government were not acting as she had assumed they would.

> So I was like, "I'm going. I'm making a speech." And then I kind of ended up leading it in a way, with this other girl. We were just kind of like, "Alright, okay. We're going to do some chanting now." That was kind of crazy, and then the next [youth-led climate strike] in March came over, and then me and two of the girls just kind of started leading it again. And then [a local climate organizer] messaged us who was like, leading the movement to begin with. She's like, "Right, I think young people should do it now because it's a youth strike. So, I'm going to introduce you to each of us, but this is your movement. You have to organize it yourself. If you need any help, just let me know." And she kind of went off.

Julia's mother was not aware of her daughter's involvement in the strikes until several months later, by which time Julia was organizing the strikes herself:

> So, by the April one, I was like, "I've organized it, so I kind of have to be there. It's going to look really bad if I'm not there. You have to let me go." And my mum just went, "Well, even if I say no, you're still going to go, so I might as well say yeah." So, they're [my parents] great with it, but I think they are concerned. Whenever I went out, my mum was like, "Don't get arrested. I'm not having you getting arrested. I'm not bailing you out." She used to say it in a joking manner, but I know it wasn't in like some levels and tones. But my dad says it makes me interesting. He was like, "Oh, it gives you a bit about yourself. It's a conversation starter, isn't it?" You can just say, "Oh, I've worked on X, Y, and Z. And people will ask you questions." I mean that's one of the conversations I had with my university friends, because it's like loads of group chats going on, meeting new people. And we were like, right, how would you describe yourself? And I was like, "I'm Julia, and I organized youth strikes" and everything. And they were like, "That's so cool. Can you tell us more?" And I'm like, yes, I fit in the bag.

I had a good chuckle when Julia relayed that comment from her father. I could imagine my own working-class mother, originally from the United Kingdom, or her siblings (my aunts and uncles) who still live there, saying something very similar. Using the language of Bourdieu, Julia's father rightly recognizes the potential of Julia's activism for generating social capital – networks and connections – which could be converted into cultural capital – relevant and well-regarded cultural knowledge – in the right settings. The fact that she was able to connect with university-level peers on the topic indicates the ways in which this can happen, creating a feeling of "fit" for Julia among peers who do not share her class background. This pragmatic approach to the value of activism, as a means to connect with others, is different than that of the (generally middle-class) parents who immersed their children in political action and its logics from the beginning. Joanna (age twenty-six) in Australia, who was introduced to activism by her parents, articulates this nicely: "My parents didn't shy away from talking about politics and stuff with me even when I was a kid. So, there was always, I guess, an awareness of politics as a thing and of injustice, I think, as a thing. My parents didn't sugarcoat stuff really." My own children, if ever interviewed on this topic, would likely say something similar.

In New Zealand, Kanoa (age eighteen) also moved quickly from involvement in the School Strikes to becoming a leader in the movement, even though she had not been politically active prior to 2019. Like Julia in the United Kingdom, Kanoa had an existing interest in the environment and, more specifically, a feeling of frustration that her relatively affluent school was not even recycling:

> We thought we could be doing a lot if not just recycling, so through that we got in touch with other people who were advocating for recycling at their high schools and they happened to be the organizers as well for the School Strike for Climate here in New Zealand. So the circle here, New Zealand is very small so the circles all sort of touch each other, so through that we got involved in School Strike and through that we got involved with Generation Zero, which was the legislative sort of wing of activism and so we got into advocating for a stronger zero carbon bill. Through that I was nominated to go to the United Nations in New York for the Youth Climate Summit, which was amazing and I absolutely loved that experience and that was because of my involvement with School Strike for Climate.

In this short paragraph, Kanoa describes the leap she took from a concern with her school's lack of a recycling program to becoming involved with the School Strikes, then with Generation Zero; she then advocated for a stronger carbon emissions bill in Parliament, which led to her attending a UN Climate Summit in New York. As a mixed race Māori-Pacific Islander, Kanoa also benefited from mentorship and support offered by other Indigenous activists and organizations in New Zealand. She went on to become very involved with one of the federal political parties, running for office in the most recent federal election. I will discuss this kind of sequence of events and its implications for young people's political engagement in much greater detail in chapter five.

The March for Our Lives youth-led anti-gun movement in the United States emerged after the shooting at Marjory Stoneman Douglas High School in Parkland, Florida, on 14 February 2018, which left seventeen students and staff dead and wounded seventeen others. March for Our Lives quickly expanded to encompass marches in 800 other locations in the United States and around the world (Laughland & Beckett, 2018); the organization continues to exist, with their stated mission being, "To harness the power of young people across the country to fight for sensible gun violence prevention policies that save lives." Rebecca (age twenty) in the United States described the March for Our Lives movement in terms very similar to those used by others to describe how the School Strikes for Climate brought them into activism. She told me that prior to this movement, she had not considered herself political despite having long been associated with theatre and the arts, which exposed her to people who are "being very free and progressive." These relationships led to her attending annual Pride marches, and then becoming involved in the Feminist Club at her high school, with whom she did the Women's March in Los Angeles shortly after Donald Trump was elected. Despite attending such events, she says, "I really didn't see that as like I'm being an activist. It was just kind of me, you know, knowing that this is right. And I'm just kind of doing this with me and my friends." This changed in her final year of high school, which was when the Marjory Stoneman Douglas school shooting happened:

> I remember just standing in my bedroom one night and watching YouTube videos of the kids being interviewed and like this awful footage they took during that time, and I was overcome with just sadness and I was just crying and then I had like this switch for a second and I was like, "what am I doing sitting here and watching these videos and crying? I should do something." And, so, then that night I drafted an email to my school administration about me wanting to raise funds for March for Our Lives and I wanted to put on like a theatrical performance in the performing arts centre.

Although her own school administration was supportive, the school district had already issued an edict prescribing formal consequences for students participating in the walkouts or openly discussing gun control. The rationale for this, as told to Rebecca by her school principal, was that it was "not a bi-partisan issue" and that they "didn't want to make it political." This suppression of progressive activism on school grounds is not uncommon, sadly, and reflects the (small-c) conservative and legalistic approach to citizenship education occurring in all five liberal democracies within this study, discussed in more detail in chapter six (see also Erdal & Kennelly, under review). Rebecca, however, was unphased by this response: "I was like, that's fine, I'll put on acts that are like, song, dance, poetry, and movement that is pertaining to the effects of gun violence or bringing world peace, things like that, and just donate funds for March for Our Lives." While she was busy organizing the fundraiser at her school, and despite the warnings from the school district, Rebecca started to participate in school walkouts. She helped organize the first one on her high school campus, to avoid the distribution of "tardies" (late slips) and detentions that were part of the consequence for students marching off campus. But she decided to take the risk and organized the second one off campus. When I asked her whether the threat of punishment being handed out by the schools affected turnout, she said that she thought yes, because:

> I think there were a lot of people that are overachievers in a sense and really good kids that that would just scare them. They weren't against it, they were just like, "I just don't really want to go through that." I remember at that first on-campus walk out, I was passing out pins and it was things like #neveragain and I would go round and people would take it, but some people were like, "I don't want to wear that." So there is a combination of, yes, that was our political view, but also at the same time just a lot of people were afraid of being bold in case they were targeted.

Public schools are one of the main ways in which the state is able to communicate its norms and expectations to the population, through both formal and informal, or "hidden" curricula. This is an excellent example of the hidden curriculum so commonly experienced by young people in liberal democracies – not only in the United States, but in every country under study – regarding the acceptable limits to young people's citizenship behaviours.

After completing her final year of high school, Rebecca moved to New York to study theatre in university. Growing up in relative poverty with a single mother, by the end of her first year she decided that the tuition fees were not sustainable and instead shifted her attention to building her theatre career from the ground up. Simultaneously, she continued the organizing work she had begun with March for Our Lives:

> [After moving to New York], I got connected with someone from March for Our Lives from the national level and then someone appointed me New York State Action Director, which is like essentially what I was doing before, of putting on events and they could be performance events and raising money for the organization. So since then I've done a couple of those. I went to the conference they [March for Our Lives] had, the national conference in Texas last summer. And that was actually really incredible because I've been doing all of this activism work and I've been combining it with my performance skills, but then I was in a set-

ting where they were formally teaching you how to be an activist. [There were] workshops, like how to check your privilege in activism and all these things that you don't really technically get anywhere else. And I feel so lucky that I got that because it's something that I feel should be taught in schools because it's such a big thing for our generation. You really have to be careful with being involved in these movements too because [of the need to be] like checking your privilege and using the right language to include everyone.

Across three different countries and two different movements, the stories of Julia, Kanoa, and Rebecca help reveal several important elements that contribute to moving young people into activism. All three of these young women had pre-existing interests in the issues at hand, but none of them came from families that could help them direct those interests into activism, nor were their schools of much use in encouraging them to act on their concerns in the public realm. None of them were yet at university, where they may have encountered social justice groups, social movements, or justice-oriented classes. They each took the initial step towards the movements in question, and then were welcomed, mentored, and exposed to networks that allowed them to deepen their involvement and participate in national and international opportunities. This happened because there were organizational apparatuses in place to bring them along in this manner, likely paid for by charitable donations and through grants and fundraisers. These types of organizations are essential to creating space for young people who would not otherwise receive any form of political education, to bring them into activism and become part of larger movements. Despite the purity politics within certain activist circles that continue to create hostility towards such institutionalized forms of activism, it is organizations such as Student Strikes for Climate and March for Our Lives that open up a broader progressive space for young people to become politically engaged in issues that matter to them.

Origin Story 3: Mentored by Trusted Adults outside the Family

The third pathway into political engagement described to me by young activists involved encountering and then being mentored by a trusted adult or adults outside of the family. Sometimes this was a teacher, sometimes an adult connected to a community organization. Typically, the adult mentor(s) did *not* introduce the young person directly to activist organizing. Rather, they helped support the young person in pursuing their political interests through more conventional means, although always beyond simple voting. It was from these introductions into alternate political realms that the young people would then develop the networks and dispositions that permitted them access to activist organizing and a broader understanding of their potential for effecting social change.

I began to get a sense of the important role played by adult mentors in Alejandro's life early in our interview. Despite being an undocumented migrant whose parents worked low-wage, under-the-table jobs, Alejandro (age twenty) was entering his third year at one of the "elite" or private universities in the United States, with a 2020–1 annual tuition fee of US$59,072. He told me he was there on full scholarship, covering his housing, meals, books, tuition, and transportation costs. I quickly asked more questions, trying to make sense of how he had managed to access such opportunities in the context of neoliberal cuts and extreme inequality. He told me about volunteering at a free clinic during high school, which helps to provide health care to low-income and uninsured people. There, he met several mentors, including the executive director of the organization, who also happened to be a college advisor. Through her coaching and support, Alejandro learned invaluable information about how to navigate the complicated American postsecondary system:

> I would say, "I want to go to college," just because I've seen it through different films, movies and stuff, and just kind of how they portrayed it just made me really want to go and pursue something better for myself and help out my family. So she ended up guiding me through the college process. She does admissions for UC Davis. She's already trained for that. So we ended up applying, I think, to sixteen schools. Yeah, sixteen or seventeen. And then I end up getting into ten or eleven of those which were UCs [University of California campuses], Cal[ifornia] States, private schools. When she was helping me apply, she taught me about, in colleges, there's a nonbinding and binding school. So when I was considering schools, I obviously considered financial resources, like a big necessity and part of my decision, like where I ended up going. So from there, I ended up applying to the private schools. I applied to Stanford, USC, Pitzer and, there is another one. Redlands. So I ended up getting into full rights from USC and Redlands University and that was because she helped me apply, and some of those schools are all I need. They don't look at your financial [needs], I mean when they accept you as a student. She told me, that's the difference between Cal States, UCs versus privates. That's why I applied to private schools [because they will accept students on full scholarship no matter their financial situation]. And then also at the same time, I was applying to external scholarships that I could find, but it was hard because of my [non-citizenship] status. So I was trying to figure out, OK, what scholarships that I do want. Even though I did qualify, the only eligibility I didn't meet was like, citizen. So that was kind of another manoeuvre, how to overcome. But that's how I was able to like . . . I just applied and then I just did a lot of essays and worked with her a lot, like, to write my essays. I think I spent, on my application for USC, like over a month. Just writing them.

The same mentor who helped Alejandro get into a high-quality, private university on a full scholarship also helped connect him with opportunities in the community that would eventually lead him into his activist networks. Alejandro's mentor, as the ED of the free clinic, would apply for grants that allowed him and other students volunteering at the clinic to attend leadership camps:

> And so she ended up sending me to different groups of camps that I applied to in leadership, like there is one called CLYLP, which is the Chicano Latino Youth Leadership Project, which is in Sacramento. I got into that one. I went to RYLA, which is the Rotary Youth Leadership something. And then there's also one called CLI, which I went to in my sophomore year going into junior year [of high school], and that one's called Community Leadership Institute. And through that camp, we talked about, CLI specifically, isms, different types of isms, like socioeconomic, socialism, as well as like classism and racism, homophobia, different things like that. That's why I kind of learned . . . When we go to those camps, like this one specifically, we're supposed to bring back a project, community service project, so the year before they started the outreaches for health education. And then when I went for my year, we brought in education equity, so that's back to our community. So that's kind of how I started education equity [activism] within [my community].

Similar to Rebecca, Julia, and Kanoa, who received activist training via conferences they attended after becoming involved in the Student Climate Strikes and the March for Our Lives movement, Alejandro was exposed to key ideas that are central to progressive organizing (such as anti-oppression training, understanding capitalism, and organizing with the community) through these leadership camps. This provided him with the language and skills needed to develop a democratic disposition that allowed him to "fit" in and begin to participate in the field of left activism.

Karen's entrance into activism in New Zealand occurred with the encouragement of a teacher. Like Julia and Kanoa, Karen (age twenty-four) remembers being concerned about the environment from a young age; this interest was noted by a teacher who put her name forward for a conference when Karen was about fourteen. As she describes, "And then that conference led to another one. And that was Rio+20 back in 2012. It was one of the big UN sustainability conferences." It was at the UN conference that Karen got her first experience of direct-action activism: "And there [at the UN conference], it really tied together in terms of climate change activism and the importance of having good science and good laws and good policies. But, also, that was my first experience of protesting and getting UN security guards to throw you out of the conference. A lot of that was a lot of fun and a good first exposure to activism." Karen continued her work with environmental organizing, which led to other opportunities and involvement in formal left politics in New Zealand. With first-hand experience of being in the foster system, Karen later applied the activist skills she had learned through the environmental movement to try and improve the foster system (discussed in more detail in chapter five).

From my interviews with both Karen and Alejandro, I got the impression of individuals who are highly motivated, charismatic, and intelligent. Upon receiving a nudge from adult mentors into opportunities such as conferences and leadership camps, which led to greater learning, building activist networks, and gaining activist skills, it was their energy and motivation that drove them ahead to apply these skills to issues about which they were passionate. As was true for Julia, Rebecca, and Kanoa, neither Karen nor Alejandro came from families that had the resources or knowledge to guide them into activist opportunities. They were lucky enough to encounter mentors or youth-led movements that helped them cultivate those interests and expand their knowledge and networks, so as to develop democratic dispositions that allowed them to move far beyond the simplistic and highly individualized accounts of democratic action available through civics curriculum in school.

Conclusions

The stories of activists' pathways towards politicization are both personal *and* reflect the structural effects of neoliberalism and wealth inequality on the acquisition of democratic dispositions. As I hope is clear from the detailed accounts contained in this chapter, each individual had their own pathway into activism, often driven by a passionate desire to create a more just society. As I hope is also clear, this passionate desire could be fanned into the flames of activism and the concrete knowledge required to effectively shift liberal democratic systems only under specific, class-bound biographical opportunities. That the majority of young activists came from activist families was not surprising to me; this was the same finding in my Canadian ethnography of young activists over a decade ago (Kennelly, 2011a). That most of these families were middle or upper middle class was also not a surprise. In my 2011 book, I trace in great detail the deeply embedded classism, racism, colonialism, and sexism that has shaped Canadian society and its education systems and left their traces through inherited ideas about the "good and productive citizen" and who gets to take up this mantle and then push it into the territory of the "rabble rousing" activist. Although I will not be undertaking the same level of historical analysis for each country in this book, the analysis of citizenship education in each of these countries, provided in chapter six, will, I hope, reveal the degree to which similar mechanisms are at play in the education systems of all the liberal democracies in this study: privileging the rational, responsible, and individualized citizen who engages with the state only through formal politics and most primarily through voting, and completely ignoring the deeply class-, gender-, and race-bound politics of this construction of the "good citizen" (see Kennelly & Llewellyn, 2011 for our detailed discourse analysis of Canadian civics curricula in the 2000s along these lines; and Erdal & Kennelly, under review, for a detailed analysis of citizenship education curricula in all five study countries).

Of course, one might argue, there are the activists who did NOT come from middle-class households, nor from politically active families. These were the activists who followed their passions into youth-led movements, or were invited along to rallies and other events, and developed their skills and knowledge in this manner. These are important examples of the possibilities for expanding political dialogue and the development of meaningful political skills in liberal democracies. Yet they remain class-bound due to their tight connection to postsecondary schooling. Even the young people who came to activism prior to postsecondary via youth-led movements like the Climate Strikes were already on pathways towards higher education. In neoliberal societies, where cuts to postsecondary education, the collapse of affordable housing supports, and the decimation of social welfare benefits has intensified and entrenched poverty, these pathways are often closed off before they are even encountered by those who are most marginalized. In other words, those who are most negatively impacted by neoliberal policy decisions are also those who are most disenfranchised from meaningful participation in democratic systems. This is clearly unjust, as a democracy is only as democratic as the space it provides for all experiences and voices to be heard. But it is also a potentially fatal flaw: by shutting down the avenues of access to meaningful politicization, those with the most intimate knowledge of the failures of the systems they must endure are also unable to share their experiences in a way that could improve the systems and help society function more equitably for everyone. I believe that the next chapter will help reveal ways in which these failures of democracy are played out, with a focus on the participants in this study who have experienced homelessness.

4 Democracy's Failures/Failures of Democracy

Very often the persons who are able to speak about the social world know nothing about the social world, and the people who do know about the social world are not able to speak about it.
– Pierre Bourdieu (in Eagleton & Bourdieu, 1992, para. 21)

So far in this book I have traced the growth of inequality due to neoliberalism across the five liberal democracies that are the subject of this book (chapter one); I have described what I mean by a democratic disposition, including specific views of what it means to "be political" (chapter two); and I have outlined in detail the manner in which individuals acquire such a disposition, substantially structured by their social location in hierarchies of inequality (chapter three). I hope that each of these chapters has delivered a sense of some of the dynamics by which inequality creates differential opportunities for young people to participate meaningfully in creating societies that meet their needs and thus are, by definition, more democratic. If that has not been clear, I hope in this chapter to make it extremely clear that *inequality is wrecking the possibilities for democracy* across liberal democratic countries that have been shaped by neoliberalism. This assertion begins from the assumption that (a) liberal democracy is in itself an inherently flawed system that (b) needs to be constantly re-worked, contested, and adjusted in order to meet the needs of its citizens. It also begins with the acknowledgment that liberal democracy is an extremely entrenched political system that is not likely to go away any time soon. Neoliberalism, on the other hand, has only been dominant for forty years or so. It can and must change.

In this chapter, I begin with the stories of Tamara (Canada), Maggie (United Kingdom), and Scarlett (Australia). These three young women each come from structurally marginalized positions within the state – that is, they were each born into communities or situations that have generated systematic disadvantages for them throughout their lives. They each have lived experiences of liberal democratic state systems that have failed them and others like them, and they all have cogent and thoughtful critiques of those systems as well as concrete ideas about how to improve them. What they do not share is equal access to a democratic disposition. In other words, despite their broadly similar experiences of structural inequalities, and despite their respective insights into how to generate more just outcomes, they have extremely varied skills and capacities to transform this knowledge into political advocacy. This access to a democratic disposition has everything to do with the degree to which they have been supported to wrench themselves out of poverty and into higher education, and the degree to which they have been able to engage with and learn from mentors or other activists.

Tamara: "You're Not Allowed to Close My File"

What is lost when young people living in poverty are disenfranchised? Tamara's story helps illustrate the painful disconnection between the political advocacy that could happen by young people for their own rights, and their lack of knowledge about how to do so.

When Tamara (age twenty-six) and I met for our interview at a youth drop-in centre in Ottawa, it was month eight of the COVID-19 pandemic. We sat across from each other with a large plastic panel separating my side of the desk from hers – a pandemic precaution – in the office the drop-in centre had provided for my use for the day. At age twenty-six, she had technically "aged out" of using the services at the drop-in, which are for youth between the ages of sixteen and twenty-four, but she was able to attend if she needed the food bank or if she had an addictions counselling appointment, as she did that day. This is one of many work-arounds Tamara has negotiated with the systems of care that she requires. Indeed, what was most striking to me throughout our interview was the ingenuity, clarity, and strategic thinking she brought to ensuring that she and her 2.5-year-old son were receiving the care they needed.

Tamara had been adopted at age two into a family in Canada, after having been born in the United Kingdom. She does not know her birth family or the circumstances surrounding her adoption. At age ten, she was surrendered by her adoptive mother to the Children's Aid Society (CAS; Ottawa's Child Protective Services), "because my mother couldn't handle my behaviour, but she didn't realize my behaviour was because of my father abusing me." At the group home where she lived until age thirteen, her behaviour only worsened and her mother eventually made her a Crown Ward (a ward of the state) rather than take her back. At age nineteen, Tamara moved out of the group home and in with a friend until her suicide attempt resulted in her losing that housing. From this time on, she circulated between different shelters in Ottawa until around age twenty-three, when her son was born. She has been housed since that time, with government-provided rent supplements in the private market; however, CAS apprehended her son at birth and she did not get him back until he was twenty-two months of age (about eight months before our interview). He had been apprehended because her own CAS worker thought that Tamara would not be able to care for him, due to his many complex health issues. But, as she told me, "I fought and fought and fought the worker that I had before. She did not want him coming home. I got a new worker and within four months he was in my care." Our interview was periodically interrupted by calls from CHEO, the Children's Hospital of Eastern Ontario, where her son is a frequent visitor. Tamara monitored the calls carefully, in case there were any urgent issues arising to which she needed to attend.

Tamara's fighting spirit, her intelligence, and her ability to form strong bonds with people are part of what allowed her to get her son back. As she explained to me, she had been assisted by an organization called Family Supports Ottawa[1] – of which I had never heard, despite my many years of research and volunteer work in Ottawa's homeless youth-serving sector. Working with them also requires an exception to be made for her, due to her current age:

> So they generally work with people from the ages of sixteen to twenty-one. Now, I kind of felt like I got special privileges, but the person who is the regional director has known me since I was thirteen. So she has been in support of [my son] coming home for me since the day he got apprehended. She was at all my CAS meetings, at all my court dates. She fought to get him home with me because she also worked for an organization called Future Hope Adoptions. So, if my kid wasn't to come home, we were going to go through her for the adoption, but then she got this job [as regional director of Family Supports Ottawa]. And with her getting this job, CAS was like, okay, she [Tamara] has more supports now. We can send him home. Because once a month on like Friday to Saturday, Family Supports Ottawa will take [my son] for those days to give me relief.

Tamara's knowledge of the CAS system is breathtaking. I had the very stressful experience of having my child's school call CAS about a month prior to meeting Tamara – my precocious and gregarious seven-year-old had been making up a story for her friends, claiming that her father threw her around. This was overheard by a teacher on the school yard, who called CAS. I wish I had known Tamara during this time, so she could have explained to me the various processes and people we would encounter.[2] As she told me in relation to her own case:

---

1 I have changed the names of the organizations for the sake of maintaining Tamara's anonymity.
2 Our upper middle-class privilege protected us from the worst of the possible outcomes of this scenario, and our child was not immediately apprehended, unlike in Tamara's experience. After a social worker came to meet with us and had individual conversations with both of our children, she thankfully closed our file.

So the way it is with CAS is they have the intake department and they have the actual workers. So, the intake department will get the phone call about the child. The intake worker will then apprehend the child. After two months of the intake worker working with the family, they transfer the file to a main primary worker that would work with them for the next year or however long. Now in my case, I've been switched [workers] four times. One worker left the department, another worker was just moving departments, and then I just got this worker and I told her that she's not allowed to change workers on me. [laughs]

Tamara's deep understanding of how the system works allows her to make it work better for herself and her son. Now that she is stably housed and has the supports in place for her son, CAS is expecting to "close her file" within the next six months, meaning that they will no longer be monitoring her capacity to be a good parent to her son. Tamara does not want this to happen, because she knows that she is vulnerable to having others call CAS on her – as my child's school did on us – and she does not want to be shuffled through several more workers who do not know her or her son. As she explained to me:

> TAMARA: Well, yeah, my CAS worker, she's like, "So in six months when we close your file are you going to be okay with that?" And I looked at her and I'm like, "You're not allowed to close my file." She looks at me and she's like, "Why can't I close your file?" And I looked at her and I'm like, "You're not an asshole." And she's like, [laughter] "I'm not an asshole? What does that have to do with anything?" And I said, "Well, Andrea, you know me. You know my file. You know how I am with my kid, so if I get a phone call right now on me [to CAS] from someone saying that I'm doing drugs or I'm partying or this and that, you're not going to believe it. You're just going to call down, do what you're supposed to do, follow up on it. But that's all. It won't mean an apprehension. Versus someone who doesn't know me, does not know my file, and they get a phone call about me. Boom, my kid could get taken." And she's like, "You've thought a lot about this already." Yes, yes, I have.
> JACKIE: And so will she not close your file?
> TAMARA: So in six months, they might want to close my file but I told them I'd prefer it if they kept it open. So she's going to see what she can do to keep it open. Because if there's really no parenting concerns anymore, they close the file. Right? So.

Tamara's fluency with the systems she relies upon could easily, under the right circumstances, translate into political advocacy to improve those systems. But the disjuncture between her intimate knowledge of these systems – which include CAS, the shelter system, affordable housing, and the supports she could access as a young person on ODSP (the disability benefit in Ontario) – and what role government played in mandating and funding those systems, was stark. When I asked her about voting, she told me that she had not yet voted, although a friend had suggested she should. In response, she had told her friend, "Well, considering the fact I don't know what I'm voting for, what's the point? That's literally my wording because I don't know anything about voting, I don't know anything about democracy. I don't know anything about any of the stuff that goes on like that, right? Because I don't pay attention or follow it." When I asked her what information she thought she would need in order to vote, she said, "What is the purpose of voting? Why do we need these people to represent us? They do a horrible job half the time anyways. That's why there's no point of voting for me."

This was a common response from homeless young people about why they do not vote, and I think it is an entirely fair point. However, what has been striking in this study is that often activist youth would say the same thing – voting is flawed, the system does not represent my views, politicians are corrupt – yet they would vote anyway. The key difference between these two groups of young people is not so much their views on voting and politicians, but their knowledge of the political system. When I asked Tamara what she thought the three most important issues were for government to deal with, she responded: mental health, drug addiction support, and housing. She has experience with all three systems, and extremely acute insights into their failings and strengths. After providing her thoughtful analyses of these systems, we had the following conversation:

> JACKIE: You're so insightful because you're going through this and living it and analysing it. So what if I were to say, the political party that's in power provincially has the power to fund or not fund housing? Does that then, like has that connection been made for you ever?
> TAMARA: Please repeat what you just said? If you can kind of word it in something that I might –
> JACKIE: Sure, so: We live in the city of Ottawa.
> TAMARA: Yes.
> JACKIE: And the province of Ontario.
> TAMARA: Yes.
> JACKIE: And then the country of Canada.
> TAMARA: Yes.
> JACKIE: So there's different levels of government. You've got the city, the province, the country.
> TAMARA: Okay.
> JACKIE: So, housing is a bit complicated. I'll try and make it less complicated in terms of who provides it. Housing is provided by the City of Ottawa.
> TAMARA: Yeah.
> JACKIE: You know that – you're dealing with them.
> TAMARA: Yeah.
> JACKIE: But is funded by the province of Ontario.

TAMARA: Okay.

JACKIE: Yeah. And who is running the province, like, who gets elected to be premier and the members of provincial parliament, they have the power to decide how much money goes into housing.

TAMARA: Oh, okay.

JACKIE: Yeah. You didn't know that?

TAMARA: No.

JACKIE: Because how would you know that? Because it's specialized knowledge and it should not be.

TAMARA: Yeah. I mean, they should still at least get some more funding in at least or raise some of the like, increase [the shelter allowance] for the people on ODSP or OW. You know what I mean? And I'm not asking them to do miracle working, but at least instead, have it be like $1400 or $1300 for a one bedroom, [right now] they get $900. A lot of people couldn't afford that on OW or ODSP because that just means we starve ourselves. But we have places like this [the youth drop-in centre] that will give us food bank. You know what I mean. If I wasn't on a market subsidized [rent subsidy] thing, I'd be paying $1600 for my two bedroom.

JACKIE: I know. Which is actually cheap for Ottawa.

TAMARA: It is, it is very cheap for Ottawa but it is like –

JACKIE: I know. If you're on ODSP, how would you pay it?

TAMARA: Like you can't afford that at all.

JACKIE: That same, that province. They set the ODSP and the OW rates.

TAMARA: Really?

JACKIE: Yes. They've been keeping [the rates] low for years. Knowing that, I can see the wheels turning. Are you like, "fuck yeah, I'm going to vote next time" [laughter].

TAMARA: I don't know. It's just weird. Because you'd think that like, more people would be off the streets or this and that and really there's a lot, like, if you really look at it, there's like thousands of people that are homeless every year.

JACKIE: Oh, yeah.

TAMARA: Like, and the numbers are going up.

JACKIE: They sure are. Yeah. For sure.

TAMARA: And a lot of families are now homeless and like, oh, yeah. The numbers are going up. There's almost never any space at the shelter anymore.

Due to her behavioural and health issues, combined with poverty and no parents or guardians to advocate for her, Tamara was not well accommodated in school; she believes she has the equivalent of about a grade six education. She has received no civics education of any sort. The very brief political education that I provided during our interview is unlikely to have a lasting impact, although I can hope that she might use that information as a jumping off point to learn more about the provincial parties and use her intelligence and charisma to become more politically engaged, even if only in conversations with peers in the community.

That said, it is important to recognize that it will take much more than a belated and well-intentioned political education to generate meaningful opportunities for young people like Tamara to contribute democratically. Given the extremes of wealth inequality that shape our social and political worlds, asking young people who are positioned at the bottom of this opportunity structure to "sit at the table" and advocate for social change is to put tremendous and unfair additional burdens on them. Maggie's experience helps us better understand the dynamics that lead to this.

Maggie: "I'm Not Having This"

When Maggie (age twenty-four) and I met over Zoom on 31 July 2020, the United Kingdom was getting its first taste of what the Meterological office would later call the "August heat wave" of 2020; 31 July was actually hotter than this heat wave, with a temperature measured at Heathrow Airport of 37.8 degrees Celsius (Met Office, 2020). Sitting in a Traveller's trailer for our interview, Maggie's long brown hair was pulled back in a tight ponytail and her brow was beaded with sweat. Our interview was periodically interrupted by young children who would pop in briefly to ask a question, which Maggie would field patiently before sending them off. "I kind of describe it as family-rearing practices," she told me. "The whole family rears the child essentially. It's kind of what it feels like. So if I'm disturbed today, that's why. There's like ten kids at my door almost every day. They've already been in six times today. I'm the pied piper so I bring them to the park. Or buy them an iced lolly." Maggie was born and raised in a Traveller community with roots in Ireland, although she herself was born in the United Kingdom. Her activism, master's dissertation, and paid work all circulate around the stigma, persecution, and prejudice experienced by Gypsy, Roma, and Traveller communities and how to change it.

Like the rest of her community, Maggie grew up quite poor and without the expectation that she would go to university. She attended the United Kingdom's public school (state-funded)[3] system and found some teachers there who inspired her, but more who mistreated her and left her feeling that she did not belong in the education system. Nonetheless, a series of experiences and encounters with mentors eventually nudged her first into community college, and then into university. When we met, she was developing a theory for her MA dissertation that explained why education policy typically did not meet

---

3 Confusingly, the term "public school" in the United Kingdom is typically reserved for what other countries would refer to as "private schools," that is, funded through high tuition fees paid by individual students and their families. Maggie did not attend one of these, but rather a government-funded school that is available without tuition fees for all young people – what other countries call the "public school" system.

the needs of Gypsy, Roma, and Traveller communities. She was also working as a policy analyst for a small charitable organization that focuses on Traveller issues; she is the only Traveller employed there. As she noted, the confluence between her lived experiences, school research, activism, and paid work could be beneficial but also exhausting:

> For my colleagues I guess they can go home. You can leave the job but actually there is no clear line for me from what I'm doing professionally to what I am personally. My activism spills over into everything. Like, although I work at [the charity for Traveller communities], I also do stuff for Labour charity, which is like a collective of Labour-leaning Traveller activists who lobby Labour [the political party] and stuff. I then do stuff with Traveller Pride, which is like a collective of LGBT folk. So you kind of, you do this, but then also like you're a social change maker for this organization and you do this for this. And like I said, there's sometimes no clear boundary.

In her paid role at the Traveller charity, Maggie recently attended a presentation by a government "policy lab," which was seeking feedback on the work they had been doing on a recently announced national strategy to improve the lives of Gypsy, Roma, and Traveller communities in the United Kingdom. Although her manager was meant to be there, in the end Maggie was there alone: "I was the youngest person at the table and the only Traveller sitting at the table talking about Traveller issues." Maggie happened to know one other person there: "I'm friends with one of the women that works in that [government] department. And although her manager knows that we talk, I don't think she realizes we're actually friends."

At one point, the presenters, "put all this research up on the walls and it was like education, crime, housing, health. Right?" Presenters asked attendees to walk around the room and add their thoughts to the posters on the walls.

MAGGIE: And I walked, there were like five or six sections and I walked to the first two and I was like, "oh, this is awful." Like, awful.
JACKIE: Like the research was wrong or what was it?
MAGGIE: It was really poor.
JACKIE: Okay.
MAGGIE: Their research approach was problematizing the people. There was no critique of the system. And there was so much that was missing. So I went to the second [poster] and I walked half-way to the third one, then I was like, "I actually can't, so I'm just going to sit back down." I was like, "Until this is over I'm just going to get really annoyed." And really because I know the research inside and out. I can reel them off to you, facts, and stats, and numbers. I'm thinking, "please tell me you just started this [research] this morning!" But, anyways. So I sit back and the member of staff [who Maggie knows], so she works in that department and

she's beside me. She kind of turns her head and whispers, "I don't agree with this. I've tried to tell them this is all wrong but they're not listening. I've been saying this for months." I was like, "Okay. Leave it to me."

Maggie waited while everyone finished going around to the posters and gathered at the table, and then she let "other people feedback first because once I start I'm not going to shut up." When it was her turn to speak, she let them have it: "And then I was like, 'Did you start this this morning? Because if I showed that to my [master's] tutor, she'd tell me out of her office and stop wasting her time.' I was like, 'This is, in the nicest way possible, it's abysmal. The whole thing here is about the people. There's no critique of the system. Yes, we know education outcomes are poor – there's no understanding of why. Other than [you say] for cultural reasons.' And I was really like, really trying to hold back a lot." After her feedback, the presenters moved on to show the group a video: "And the only way I can describe it is they wanted to follow Travellers around with cameras to learn more about Travellers, for the policymakers to have a better understanding of the people there. So I'm watching this video and the more it goes on, the more stressed I'm getting because I'm thinking, have you not seen any of the documentaries on Travellers?" Again, Maggie allowed others to provide feedback first, but she noticed that nobody else was speaking up against it, and she thought to herself, "If I don't say something, this is going to happen." So she spoke up again:

I was like, "It's not a zoo. Like, we're not zoo animals. Are you serious?" They're like really demeaning [to me]. She's [the presenter] trying to be like, you know, "[This is] from a research perspective." And I'm like, "Do not come at me, I have worked on loads of different research, in different areas. Please don't even come at me. I'm not a stupid Traveller you have sitting at the table, so that's not me." I was like, "I know policies." I was like, "Okay, let's do this: so how many of you have been followed around with cameras?" And you could tell every one of them was really uncomfortable. No one had answered. And I was like, "How about you, and you, and you?" I made them all answer and they were like, none of them, and I was like, "Exactly. Like, you're missing my whole point." And they kept trying to lead me into an agreement of this and I was like, "I'm not having it. Basically, if you think I've started today, I've not even got warmed up. I will singlehandedly ensure that this does not take off, that no one takes part in it." I was like, "You don't understand the risks of this for the people that are involved with this." I say, "It's okay for people like me with an education – I can mitigate some of the stigma that comes with being a Traveller because I have a good education. Because I've done really well academically. But not everybody can mitigate those." I was like, "We've been researched, we've been documented since we were children. I remember people coming onto the site when I was a kid, researching us." And I was like, "I don't understand what this would add that all of the other research, like there's so much research, we don't need any more. What you actually need to do is to just do something." And I was blunt: "Listen. I know how this goes. You're going to spend a year to six months doing the research. Six months to a year writing it up. You know, come in with some policy recommendations. Then you might talk about it," I said. "By the time you even get anywhere, we've got a new government in. And we're all going to have to start from the ground up again." I was like, "How much have you spent on this? This is ridiculous." And I managed to get a figure out of that. And I was like, "Do you know what that money could do for people?" And I literally wouldn't let it go and they kept trying to, kind of like reel me back in. And I was like, "No, no, no. Like, I'm not an idiot. We're not having this."

Maggie's fierce and well-informed critique of the research and proposed film was exhausting for her. "It was so stressful," she told me. "It was mental. And we left the meeting like, I was so stressed. Like, I slid, the emotions, it was emotionally very draining." She and her friend from the government department went to the pub after the meeting to decompress. While they were there, her friend received a call from her manager, who said, "If Maggie's still there can you tell her we've basically pulled the plug. We're not doing it."

At that particular table, in that specific moment, Maggie happened to be a Traveller at a table of policymakers speaking about Travellers. Her refusal to accept their middle-class logic of practice when dealing with her community stopped them in their tracks and forced them to reconsider their plans. But she was not supposed to be there. She had stepped in for her non-Traveller manager at the last minute. Her manager had been invited to the table, Maggie believed, as a gate-keeper to Travellers, as "someone who has access to Travellers who could have taken part in that policy research, right? [Travellers] who might consent to being followed around with cameras." In other words, it seemed as if it was mostly luck and timing that had Maggie at that table in that moment, giving her the opportunity to stop a bad policy decision from being enacted upon her community.

But we need to back up. It is too simplistic to attribute only luck and timing to Maggie's ability to both be at that table and speak back to those middle-class policy actors. She has practice at creating positive change for Travellers through intentional, strategic, and creative activist work. These are not just happy accidents that allow her to wield influence, even if it was a bit of luck that had her at that particular table. Maggie has honed these capacities. Through her activism, she has practice at addressing politicians, engaging the media effectively, and speaking back directly to power. This has allowed her to hold others to account in their engagements with her community. In other parts of our interview, she told me about her successful efforts at stopping unscrupulous filmmakers from creating yet another damaging documentary of her community, and about calling out a Labour MP for NIMBY[4] comments he made about Travellers over Twitter. Maggie has found comrades and allies in her activist work, particularly through the group of Labour-leaning Traveller activists with whom she organizes, and this is in part what allows her to keep doing the exhausting advocacy that she does when she happens to be at a table of policymakers for work. But she would not be at that table, nor capable of speaking back to power, without having an atypical biography for a Traveller: of receiving graduate-level university training and being introduced to activism through a conference about the Roma Holocaust attended by other young activists. As she told me, "before that I'd been really hesitant around the label activist," because she felt that, "I wasn't doing enough of it, you know. I was a bit like, I don't really do [activism] – yeah, I think that was my hesitation."

The hesitation over claiming the title of "activist" is one I have heard reiterated several times by young people, particularly those who do not come from a (typically white and middle-class) activist family and thus have not been socialized into comfortably claiming that label for themselves. In my 2011 ethnography, Conrad, a South Asian young person living in the suburbs of Vancouver, expressed a very similar hesitation:

> *Conrad*: It's political, right? Always. And, that's the box though, is that it's about rallies, protests, and your complete refusal of things. That's why I have a hard time accepting it, because my youth activist [identity], is like [different from] those people that are in those [protests] that I go to, or I have a meeting with them all the time, so yeah, I guess I am [an activist], but I don't look like that, I'm not dressing like that, I'm not there, I have my car, all those things. So it is this total identity. And not just like what you're doing.
>
> (Kennelly, 2011a, p. 105).

Although Maggie found her way into claiming the label of "activist" by meeting other young people like herself who also proudly claimed it, the barriers that prevent some young people from taking up that identity for themselves are real and are bound to social markers such as higher education, race/ethnicity in white-dominant societies, and family of origin. As I have been at pains to demonstrate so far, one does not simply "become" an activist – that is, someone with the skills, knowledge, and capacity to challenge unjust systems – even if one has important insights to share, or even if one has been invited to be "at the table."

Maggie was keenly aware of this dilemma. When we were discussing what she associated with the word "democracy," her response was: "Freedom. Like

---

4   NIMBY = Not In My Back Yard: referring to the common middle-class tactic of saying that such and such an option ought to happen, just don't do it near me and my neighbourhood.

the freedom to be, without being problematized, [to have] a fair representation. And yeah, just true freedom – not like a pseudo-freedom." When I asked her what "true freedom" means to her, she said:

> I think some of that comes from my work. So, I know that we take part in things and it feels like you have a say, but often things are done deals. If that makes sense. So like for example, there was a conversation that went out before Christmas about making trespass a criminal offence and increasing police powers, specifically against Travellers. And it was really, like a *really* clever consult. And they thought, "Ah, we're a democracy. We're going to ask people's views in this consultation," and you know, "We'll take the public's opinion." But it was really, really clever policy because the way they phrased the questions meant that whatever you answered, it produced policy agreement as an effect. So then I'm like, do we have true freedom? And I go through, like, I seesaw all the time. I yo-yo from one idea to another where I'm like, "Yeah, we can reform the system." Then half an hour later I'm like, "We need to burn the whole fucking thing down." And the way I view policy is a little bit like a chessboard. You make one move and then sometimes you're knocked back and it's about the long-term game and sometimes you make a gain and sometimes you don't, but it's like whose game are we playing? You know?

This question – "whose game are we playing?" – is a beautiful way to capture one of the central dilemmas of the acquisition of a democratic disposition. Bourdieu is well known for using the metaphor of a game when describing his social theory, where the players involved all have "stakes" in the game that are defined by their own specific social dispositions (or habitus) as well as their respective acquisition of different forms of capital. This game always has a set of rules, or illusio (also described in chapter two), which players within it take for granted. But those players who have not come to this particular political game through a middle-class history are able to catch some glimpses of the taken-for-grantedness of this illusio. This is because *the rules of the game required for advocating within political spaces are middle class rules.*

Playing a game with middle-class rules when you do not come from a middle-class background can be exhausting. It requires a performance of middle classness, often, that is used to shore up one's sense of belonging and legitimacy within the space. For Maggie, she learned to do this through modifying her accent, which allowed her to claim space in postsecondary schooling as well as around middle-class policy tables:

> In my day to day, I can change my accent. I can do an English accent that sounds fairly well-to-do. And I don't sound like I'm a Traveller. I live in a rough area of London, and I don't sound like I come from there. You know, I learned as a student when I was at university, spent a lot of time expanding my vocabulary, ensuring

that actually you could never turn me down for any of those reasons. For me, my biggest fear is that – it isn't failure – I get failing. That's fine. My biggest fear is not being good. Like, someone telling me like you're not enough. And I think this is part of it, the activism. You keep pushing so that no one can say it. Like, no one can say "well, actually you're not enough." And this for me is a big part of why I push academically.

Maggie's fear of being seen as "not enough" when playing the middle-class games of academia and politics is very much grounded in a classed disposition that has been inexorably shaped by neoliberal logic. Despite her insights into the systemic unfairness of the policies she is working to change, Maggie must daily face the class injuries that occur from within a neoliberal cultural logic that insists that one's hard work is the only thing separating her from the unrelenting grind of poverty. To "be enough" is not only about a sense of self-worth, although it is certainly partially that: it is also fundamentally about being able to survive in a world that does not expect her or her community to be capable of survival. It is to prove herself capable, over and over and over again, at enormous personal and emotional costs, in order to continue to participate in the middle-class worlds of politics, academia, and activism. To straddle the worlds of activism and marginalization is, in the words of Stephanie (age twenty-two, United States), who is similarly positioned across both of these locations, to "turn from lived experience to lived exhaustion. By the time you get in a place that you can be an activist, it's like, I'm just so tired."

Scarlett: "I'm a Very Political Person"

Scarlett (age twenty-four) was the first Australian participant I interviewed for this project who had experienced homelessness. She responded to the recruitment notice she had received from one of the largest homeless-serving agencies in Melbourne, distributed by my Australian research assistant. As was true for all of my Zoom interviews with participants in Australia and New Zealand, it was my evening and Scarlett's morning of the next day when we spoke; our interview was the first event of her day, and she was still waking up as we began. Scarlett appeared on Zoom with a shaggy brown beard and curly hair that brushed her shoulders. Wearing a black tank top, she scratched her arms frequently as we spoke, leaving red lines on her skin.

I gave a brief overview of Scarlett's life circumstances near the beginning of chapter one. Like all of the homeless young people I have interviewed over the course of my career, Scarlett is a survivor. She is regularly forced to make strategic choices to protect herself from violence and abuse, to the extent that she can. For this reason she opted not to come out as trans until age eighteen, when she was legally free of the foster care system: "There's a lot of people in foster care and resident care that are really transphobic and homophobic. And like I almost got bashed for being gay in resi (group home), so. I just didn't feel safe coming out as trans. Like, I knew I was trans, but I just didn't feel safe coming out." Born into an incredibly abusive but also politically left family, Scarlett was exposed to lefty ideals from a young age. She honed her analysis through her encounters with the foster care system, the police, and the city's homeless-serving agencies, ultimately landing on a well-developed critique of the Australian Labour Party and its limits:

> I mean, Labour is one of the better ones [political parties]. They're still pretty horrible, like, they kind of ignore homelessness, pretend it's not a big issue. It's the same with mental health and like, due to that I'm leftist but one of those extreme leftists. I believe everybody should have housing. Um, like, access to food and food should be free, the same with water, and the same with housing. And that sex workers shouldn't be prosecuted. Drugs should be legal. Um. Like, a lot of that leftist ideology. And, like I believe women should have the power over their bodies and I don't really think it should be up for political debate. And like human rights shouldn't be up for political debate and stuff because they're human rights.

When I asked her where she had developed her ideas, she said, "I taught myself. Um, like, and I just have empathy for a lot of people so like, my purpose in life is to help as many people as possible." Scarlett spent a lot of time educating herself through reading online, and also engages in online activism via TikTok and Twitter, directing her critiques at politicians in the United States and Australia. Her pre-existing left leanings were deepened when she joined the youth advisory committee at one of the youth-serving agencies for homeless young people. There she helped to fundraise for the organization, "because they don't get a lot of government support," and learned more about the political work they do: "they want to build more youth refuges [shelters] and they do amazing at speaking out against how homeless people in general get treated like shit by the general population of Australia." The agency uses their social capital, particularly their connections with regional governments, to arrange for members of their youth advisory to engage with policymakers: "When I was homeless I worked very closely with the City of Melbourne council, on like homelessness and how their parks could be better run and better maintained. And trying to get, to raise money for them so that they can build more affordable housing in the city of Melbourne. I've met the mayor of Melbourne a couple of times. She's heard one of my TikToks." These opportunities led to others, including joining a campaign run by the Salvation Army, called "Walk the Walk for the Homeless" (The Salvation Army, 2017). The Salvation Army "took a bunch of homeless people up to Canberra to finish the walk. Um, just to raise awareness and like bring the spotlight on homelessness in Australia as a whole. Because it gets ignored quite frequently. And so I met Bill Shorten [then official leader of the opposition Labour Party] there. I shook his hand. I even have a photo of him and I on Facebook." With the ongoing support of the youth-serving agency, Scarlett continues her advocacy work, particularly by doing presentations to other youth organizations and companies, "about homelessness and about LGBT issues and domestic violence and sexual harassment and all that sort of stuff."

Scarlett's pre-existing left leanings, begun with her family of origin and then further developed through self-education, was transformed into a democratic disposition via her involvement with the youth advisory committee. Because of the opportunities created by the youth advisory, she was able to take her political knowledge and apply it strategically to attempt to directly influence political actors. Her acquisition of a democratic disposition is signalled by the fact that Scarlett was one of only a few young people I interviewed who had experienced homelessness to describe "being political" in a way that echoed young activists (see the discussion in chapter two), as a total identity and way of being in the world: "Actually I'm a very political person. Like, every single thing that I do is political. Like, just living is a political statement. Like, as a trans woman. Every move I make is a political statement. Every letter I say is a political statement, so."

Where Tamara had important knowledge about the gaps in systems but no way to bring that knowledge into political use, Scarlett was able to engage in political social change work, largely because of the mentorship and support she received through the youth advisory council of an agency where she had accessed services. This signals the mutability of a democratic disposition: it can be acquired despite major structural barriers, with appropriate support. Two other young people in the study who had experienced homelessness similarly articulated a more politicized identity and strategic knowledge about achieving democratic change; both of them had been involved in similar types of youth advisory groups offered through youth-serving agencies. However, as will be discussed in the next chapter, while such mentorship can be an important first step for young people to develop a democratic disposition, there remain multiple structural barriers to becoming more deeply embedded in political social change efforts, largely due to the hidden class cultures of political activism and engagement. It is not a coincidence that Maggie has been able to take her political advocacy and activism work directly to the tables of middle-class policy actors and forced them to back down on ill-conceived plans for working with Travellers. Maggie has become fluent in the middle-class language of politics, largely through her academic research training. Scarlett, by contrast, while meeting the mayor and the leader of the Opposition Labour Party, seems rather to have been engaged in a tokenistic manner that lends itself to the optics of meaningful youth engagement by political actors. Unlike Maggie, Scarlett did not relay to me any ways in which her involvement made significant changes to political outcomes. The bulk of Scarlett's energy continues to be taken up by her efforts to establish a reasonably sustainable life and livelihood for herself: although she is finally housed, she is now trying to access funding to attend postsecondary training as a youth worker. Her ultimate ambition is to be a politician; I hope, for her sake and that of Australian society, that she is able to make that a reality. But the path from where she is to that goal is a long and arduous one, and I remain pessimistic about the likelihood that she will be able to get there – unless she is lucky enough to find some powerful mentors with funding who are willing to work with her to achieve those dreams. This is not a comment on Scarlett's determination or her skills; it is rather a reflection of the current structural inequalities that perpetuate marginalization, a theme I explore in greater detail in the following section.

State Failures

In the previous chapter, I described the biographical conditions that enabled young activists to develop democratic dispositions, rooted in their families of origin, their exposure to mentors and/or student-led social movements, and their postsecondary training. For the second half of this chapter, I focus on the barriers to democratic engagement experienced by young people who have been homeless. I organize these around the three domains of neoliberal state retrenchment that I examined in chapter one: stratification of access to high-quality, publicly funded schooling that can lead to affordable postsecondary education; loss of affordable housing; and cuts to state benefit systems.

People live complex lives. It is rarely true that *this* one specific circumstance created all of the conditions that led to such and such an outcome. Rather, as is true for all of us, one circumstance combines with another, and then another, is countered by something, then reinforced by something else, leading an individual towards a positive or negative outcome. This is how we need to understand the effects of state retrenchment. It is not *only* that a young person had inadequate housing (although housing is arguably among the most foundational factors), and it is not *just* because their family's or their own welfare benefits were inadequate, and it is not *entirely* because they could not afford to attend university, or their public school failed them in some way or another. It is generally *all* of these things, in combination, building upon and reinforcing one another, combining with other state-influenced structures, such as access to adequate health care, migration experiences, and the condition of foster care in their respective countries. This is why there are always exceptions: the young person who comes from difficult circumstances yet manages to succeed, like Maggie in the United Kingdom, or Alejandro in the United States, or Karen in New Zealand. Unfortunately, these exceptions are often held up as examples of how the systems are not *that* broken. Mainstream media loves the story of the young person who left homelessness or poverty behind and then made something of themselves. It is a simple story, and a reassuring one. But it is not the whole story, or even really a true story. Rather, it is a story that serves to reinforce the mystification of (neo)liberal democracies: that one's individual effort can pull one out of poverty, and that the state has little to do with any one person's successes or failures.

In what follows, I try to demonstrate why it is that failures of the state, often stemming from neoliberal policy measures, are resulting in failures of democracy. Keeping in mind that these are vignettes from much more complex lives, I narrow my focus to the impacts of one or more of the three state structures that I described in chapter one – education, housing, and state benefits – beginning with schooling.

Neoliberal Education Systems

Frankly, my challenge in this section is to prevent it from becoming a book of its own. Almost every young person I spoke with who had experienced homelessness had a difficult experience with schooling. Because of challenges in the K–12 system (from ages four or five to seventeen or eighteen), few had been able to proceed to postsecondary. Those who made it to postsecondary would find their challenges compounded by being evicted from college or university residences/dorms into homelessness, being forced to engage in multiple part-time jobs, including sex work, to be able to afford sky-rocketing tuition, and/or being limited in their choice of studies due to poor secondary school grades, which were a direct result of not being accommodated for housing insecurity and/or learning disabilities. I will share the experiences of Armin (Australia), Tiffany (United Kingdom), and Chloe (Canada) to give readers a sense of how these issues play out in young people's lives.

"Fell through the cracks" is a phrase that is often used to describe what happens to individuals as the social safety net erodes under neoliberalism; it is the phrase that came to mind as Armin (age twenty-two) told me about his schooling experiences in Australia. I shared some of Armin's story in chapter two, comparing and contrasting his views on democracy with that of Noor, another racialized young person in Australia who grew up in a stable, middle-class family. Armin's experience of family was quite different. He arrived from Iran at the age of fourteen, sponsored by his father who was already living in Australia. Armin's relationship with his father was clearly difficult for him to speak about; I did not ask for many details. Armin described him as a stranger: I assume this meant that Armin did not really know his father, presumably because he had relocated to Australia when Armin was still a young child. Armin told me that he had moved to Australia with two older siblings, leaving his mother and grandparents behind in Iran, where life had been good for him. He had lived in a comfortable home and been attending a "top selective school," where he was quite successful. When his father offered to sponsor him and his siblings, Armin's mother insisted that they go. Although Armin did not discuss her reasons, perhaps she was concerned about the political unrest in Iran and believed that her children would be better off in a Western liberal democracy like Australia.

Armin's arrival in Australia was not a smooth one. He would not go into detail about this time in his life, describing it as "just dark, very dark." He told me that he has been on his own almost since arriving at age fourteen, having cut ties with his father. He spoke frequently of the racism he encountered in Australia and the misperceptions people have about his home country of Iran: "But, yeah, life back home was, it was really warm. It's nothing like unfortunately what people see in the media because if I see the media I'll think, you know, it's a terrorist country. I'm Iranian. If I look at the news, because if you search Iran in Google, all you see is ballistic missiles. Bombs. Wars. Threats. That's all you see. But, that's the government. That is the government. You know, just like with the US. You know, people here, like they hate the US, but I know that Americans are lovely people." Armin would consider returning to Iran if it were not for the economic sanctions imposed by Western countries, which have crippled the economy there. Also, as a male over the age of eighteen, if he spends more than three months there he will be conscripted into the Iranian army. So he continues to try and eke out a life in Australia, where he may be free from military conscription but has otherwise been failed by almost every government system he has encountered while experiencing racist bullying and harassment by Australians since his arrival.

When Armin arrived at age fourteen and was unable to live with his father, he still did his best to register for school. This was, after all, the reason he had moved to Australia: to get an education and have better opportunities for his future. However, without a parent to sign the paperwork, Armin found it difficult to navigate the educational system. "They didn't really know what to do with me," he told me, "they" in this case being the schools. "They didn't want to enrol me. There was a lot of beef, there was a lot of problems, you know." In the end, Armin was either not able to enrol in school or else he enrolled and found the racist bullying so difficult that he dropped out; when I met him at age twenty-two, he told me he was "in a transition to hopefully be able to enrol for study next year," to finally be able to complete his secondary school diploma.

Armin did not provide me with enough details to get a clear sense of whether these systems failures could be directly attributable to neoliberal policymaking or retrenchment; my guess is that the under-funding of schools has done few favours for young people who do not fit neatly into the existing bureaucratic categories. Accommodating individuals requires extra time; extra time requires extra people; and extra people requires sufficient funding. According to Adam Rorris (2021), Australia's public schools have been under-funded by

AU$27 billion over the past four years, a trend that began in 2013 – the year Armin arrived in Australia – under the right-wing Liberal-National Coalition government. By contrast, tuition-charging private schools in Australia have been receiving more and more public funds, generating a more or less direct siphon from the public education system to the private one (Rorris, 2021). This is pure neoliberal ideology at play.

In the United Kingdom, Tiffany's schooling experiences have the fingerprints of neoliberal policymaking all over them. Her story is also about the deep cuts that have happened in UK public housing since the 1980s. When Tiffany (age twenty-three) and I spoke in early 2021, she and her family had already been living in "temporary" accommodations for five years. This began shortly after her mother left the United Kingdom to return to Germany for addictions treatment, where it is covered by public health care. Her father was unable to keep up with the rent, and they were evicted in 2016.

> So, when we were first evicted, we had like an emergency room in a hostel. I think that's what it was. It was the four of us in a room with three beds. Um, two blankets. So, I literally slept with my jacket. So that, there was that. And then we were moved to a temporary accommodation, which was supposed to be better. But it was actually – it was easy to get to by bus, but there was like no reception, no Internet, and that's when I was doing my A-levels, which you get to go to university. So there was that. We had to share, so you get the room and you share it in a house of like four other families, where each family has one room. And we all share one shower. We all share one toilet. We all share one tiny kitchen.

Not surprisingly, all of these disruptions had an impact on Tiffany's grades: "So around when my mum was becoming an alcoholic is when I failed school. And then when she left, it was like a relief and I did really well. I had like A star, A star, A. And then we got evicted and then I had D, D, C. Luckily enough I had good enough grades for it to even out for me to get into a good uni. But I do sometimes think if that hadn't happened, I would have probably gotten much better grades." To further add to the instability in her life, her public secondary school expelled her when her grades dropped, and she had to begin her A-level courses over again at a different school. I spent quite some time exploring this with her during our interview, trying to make sense of how this came to be. My shock and outrage grew stronger the more she told me. When I asked her why she thought they had expelled her, she said, "They did it just because they need to be able to say 80 per cent of our students pass. But then they basically, all the students that don't pass, they just kick them out. So then that way it won't affect their percentages." I knew about the UK league tables, which rank the so-called quality of schools based on student performance. League tables and school rankings have long been critiqued by educational scholars as a neoliberal project that ultimately increases inequality between poor and rich students (Lucey & Reay, 2002a, 2002b). But Tiffany was reporting on something more than this.

> TIFFANY: The secondary school I went to, before, so it actually changed, like, it was bought by this, um, I don't know if they're called franchise, but they're basically, this guy Henderson. And he buys schools and then basically just makes them businesses.
> JACKIE: What? How can he buy the schools? Aren't they public? How does that work?
> TIFFANY: So they're called academies. So, the school used to be [name of school] when I joined and then halfway through they changed to Henderson[5] Academy.
> JACKIE: Oh my god.
> TIFFANY: And that was a huge difference. At [former name of school], it was, you know, we were all poor. It wasn't necessarily the most cultured environment, but we did have good teachers and we had like, people weren't getting detentions all the time for no reason. And people were allowed to express themselves and be themselves. We had rules but they weren't extremely rigid, and the focus was more on education. Whereas when Henderson came, it was like if you're wearing nail varnish, you get taken out of class. You'd get taken out of class, into isolation.
> JACKIE: What?!
> TIFFANY: It makes no sense because how are you meant to do work? It was basically just teaching us to comply. We changed uniform. You weren't allowed to wear your skirt a certain length. If you rolled up your skirt at all, you'd be punished for that. We'd always get detentions. And then another thing that happened is a lot of our teachers left. I'm not sure why. It could have been pay or rules, but a lot of our teachers left. We had really good, experienced teachers before who were old, but they were very experienced and very like intuitive almost. But then after they left it was just a bunch of new teachers. As in people who are teachers because it's their in-between job for when they actually want to become a teacher. Which, you know. Definitely was evident.… So our education was completely thrown out the window.
> JACKIE: Wow. And so, sorry, my brain is blowing up here. So this guy buys your school and then –
> TIFFANY: Monetizes it because the government gives you money. The more people you have at your school, the more money you get from the government. The more students. Like, the more students you have. And obviously when you have the good grades and the excellent reviews, more people come to your school. However, I mean, I don't really know what the goal was or how they were making more money. Maybe they were making more money because they were paying teachers less. I don't think school was really this man's passion. I don't know. I don't know him that well. But, you know.

---

5 Henderson is a pseudonym.

JACKIE: So this guy buys the school. Sorry, I'm still trying to make sense of this [laughter]. He buys the school that is still being funded by the government, but he can now make money off of it. Like, it's like a private, but you guys aren't paying tuition now – it's still public – so-called public school. But he's trying to make money. Oh my god. That is horrifying. When, sorry, what year approximately did this happen?

TIFFANY: Um, so that happened. [pauses] Uh, seven, eight, nine. [pauses] Yeah, so it was when I was, it was about seven years ago.

JACKIE: Okay. So what are we now? So like 2013, 2014. Yeah, David Cameron [was prime minister then]. Oh my God. I had no idea. I didn't know about that happening in the UK. That's, wow.

After my interview with Tiffany, I dived into the academic literature in order to better understand what she was describing. I learned that her account of what had happened to her secondary school was quite accurate, even if she did not have all of the relevant language to explain it. Tiffany's impoverished and likely "under-performing" school had either opted or been forced by central government to integrate into a Multi-Academy Trust. Academies had been established by federal legislation in 2010 in the United Kingdom as a form of "independent school" – similar to charter schools in the United States and Canada (Simon, James, & Simon, 2021). This allows them to withdraw from their Local Authority (the regional level of government who formerly funded schools via money received from the national government), and instead receive funding directly from the national government; it also provides them with much greater autonomy in terms of curriculum design, term dates, and the hiring of school staff (Simon, James, & Simon, 2021). The Multi-Academy Trust structure emerged slightly later; this is a formal grouping of academies, managed under one CEO and board of directors – rather like a franchise, as Tiffany described it. The drive to form these Multi-Academy Trusts (MATs) is a financial one: Simon, James, and Simon (2021, p. 113–14) explain that they are motivated to expand largely because of the "'funded invitation' they receive [from central government] to 'sponsor' schools judged as inadequate following inspection by the Office for Standards in Education and Children's Services and Skills (Ofsted)."

Simon, James, and Simon (2021, p. 113) suggest that "Academization ... provided a mechanism through which parental choice, competition and autonomy were enhanced in the state-maintained school system in England. In many ways, a 'branded' education system has emerged that enables schools to turn their pedagogical beliefs and values into marketable commodities." Christy Kulz (2021) is more blunt: she argues that not only are MATs shaped entirely by neoliberal political rationalities, but also that this structure inherently erodes democracy. Other scholars agree. Andrew Wilkins (2017) notes that MATs are accountable only to the national government that funds them, and that this accountability extends primarily to the MAT meeting its obligation to "improve" school performance, as measured through "standardised tests, performance monitoring and expert evaluation" (Wilkins, 2017, p. 179). Rather like the responsibility a corporate CEO and board of directors hold to maximize profits for their shareholders, the MAT system is designed to "streamline" results in order to maximize "economic efficiencies and quantifiable outcomes" (Kulz, 2021, p. 69).

The neoliberal, corporate, and anti-democratic logic of Multi-Academy Trusts is fundamentally changing public schooling in the United Kingdom. Simon, James, and Simon (2021, p. 112) describe the emergence of the MAT system as a "radical reorganization" of the education system in England; Kulz notes that, as of 2019, over half of England's student population was enrolled in an academy, and over 80 per cent of all academies were part of a Multi-Academy Trust. Luckily for Tiffany, after her MAT-run school expelled her for dropping grades, she was able to attend a non-academy school which supported her to complete her A-levels, the university preparatory courses. The experience delayed her graduation, however, and also narrowed her options for postsecondary schooling, as she scrambled to take classes in which she knew she would succeed. If MATs continue to expand at current rates, soon there will be no traditional public schools left to rescue those students deemed unworthy of continuation in an academy. This will undoubtedly affect impoverished, racialized, and otherwise marginalized students the most.

Chloe's story in Canada is also marked by failures of state systems for both housing and education. When we met, Chloe (age nineteen) was in her first term at a private career college in Ottawa, where she was paying CA$10,000/year for tuition and textbooks. Chloe had been attending one of Ottawa's largest public colleges until earlier that year, when she had been abruptly evicted from her college residence directly into homelessness. The eviction occurred on the heels of Chloe's drop from full-time to part-time student status, a choice she made in the context of worsening disabilities that had confined her to a wheelchair. She had been finding the full-time load too much to manage when combined with her medical issues, and so, with the support and full knowledge of the college administration, she had shifted to a part-time course load. Nobody told her, however, that such a shift would also result in her losing her room in residence: her only viable housing option at the time, which she could only afford with student loans. She was given no notice of her pending eviction; her residence manager called her to the office at 4:00 p.m. on a Friday in the middle of a February snowstorm and told her she had to pack her things and leave. This public college offered absolutely no support to Chloe in her transition out of residence, nor even seemed to consider the implications of evicting a young woman with a disability into the subarctic winter weather typical of Ottawa in February. Chloe was unable to secure a spot in the relatively safer young women's shelter at such short notice, so she had to go into the extremely unsafe adult shelter in downtown Ottawa. The COVID-19 pandemic had decimated the shelters, leaving them scrambling to find enough space for people to sleep with sufficient distance between them to prevent the spread of the disease. Because of her disability, Chloe was unable to climb stairs and so was placed in the only wheelchair-accessible space, which she described as "where the people that are like drunk and under the influence are." When I asked her if there was enough distance between her and the others sleeping there, she said, "No. Furthest away that we ever were was like, well, close. So there's usually two bunkbeds in a room and the bunkbeds are maybe two feet apart. And then they usually put a couple of mats on the floor, too, so people are really only a few inches apart."

Because of her new location downtown, combined with her disability, Chloe found it impossible to get to her 8:00 a.m. classes by public transit, located at the college campus far from the downtown core. She was thus forced to drop out of college, where she had been studying to become a developmental services worker, which she described to me as a personal support worker for people with disabilities. To add insult to injury, Chloe was placed on academic probation due to dropping out of her classes halfway through the term. Although I did not get full details on this, I presume she failed the classes once she was no longer able to attend, and before she was able to complete the administrative paperwork required to formally withdraw. One can imagine that she may have had other things on her mind while living nose to nose with inebriated adults in a homeless shelter in the midst of a global pandemic. Unable to advocate for herself, she thus bore the bureaucratic aprobation of a system that had utterly failed her.

Despite this experience, Chloe remained determined to complete her education. After her terrible treatment by the public college, Chloe turned to a private career college to get her qualifications. Proponents of the privatization of Canada's higher education sector would likely hold this up as a triumph of "consumer choice" supposedly made possible by the private market. This simplistic reading of the dynamics of inequality overlooks a number of realities that have been exposed through research in other countries where private career colleges have emerged as part of the marketization of the higher education system. While Canadian research has not yet caught up with the phenomenon of the private higher education marketplace and its implications for students, researchers in the United States have already laid a powerful critical foundation for understanding the manner in which this private market can further marginalize already disadvantaged students.

Although some form of private higher education has existed in Canada since its inception as a settler-colonial country (Li & Jones, 2015), the role of so-called private career colleges as meaningful competitors to publicly funded colleges in Canada, particularly in Ontario, dates from the year 2000 under the Mike Harris provincial Conservative government. The increased presence of private career colleges in Ontario is thus directly attributable to the rise of neoliberal policymaking. Pizarro Milian and Hicks (2014, p. 4) describe private career colleges as small, generally for-profit businesses, which "focus predominantly on vocational training at the diploma and certificate level." They overlap considerably with the offerings of public colleges, although they remain quite distinct from universities in Canada. Private career colleges must be registered with the provincial government, and they are subject to consumer protection requirements and external, third-party reviews of the quality of their offerings. Although their annual tuition fees tend to be higher than their public college competitors, they offer shorter programs due to the fact that they are not required to include "essential employability skills (communications, numeracy, information management, critical thinking, interpersonal skills, etc.)" as are public colleges (Pizarro Milian & Hicks, 2014, p. 4). Private career colleges offer "sub-degree credentials in many of the same vocational program areas" as public colleges, "such as hairdressing, massage therapy, and social services" (Pizarro Milian & Quirke, 2017, p. 79). The most heavily enrolled area in private career colleges in Canada is Health Services (28 per cent of students); of the Health Services offered, 36 per cent of students – like Chloe – are enrolled in programs for personal support workers (Pizarro Milian & Hicks, 2014).

Not surprisingly, given the early adoption of this neoliberal policy measure, Ontario has the largest number of private career colleges in the country, with 601; the nearest competitor is British Columbia, with 317. Ontario's private career colleges have over 67,000 students enrolled as of 2014 data (Li & Jones, 2015). Marginalized groups are "over-represented" in private career colleges (Pizarro Milian & Quirke, 2017, p. 79). with students more likely to be racialized, female, and from low-income backgrounds (Pizarro Milian & Hicks, 2014).

Although Canadian scholars state that "we generally lack data to compare costs and outcomes meaningfully across the college sectors in Ontario" (Pizarro Milian & Hicks, 2014, p. 21), American scholars have been able to do detailed analyses of these factors. The most comprehensive study I could find draws on population-level administrative data from the US Department of Education and the Internal Revenue Service to "compare the earnings of students before and after attendance at for-profit versus public institutions, after matching by demographics, prior earnings, field of study, geography, and age group" (Cellini & Turner, 2019, p. 343). The researchers also generated "a control group of young individuals who do not attend college in the time period we study to measure employment and earnings relative to no college" (ibid.). This massive study includes data from over 840,000 for-profit college students in the United States, allowing them to explore through their data, "heterogeneity of returns by gender and field of study" (ibid., p. 344). Their findings unequivocally demonstrate that "the vast majority of for-profit students experience both higher debt and lower earnings after attendance," and that across all fifty states plus Washington, DC, "students from public institutions have higher earnings and lower debt than their counterparts from for-profit institutions." Further, in comparing private career college students to the control group who did not attend college at all, for-profit college students are slightly more likely to be employed, but their earnings are on average lower than individuals with no college. When comparing the average debt of a career college student to their likely earnings, they come out in the red in relation to those who did not attend private or public college at all. Not surprisingly, women fare worse than men in relative earnings with a private career college certificate, in addition to faring worse than their public college–educated counterparts. Further, the health-related fields are among the worst for comparative salaries when considering students who attended private career colleges versus public colleges (ibid.).

Key performance indicators for Ontario private career colleges are now collected by the Ministry of Training, Colleges, and Universities, and are openly available as downloadable CSV charts on their website. I could not find any Canadian studies that make use of this data to assess the comparative outcomes of private career colleges to public colleges; such a study would need to link administrative datasets from the Canada Revenue Agency, the Canadian equivalent to the US Internal Revenue Service. Although there does not appear to be a comparable Canadian study of private career college outcomes, there are reasons to believe that the American findings will hold true across both countries. Even before other key performance indicators were being collected, loan default rates were recorded in Ontario. These data show that private career college students have a much higher student loan default rate (21 per cent) than either public college (13 per cent) or university (5 per cent) students (Pizarro Milian & Hicks, 2014, p. 24). This suggests that rates of employment – and thus ability to repay loans – are lower for private career college graduates. A survey of 2007–8 private career college graduates in Ontario found that their average income, six months after graduation, was CA$26,000; for public college graduates, the equivalent income was CA$34,000, and for university graduates, it was CA$42,000 (as reported in Pizarro Milian & Hicks, 2014, p. 28).

Now let us return to Chloe's story. Estranged from an abusive foster family, living with a disability stemming from an earlier car accident, Chloe was doing her very best to yank up those bootstraps and transform herself into a good citizen of the neoliberal Canadian nation-state, in order to make money and contribute to the economy. Despite the barriers she faced, she had managed to enrol in a public college, secure a spot for herself in residence, and start earning a college diploma that would allow her to enter into her chosen field of work. Remembering that "choices" are always constrained, we ought not to overlook the fact that Chloe is "choosing" a low-paying and feminized field of work – as a personal support worker – but at least with a public college diploma she would be likely to get a better-paying job than she could without the diploma. Due to a number of bureaucratic failures on the part of that public college – which, as with Armin above, we cannot be sure are due to neoliberal cuts but we might guess that having less funding means that public colleges may well be less accommodating to their students than otherwise – Chloe is essentially thrust into the arms of a private career college. Here we can track the fingerprints of neoliberalism quite clearly. Offered as a private "alternative" to public colleges, Chloe is now firmly on a path to greater debt and lower pay – a reality that is, of course, not advertised on the websites and shiny brochures of these career colleges (Pizarro Milian & Quirke, 2017) – thus reproducing her impoverishment and that of any children she may have in future.

Neoliberal Housing

It is no surprise that the education journeys of Armin, Tiffany, and Chloe, described above, are also stories about failures of the housing systems in their respective countries. Housing, like education, is supposed to be a fundamental human right, enshrined in the UN Declaration on Human Rights, as well as in the UN Declaration on the Rights of the Child. It is also recognized as one of the fundamental factors in the social determinants of health, leading some researchers to call for policy recognition of high-quality, affordable housing as a public health measure (Rolfe et al., 2020). In what follows, I trace the stories of Jillian (New Zealand), Isabella (United States), and Daraja (United Kingdom) to demonstrate how neoliberal policy measures that have decimated public and affordable housing in each country play out on the ground for marginalized young people.

Jillian (age twenty-two) was twenty when her son was born. I could have included Jillian's story in the section above, about the failures of the education system; growing up in poorly maintained New Zealand public housing with parents who were doing their best but were not able to advocate for her very well, Jillian had learning disabilities that went undiagnosed for years. This made schooling a nightmare for her, leaving her feeling like she was not smart enough to succeed, and ultimately leading to her dropping out entirely. Schooling was also complicated by the instability in her life, another common thread among young people who have experienced homelessness. She attended three different high schools and five different primary schools, due to her mother moving around for work, and also because of family violence, which induced her to leave home at age twelve. From there, Jillian lived with friends for a while, then moved in with her father, then moved back to her mother's home, and then back to her friends' place. As described in the Introduction to this book, this kind of "couch surfing" is a common way for youth homelessness to manifest, and is considered a form of "hidden homelessness," as it is not as easily captured within measures of homelessness.

Jillian was living independently by the time she was pregnant, in a private rental unit. Shortly after her son was born, the landlord informed her that he was selling the house and she would have to move. With little notice and few resources, Jillian approached the local benefits office to explore her options:

> I went into welfare to ask for help because I had nowhere to stay and because of the current situation, which was then on our first [COVID-19] lockdown, and like the emergency housing and everything was really full. They pretty much would have made me give my son away. I told them that I have absolutely nowhere to go. Like, the only place that I can go to is a house that, which is a Housing New Zealand house, but the house is so bad like it's got black mould growing in there and like, it's just not good for your health. This is my dad's house and I've lived there my whole life on and off with, like, because my mum and him aimed to give us a life. Over the holidays, I'd live at my dad's but I'd get really sick because of like all the black mould and stuff and that's the only place I could go with my newborn baby. And I had told them [the benefits office] this, I told them that I had nowhere to go and if they didn't help me, I would be sleeping in my car because that's my only option. And they said they would take my son away.

Rather than face losing her son, Jillian started calling up local hotels, where she could be temporarily housed with the help of a state benefit. "I rang from Wellington to Palmerston North and like all the hotels within their area code and none of them would take me. Knowing my situation and what I had, you know, been going through. The people that wanted to take me were just full, so. Like, it was really hard." Forced into the impossible choice of living in her car with her infant son – and risk having her son removed from her care – or living in her father's public housing with its black mould, she chose the black mould.

> So I ended up going to my dad's because it was the only place I could go and also we were in the middle of a lockdown. And he was also, you know, did everything he could but his house was just too, it was too bad. Like the black mould and the rain coming in and it was – me and my dad have been living in that house since I was three and he's been calling Housing New Zealand ever since I was three to get that house fixed. Now that my son's born and three generations have been through that house, they're finally fixing the roof. [It took] twenty years.

At the time of our interview, Jillian had just moved into her own rental unit, with a rent supplement from the government, after more than a year on the housing waitlist. As a single mother experiencing homelessness, I know that Jillian would have been ranked as high priority for housing in Ottawa, where I live; I do not know how she was ranked in New Zealand, but the one year wait suggests she was not at the very top of the list. As of July 2021, New Zealand news outlets were reporting a six-month wait for those at the very top of the priority list for housing (Lynch, 2021), a substantial increase over the pre-pandemic wait time. While the COVID-19 pandemic has made the crunch on affordable housing in New Zealand even more pronounced, the beginning of the crisis can be traced to neoliberal policy measures that cut public housing spending substantially, starting in the 1990s. This is the root of the issue with Jillian's father's public housing unit, which had been in a state of unhealthy disrepair for two decades.

Depending on what state they live in, American young people who have experienced homelessness have varied access to state-funded housing or rental supports. For Isabella (age twenty-one), who grew up in Texas, state-funded housing was not part of the story for herself or her low-income Mexican-American family. Instead, they scraped by with crumbling, privately owned housing and barely affordable private rentals. Private ownership appears to be seen as the solution to the affordable housing crisis in Texas, as reflected in the mission statement of the Texas State Affordable Housing Corporation, a non-profit, charitable organization established by the Texas Legislature in 1994 "to serve as a self-sustaining, statewide affordable housing provider" (Texas State Affordable Housing Corporation, n.d.). By "affordable housing provider," they do not mean that they provide affordable housing, in the sense that publicly funded housing is directly provided by the government as in other parts of the United States and the other countries in this study. Rather, they "provide a variety of affordable housing programs" that aim to support private developers (both for-profit and non-profit) to build "better housing for working families," and to help "homebuyers achieve the American dream of homeownership" or to "sustain homeownership" by existing homeowners (ibid.). As discussed in chapter one, this is typical of the American approach to housing, which has always privileged private ownership over public housing, an emphasis that became even more pronounced from the 1980s onward.

I could not find any programs offering standing rent supplements for Texans, although there was a COVID-19-specific "Texan Rent Relief" program, which stopped accepting applications in November 2021 due to the overwhelming demand. While there are city-specific public housing authorities in Texas, the one in the city where Isabella was homeless boasts only 1839 units in a city of almost 1 million (Housing Authority City of Austin, n.d.). As a point of comparison, in Ottawa, Canada, also with a population of about 1 million, there are about 22,500 public housing units (City of Ottawa, n.d.) – and a waitlist of at least twelve years to get into one. In other words, it is not surprising that Isabella's housing story includes no mention of public affordable housing, since it is virtually non-existent where she lives.

Isabella became homeless as a result of losing her scholarship to attend a music education program at a prestigious university. The scholarship was linked to employment with a performing arts centre; as an aspiring opera singer, this had seemed like the opportunity of a lifetime for Isabella. Sexual harassment by her employer ended this opportunity, leading Isabella to attempt suicide three times, losing her job and then her scholarship in the process. She kept all of this hidden from her family, who lived in another city in Texas, trying to make everything work on her own. After losing her job and her scholarship, Isabella could no longer afford the expensive rent she had been paying; instead, she couch surfed for several months, staying with friends and colleagues.

Despite all that she had been forced to deal with, she stayed on in the city where she had moved to attend university, in order to take advantage of another opera opportunity: a paid gig in a Gilbert and Sullivan production. Unfortunately, rehearsals happened at a site that took two hours for her to reach by public transit; because rehearsals were at night, this often left her travelling alone on transit well into the night, an experience she found terrifying at times. The only reason she could afford public transit was because of the student bus pass she still had; the rest of the cast attended rehearsal by car. Isabella eventually learned that everyone else in the cast was in their forties and had other, full-time jobs. She was the youngest, at age nineteen; she also found out she was being paid less than the other cast members.

After this series of difficult experiences, Isabella returned to her home city and moved in with her grandfather, who lived in a family home purchased when housing was more affordable. Located in a designated "heritage" neighbourhood, Isabella's grandfather was unable to pay for the repairs and restoration costs that were approved for housing in the area; the house was thus in terrible disrepair. This was where she was living at the time of our interview. She was working two part-time jobs at performing arts centres, still trying to pursue her dream of working in the sector, with plans to re-start her postsecondary education in the fall. There was no way she could afford a private rental on her current wage; with rents averaging US$1192/month (Rent Café, 2022), her two part-time wages of US$11/hour and US$10.75/hour were nowhere near sufficient for her to move out on her own. Still, Isabella characterized herself as "lucky" – minimum wage in Texas is US$7.25/hour, and she was grateful to no longer be homeless. As she told me when I asked if she had anything she would like to add at the end of our interview: "I think that in terms of people, it's very easy to fall into homelessness. Even if, I was lucky – I only had like a summer. And I think people should keep an eye out more for early signs of homelessness. I lost my scholarship in one day. It was that easy. Or, just, like, don't mock people for not being able to afford a car until they're thirty. You know? It's harder for some. Not everybody's gifted cars and it's just – I don't know, don't knock public transit or stuff like that or just, don't be disrespectful." As Isabella is pointing out here, under neoliberal conditions and extremes of wealth inequality faced in particular by this generation of young people, it can be quite easy to "fall into homelessness" – particularly if you do not have a wide family safety net to catch you. Without a state-funded safety net of affordable public housing, non-stigmatizing state benefits, and accessible higher education, it is only families and friends that young people can turn to when things fall apart. Luckily for Isabella, she was able to draw on these resources to pull herself out of a very difficult situation. But the combined trauma of homelessness and being the victim of workplace sexual harassment, plus the increased debt load she will be taking on to complete her schooling without her scholarship, will likely take their toll on her life chances and future opportunities.

Daraja (age twenty-nine) joined me over Zoom on her mobile phone, moving around her tiny unit in East London, United Kingdom, as we spoke, trying to get some privacy and space from her two young children while answering my questions. Giant dark smudges were visible below her eyes, and she yawned throughout our conversation. Daraja was working part time as a personal support worker and hoping to start her education in nursing in a few months' time. Woefully under-housed with two small children (six months old and four years old), Daraja subsisted on very little sleep. As a single mother and relatively recent migrant from Nigeria, Daraja had few supports in England, beyond connections she had made in the charitable sector and with an advocacy group working on housing issues in East London. The "temporary accommodation" in which she had been placed by the local borough was inadequate, to say the least: a former youth hostel, her unit had one room in which she and her two children could live, eat, and sleep, with a tiny kitchenette and private bathroom. The building was filled with people in similar situations as her own: there were no "proper British," to use Daraja's phrase, which she explained to me as, "[T]he white ones. British. What I mean is the white British, not the Black British." Daraja witnessed and experienced racist discrimination on a daily basis; for this reason, she told me she did not feel that England was a particularly democratic country, even if it was less dangerous and corrupt than her home country of Nigeria. "There are very few people, that their voice has been heard. People like me. People like a lot of people in these buildings."

Daraja had moved into her current unit one year prior, pregnant with her son and caring for her then three-year-old daughter. She was given the unit furnished with a double bed and told, "[that] is going to be enough for you and your daughter." After her son was born, the building managers provided her with a cot (or crib), which had to be squeezed into the same room as their bed. As Daraja explained to me,

> These accommodation is designed for singles, not for people with kids, family people. Because it's not enough. Like the kids. I could have put them to bed at seven, you know? But here, now, they haven't got any sleep. [Fussing in the background.] So they don't have any sleeping routine. Even myself, I don't have time to myself. Also the sleep at night. [I cannot] just put them to bed in time so that I can have some time to myself. Go through my emails. To go through any assignments I need to carry out and stuff like that because I can't. I'm using my phone [for this interview]. If I'm using my laptop, I wouldn't be able to do this because my kids won't let me. Like this boy [gesturing at her son, climbing onto her lap at the time] won't let me because I'm up with both of them. So, so, it's so tight here.

Daraja would not have known that she could push for better accommodations if she had not encountered a local housing advocacy organization that set up a table on the high street every Saturday. She picked up their brochure and then attended one of their meetings. After speaking with them about her situation, they told her: "You don't have to keep struggling and then you didn't tell anyone about it. You just have to say this out and then complain and let them know the situation. Because they might be thinking you're comfortable – you're just staying there, you didn't even say anything, so [they think] I don't want [anything different]." With the support of the housing activists, Daraja approached the housing manager and explained her situation:

> And I went to her and I said, "This is the way we've been managing but it's not so comfortable. What can you do for us?" Blah blah blah. And then she said to me, um, we're giving you a nice type bed. The sofa is the sofa bed so you can put your daughter on it. Sleep on it. I said, "It's a three-year-old girl. That shouldn't be." The [manager] said, "That's my advice anyway. If not, then you can go and get yourself a child's bed or a bigger cot." I said, "Where do you expect me to put that in this room?"

Without other reasonable options, Daraja followed the manager's advice about placing her daughter on the sofa bed to sleep. When her daughter fell off the sofa bed, Daraja returned to the manager, who then told her she should complain to the council's corporate office (the managing office of the local government). It was the housing activists who advised her to include the mayor on her email to the corporate office. After a few pointed follow-up emails from Daraja, the council (local government) finally agreed to come and inspect her unit. The inspection was scheduled for the day after our interview; my guess is that even with an inspection, Daraja's circumstances were not likely to change. However, with the support of the housing activists, Daraja is learning the skills and strategies that may help her secure more appropriate housing at some point.

I have researched housing issues in the United Kingdom before (Kennelly, 2016; Kennelly & Watt, 2011, 2012). From that experience, I can posit with some confidence that if Daraja had been in Canada, she likely would have been living in a homeless shelter or other, even less stable, accommodations with her young children. The previously expansive public housing system in the United Kingdom, which housed almost 30 per cent of all residents, is a shattered remnant of what it once was – and yet it is still better than the public housing system in Canada, which even at its zenith never breached 5 per cent of the available housing stock. So perhaps we could say that Daraja is lucky to have migrated to England rather than Canada when fleeing Nigeria. However, the UK housing system is broken and is only getting worse under recent governments. This broken housing system means that a young mother with high aspirations to attend university and attain her nursing degree is faced with a living situation that will make success at university a real challenge. She and her children are both under-slept, which for her children will likely have knock-on effects on their behaviour and their own school success. While Daraja has been learning from local housing activists how to fight for her rights, securing a separate bedroom for her and her children is likely to be a long, hard, and time-consuming battle.

Neoliberal Welfare Benefits

As discussed in detail in chapter one, one of the clearest signals of the advent of neoliberal ideology in government is massive cuts to social benefits, and the transformation of the welfare system into a punitive and stigmatizing bureaucracy, designed to deter people from using state benefits in the first place. The overall effect is to keep people in poverty, preventing them from accessing benefits to which they might be entitled, or structuring the benefits such that the process of getting them is humiliating and traumatizing in its own right. Indeed, receiving social welfare benefits has become so stigmatized that I found it challenging to get detailed information from people regarding their reliance on welfare payments. Always trying to be attuned to participants' non-verbal cues about their level of comfort with a given topic, I found myself skirting around the issue of welfare benefits most of the time. This means that the data I have on this topic is more limited than on either of the above categories (education and housing). This in itself is a relevant finding; as Tracy Shildrick (2018, p. 785) notes, the pervasiveness of what she terms "poverty propaganda" – "that those experiencing poverty are workshy, lazy and culpable for their own predicaments" – is reproduced with particular ferocity in representations of people living on welfare, where "political figures and the media deploy rare, unusual, and at times downright fantastical stories of supposed problematic behaviour of varying sorts that is purported to be supported by the welfare state" (Shildrick, 2018, p. 787). This helps explain why talking about welfare benefits during interviews carries more emotional risk for participants and can thus be more challenging than talking about other, less stigmatized, topics, such as education background or even histories of homelessness.

For those participants who were willing to speak openly about their reliance on state benefits, I heard, unsurprisingly, that the amounts they received were a mere pittance, not nearly enough to survive on. In Australia, Scarlett told me she was receiving about AU$40/day in welfare benefits, half of which went towards paying her rent (the rest of her rent was covered by a rent supplement). This left her with AU$20/day to live on, or about AU$600/month for groceries, transport, clothing, supplies, and any other items she needs. One estimate of monthly grocery costs for those living on low incomes in Australia, based on survey data, is $115/week, or about $518/month (Birot, 2022). This amount says nothing about the quality of the food purchased. In other words, on Scarlett's welfare payments, she may be able to afford groceries every month, but only if she foregoes almost every other possible expense. Scarlett is well aware of the limited buying power provided by her welfare payments, her poor opportunities for employment, and also the stigma attached to receiving welfare at all: "So, like, I've been on welfare since I was sixteen. Because that's the age you can get welfare here in Australia. And it's, like, you get this reputation for being a bogan and all that the longer you're on it. So, like, I've been trying to get a job and it's almost impossible to get a job, especially like when you dropped out of school and haven't really got a formal education." I had to look up the Australian slang term "bogan." Although it can have multiple connotations, one article advises that it needs to be used carefully, as it can cause harm and be degrading: "It's associated with actual poverty, actual suburbs, it can be a way of demeaning and denigrating people who are disadvantaged" (Lathouris, 2020). Wikipedia describes it as "slang for a person whose speech, clothing, attitude and behaviour are considered unrefined or unsophisticated" ("Bogan," 2022). Scarlett's use of the term is thus signalling that remaining on welfare may increase her disadvantage due to the stigma of being seen as poor and unsophisticated – not middle class, in other words.

Even young people who relied on state benefits sometimes shared the view that welfare recipients are lazy and undeserving. "Poverty propaganda," says Shildrick (2018, p. 785), is "so powerful, pervasive and persuasive that even people experiencing deep poverty often subscribe to their truth." In New Zealand, Monica (age sixteen) told me she was eligible for an "independent youth" benefit to help her pay for room and board since leaving home. As I asked for more details, I determined that this payment seems to be similar to the support that young people in other countries can receive from Children's Aid or Child Protective Services – in other words, it is not seen as a welfare benefit but rather as a form of support for children under the care of the state. Because Monica had lived with her parents until recently, both her mother and her father had to be willing to sign off on paperwork stating that they could no longer care for her; this would mean her mother's welfare payments would be reduced, as she would no longer receive the child support benefit that had been tied to Monica residing with her. Monica and her family had been relying on state benefits for her entire life; Monica had a sophisticated critique of the effects of poverty and the impacts of the lack of affordable housing in New Zealand. I was thus surprised when she expressed disdain for those New Zealanders relying on work-related ("working income") welfare benefits:

> MONICA: But like, because we have like working income, which is like throwing free money at people, makes it so much easier for everyone to just be like, awful

people in poverty. Instead of looking for a job and trying to get somewhere in life, they just like go on a benefit.
JACKIE: Okay. Is that, are you saying that that's what other people think is happening? Or are you saying that is what's happening?
MONICA: That's what's happening. When I'm phoning the benefits office, I can't even get through to it because everyone's calling it. Wondering where their money is.

The notion that people receiving welfare benefits become reliant on it and too lazy to look for work is drawn straight from the neoliberal ideological playbook, hearkening back to Ronald Reagan's claim that welfare benefits were creating "an America of lost dreams and stunted lives" (Reagan, 1986; see also chapter one). There is no evidence to support this widely held belief. Indeed, large-scale statistical studies have shown the *opposite* to be true: that the higher the welfare benefits, and the less restrictive the limits, the *more* motivated people are to return to work and the *better* they do overall (Esser, 2009; Hamilton, Wingrove, & Woodford, 2019). Although researchers caution that this finding ought not to be treated as a simple causal explanation – that is, we cannot assume that simply increasing welfare benefits will magically improve employment motivation – it remains the case that clearly there is no actual connection between high welfare benefits and low work motivation or "laziness."

Under neoliberal policy regimes, the double whammy of welfare stigma and insufficient benefit amounts combines to prevent people who might otherwise be eligible from applying. As described in chapter one, this is one of the ways in which neoliberal states "reduce" the number of people receiving welfare – not by increasing their job readiness or their opportunities, but rather by making welfare so stigmatized, administratively challenging, and poorly paid that people opt not to apply, even if they need the support. In the United Kingdom, Elizabeth (age twenty-two) grew up in a middle-class family and became homeless as a result of family conflict; when considering her options for supporting herself, welfare benefits were not even on the list:

> Even before the pandemic, knowing for years that benefits in the UK are not really enough to survive off. So if you become unemployed and you don't have savings, you're on your own basically. Having that hang over me for my whole adult life, you do have this attitude of like, again, not that voting is worthless, because it's got to be done. It feels like something you've got to do, but when it comes down to it, it's things like those community gardens and mutual aid groups that will distribute food to people and make sure the lights are still running. Because the government definitely is not going to give you enough money or enough support in any way to help you if you get unlucky like that. And that's just something I've sort of always known if that makes sense.

Elizabeth makes an explicit link between voting and state benefits here; this was part of a wider conversation we were having about what one can reasonably expect from government. Elizabeth was one of the few young people in my study who had experienced homelessness and was committed to voting; her class background and higher education provided her with those aspects of a democratic disposition, although she described voting as "a grim moral obligation" rather than something she felt would actually make change. For Elizabeth, there is no point in expecting that the government will provide reasonable support; better that she turn to local, grassroots community groups to fulfil those needs. This is the neoliberal policymakers' dream: moving citizens away from relying on the state to fulfil their obligations, and instead have them expect nothing from the state and instead become entrepreneurial actors who turn towards other forms of provision in order to scrape by. I raised this point with Elizabeth and asked her what she thought of it:

> ELIZABETH: I'm definitely sceptical of [David Cameron's] "Big Society" like thing, and the outsourcing of government's roles to community. I don't think that should happen. At the same time, I think the way things are going and how entrenched neoliberalism is, that's largely going to happen. It's been happening. And it certainly seems like a bad idea to not have those things supporting people in the hopes that it provokes the government to act when they very much could spend twenty years shrugging their shoulders and going, "It's not my problem." Um, you know? I think also I will say I am not particularly an anarchist myself, but I am drawn to the fact that a lot of these places have quite an anarchist philosophy because it means that they feel less easily exploited by a kind of neoliberal system. They're actively challenging it, if that makes sense, as well as trying to make people's lives better within it.
> JACKIE: Yeah, yeah, yeah. And that matters also, for sure.
> ELIZABETH: Yeah, I think it's just this idea that I've kind of written the government off in a lot of functional areas. So I take what I can from the community even though you raise a good point. I don't think it should be a community organization's responsibility necessarily to make sure that people have basic human rights. But it's what we have.

I am sympathetic to the anarchist organizing thrust towards community-driven social support; many of the movements with which I have been active have had a similar ideological position. Bringing people together to mutually support one another creates a sense of community and complex relational ties; it is these complex relational ties that can often be nurtured into political agency (Kennelly, 2009b, 2014). But what I see happening quite often is not anarchist organizing for the sake of widespread political change, but rather, as Elizabeth has described here, a collective response to community crisis that means providing emergency assistance in place of the state. Without a corresponding political movement that demands the state take up its responsibilities to its citizens, I see this leading to the unintentional fulfilment of neoliberal political ends, including the abandonment of the state's duties to provide an adequate social safety net in the form of decent welfare benefits.

Conclusions

The central argument of this book is that neoliberal policymaking over the past forty years has generated massive and growing inequality in the five liberal democracies under study, and that this inequality is harming democracy. This chapter, I hope, has provided some glimpses into the complex contours of how neoliberal inequality is lived at the level of the everyday for young people who have experienced homelessness in the United States, Canada, the United Kingdom, Australia, and New Zealand. Of course, it is not only homeless or formerly homeless young people whose life chances have been altered, and worsened, by neoliberalism. Seeking out homeless young people in each country was one way in which I could concretely operationalize the experience of poverty and hear from a population of youth who have been demonstrably failed by the state.

In the first part of the chapter, through the stories of Tamara (Canada), Maggie (United Kingdom), and Scarlett (Australia), I tried to demonstrate how direct experience of state failures does not necessarily translate into the ability to advocate for change to said systems. This is because the skills and dispositions required to navigate the political field of liberal democracies are resolutely middle-class ones and are generally acquired only through being born to a middle-class family or being habituated into middle classness through higher education and/or direct mentorship. Tamara had keen and detailed insights into the various systems that touched her life, including mental health care, child welfare, and housing, but had none of the skills or networks needed to translate this knowledge into political advocacy, even at the basic level of voting. Through a combination of intelligence, charisma, luck, and opportunities, Maggie acquired a democratic disposition that allowed her to speak back to middle-class policymakers and politicians and meaningfully advocate for her marginalized Traveller community in the United Kingdom. However, the experience left her feeling exhausted and overwhelmed at times, which may lead her into burnout in future. Scarlett had received some mentorship from the staff-supported youth advocacy circle at a homeless-serving agency in Australia, and this had led to opportunities for her to speak with the mayor and city council and participate in fundraising activities. From her description, however, these activities struck me as being fairly limited in their political efficacy, instead serving political leaders' desire for the optics of homeless youth participation – a tokenistic inclusion, at best. Scarlett's circumstances also continue to be extremely dire and often life-threatening, and her energy and time for political advocacy and activism are subsequently constrained.

Chapters two and three used data from my interviews with young people across all five countries to uncover some of the markers of acquiring a democratic disposition (specifically, attitudes and beliefs about politics and democracy), as well as the shared biographical pathways that can lead to such acquisition (families of origin, mentorship, and higher education). Without more effective civics education in public schooling (more on this in chapter six), those not born to middle-class, politically active families are much less likely to acquire a democratic disposition – that is, the complex set of skills and attitudes required to meaningfully create social change under liberal democratic structures. The majority of young people who experience homelessness are born into poor families (Mabhala, Yohannes, & Griffith, 2017); it is not surprising, then, that only four of the twenty-two young people who experienced homelessness and participated in this study were born to middle- or lower-middle-class families (Armin [Australia], Stephanie and Isabella [United States], and Elizabeth [United Kingdom]). Middle-class kids who become homeless due to familial conflict or violence in the home are rendered equally vulnerable to the ravages of neoliberal cuts to social spending; but kids born to poor and working-class families experience these impacts right from birth. As documented in chapter one, every country in this study has undergone neoliberal policy transformations that have stripped them of their social safety nets, leading to losses of affordable housing, lower-quality public education for poorer students, the decimation and stigmatization of welfare benefits, and skyrocketing costs for higher education. The stories in the second half of this chapter have sought to demonstrate how policy decisions are rendered concrete in the lives of young people, shutting doors and closing off opportunities, making it harder still for impoverished individuals to acquire the class-stratified skills required to participate in the political field. The result is that those most in need of policy change – those being most dramatically and vividly failed by the state – are the least likely to be able to engage with it, a condition that has become ever more extreme under current levels of inequality.

In the chapters to come, I attempt to provide some response to the question of *how* inequality of access to opportunities, stability, and prosperity leads to inequality in the capacity to participate meaningfully under our current liberal democratic structures. In chapter five, I trace what Bourdieu might have called the *homological* relationship between middle-class activism and middle-class political engagement within formal liberal democratic structures. Homology refers to likeness of form, the ways in which one's "fit" within one cultural space allows one to fit rather easily in another, and vice versa. In chapter six, I consider the lessons offered by the state, both formally and informally, about what it means to "belong" to the state via the mechanism of "citizenship." As we shall see in that chapter, the concept of citizenship is both ineluctably tied into liberal democratic state structures and also strangely distanced from the notion of democracy itself.

5 The Social Distribution of Democratic Knowledge

> Nothing is demanded more absolutely by the political game than this fundamental adherence to the game itself, *illusio, involvement, commitment,* investment in the game which is the product of the game at the same time as it is the condition of the game being played.
> – Pierre Bourdieu (1991, p. 179–80; emphasis in original)

One of the main myths about universal democratic participation, generated by both liberalism and neoliberalism, is the role of individual effort and merit as the means by which to transform both oneself and one's community. This myth of the meritocracy is generally blind to the effects of structural inequality on an individual's access to resources and opportunities; or, if inequalities are recognized, attempts to rectify them focus on providing financial aid (such as scholarships for low-income students to attend elite universities). What is missing in such an approach is a recognition of the deeper *cultural* stratification that accompanies material stratification. In other words, the classed, raced, and gendered cultures associated with distinct fields go unrecognized or unacknowledged, meaning that those without the habitus conditioned to specific elite fields will find themselves afloat in a sea of contradictory meanings. This is as true of the political field as it is of any other.

As the preceding chapters have demonstrated, activists in all five liberal democracies tend to emerge from middle-class fields of access, shaped by professional parental occupation and political interests, extra-curricular activities, and attendance at postsecondary institutions. Activists who come from working-class families share biographies that narrate a class shift occurring for each of them, generally through mentorship or access to postsecondary schooling and/or student-led activist movements. On the other hand, the shared story of the most impoverished and marginalized of young people in these same five countries – those who have experienced homelessness – is overwhelmingly marked by an absence of democratic engagement in any form, due to lack of knowledge, lack of opportunity, and/or the political disillusionment that is an almost inevitable result of witnessing the ongoing denigration of one's own worth and the worth of one's friends and family.

To understand that this is true is an important first step. This chapter attempts to theorize *why* this is true, and *how* it has come to be this way. Drawing on Bourdieu's theoretical corpus, specifically the concept of homology, here I trace the mechanisms by which a democratic disposition can hop easily between diverse but overlapping political fields, opening up further avenues of access to democratic engagement. Conversely, I demonstrate the cultural barriers that reinforce structural inequalities and prevent those without a (largely middle-class) democratic disposition from traversing these same fields, further entrenching their lack of access to liberal democratic mechanisms of social change.

Homologous Political Fields

I briefly described Bourdieu's concept of field in the Introduction to this book. I return to it in more detail here, as it is a necessary component for appreciating how homologies function. Homology is not a concept that has been widely used within English-language theory inspired by Bourdieu (Wang, 2016); I owe my awareness of its potential utility to the original work of my former doctoral student, Dr. Alex Bing (Bing, 2021). Field is a concept that has circulated much more widely.

In the Bourdieusian theoretical approach, a field is not a physical entity with strict boundaries that can be observed separately from those who move within it. Rather, it is a *social space* inhabited by social beings whose dispositions, beliefs, and habits have been developed within social milieus that began with their families of origin. The boundaries of a field are demarcated by the felt experiences of its inhabitants: the field ends where the effects of the field are no longer felt, emotionally and viscerally within the body. The effects of the field on a given individual depend on how habituated their habitus is to that field; if they were raised within a comparable field (with similar norms, expectations, and rules of behaviour), they will feel quite at ease within that field – like a fish in water, as Bourdieu has analogized. If their habitus is *not* a match for the field, an individual will notice this generally with more intensity than the fish in water, as instead they will feel like a fish *out* of water: metaphorically gasping for air, uncertain of where to turn, perhaps panicky and seeking to get back into their familiar habitat where they can breathe more easily.

All fields are not created equal within extremely inegalitarian social milieus. While everyone has a habitus that matches some specific field, there are certain fields that are considered "the norm," whether or not they are statistically more common than others. This is where doxa comes in, and also symbolic violence. Doxa, or state-mandated common sense, is "the norm" that also happens to be the field of the dominant class. In all of the liberal democracies within this study, this is the field inhabited by white, middle-class, heterosexual, and able-bodied men, at its most general level. There are fields within fields, striated by access to specific forms of cultural, economic, and social capital (e.g., education levels, access to wealth, connections, and networks), which means that not all dominant fields are inhabited by the same individuals with dominant traits. The degrees of differentiation become more subtle and nuanced the closer one gets to power.

Because we are all exposed to doxa from birth, we all, to greater or lesser extents, have absorbed the "common sense" that posits dominant fields as "normal" and thus more desirable. Liberal democratic doxa, particularly under neoliberalism, is steeply entrenched in the ideology of the meritocracy – the pull-yourselves-up-by-the-bootstraps myth that is central to neoliberal approaches to welfare and social policy – such that individuals are encouraged to believe that they are solely responsible for their own circumstances, even if their lived experiences belie that story. Symbolic violence occurs because the dominated cannot help but absorb the doxa that is generated by the dominant. Under neoliberalism, this most often looks like blaming oneself for one's own situation – by believing oneself to be not intelligent enough, capable enough, and/or perseverant enough to have succeeded in a world that is supposedly open to anyone. This is why Bourdieu (2014) revised Weber's definition of the state to be not only the legitimate arbiter of physical violence, but also of symbolic violence.

How homologous one field is to another has much to do with the forms of capital that are valued within each field. As Wang (2016, p. 354) states so eloquently: "Fields … are comparable to each other on account of homologous relations, in that agents with similar status and capital converge with each other by making consistently similar choices regarding schools, disciplines, occupations, cultural products, or political stances." This means that if one field, say, values a liberal arts education, the ability to speak knowledgeably about current political actors, and experiences of community organizing and/or international travel, then an individual with all of these traits will feel quite comfortable within it. If this individual then encounters a field where these qualities are similarly valued, but greater emphasis is put on one's political knowledge than one's community organizing skills, and there is an additional value put on the ability to speak one's mind with confidence and clarity, they will likely still feel quite comfortable within that field. In other words, these two fields – which might be recognizable by readers as resembling the field of activism and the field of political candidacy – are homologous. By contrast, if an individual's habitus has been shaped by a field in which the most valuable knowledge is rooted in avoiding neighbourhood and/or family violence, navigating demeaning social services, and countering humiliation by the education system, being plunked into a field where postsecondary education, formal political knowledge, and confident public speaking are most valued will likely be an exercise in bewilderment and shame.

The concept of homology was most extensively developed by Bourdieu in *Distinction* (1984), where he explored the connection between social class and cultural tastes. As described by Wang (2016, p. 349), "Homology refers to a morphological resemblance between the structures of different fields. Bourdieu posits that homologous structures exist across fields thanks to underlying logics of social classification." While *Distinction* focuses on cultural tastes in France in the 1960s – that is, preferences for "high-brow" versus "low-brow" art, among other cultural artefacts and activities – homology as a concept is applicable across any social fields. Indeed, Wang (2016, p. 354) characterizes homology as "one of Bourdieu's most important discoveries," and in fact a core component of Bourdieusian social theory. Wacquant (1993, p. 1; emphasis his) classifies Bourdieu's entire *oeuvre* as being fundamentally a "quest to explicate the specificity and potency of *symbolic power*, that is, the capacity that systems of meaning and signification have of shielding, and thereby strengthening, relations of oppression and exploitation by hiding them under the cloak of nature, benevolence and meritocracy." Homological relationships between fields hide symbolic power, contributing to the myth of social mobility that lies at the heart of contemporary liberal democracies.

In the remainder of this chapter, I draw on the stories of young activists to illustrate the manner in which one's social location in a stratified system can be systematically transformed through access to homological fields of political practice to open up ever more intricate knowledge of, and access to, formal structures of power. Conversely, I will demonstrate through the stories of young people who have been homeless the social effects of inequality, which block access of those without the relevant capitals to the holders of power, where such access might actually result in positive structural change that would benefit themselves and their communities and families. In other words, this chapter seeks to further demonstrate how inequality makes democracy all but impossible under current liberal democratic structures.

Homologies between Political Fields

Activism provides a wonderful example of the cross-cutting nature of fields across social space. I will speak here primarily to my own experience of this, although my observations have been confirmed by other activists I have interviewed, as captured in *Citizen Youth* (Kennelly, 2011a). To call oneself an activist is to stake one's claim within a contentious field that demands quite strict adherence to certain values, practices, and views of the world – a specific habitus, in other words. As explored in *Citizen Youth* and elaborated near the end of this chapter, the category "activist" in Anglo-American liberal democracies is often also laden with disguised social positionings, such as whiteness, middle classness, and access to higher education. There is a broad field of activism, roughly encompassing politically progressive people from the Labour movement, environmental protection and animal rights, anti-poverty movements, Indigenous rights and solidarity movements, climate activism, feminist and LGBTQ2S+ movements, the anti-gun lobby, and many others.[1] If one were to be lucky enough to attend a massive mobilization, such as was common in the heyday of the anti/alter-globalization movement in the late 1990s/early 2000s, or to participate more recently in climate marches or the Black Lives Matter protests, one would likely see many or most of these groups present in some capacity, and agreeing broadly about the importance of the issue at hand. Within this wider field of activism are many smaller, overlapping fields that alternately support or collide with one another, as the agents within each field vie for dominance in the Bourdieusian sense. Activists will not appreciate being described this way, but when I use the term "dominance" here, I always mean relatively, as enacted through the mobilization of specific capitals that mark out who "belongs" and who does not. Again, this was an issue I explored within *Citizen Youth*, identifying the specific forms of capital that were most valued within activist spaces as a kind of *subcultural capital* (following Sarah Thornton's [1996] use of the term within the youth subcultural literature). This is felt and intuited more than it is explicitly articulated; in my ethnographic research with Canadian activists, it was described to me in terms of wearing appropriate clothing ("sweatshop free" etc.), working in the right types of jobs (non-corporate), and understanding specific terms and concepts related to social justice issues (Kennelly, 2011a).

Anyone who has spent any time within activist spaces will be familiar with the frequent and sometimes painful in-fighting that can emerge between diverse subfields within the wider activist field. I have heard this referred to as "the left eating the left," where lefty movements devour each other rather than working in solidarity against a common foe. This has been bemoaned more times than I can count by activists who claim this is the reason the right have gained prominence over recent decades, as they have learned to put aside their differences and work together. I am not sure I see evidence of this on the right, certainly not lately, but I have definitely witnessed the damage that can be wrought within activist spaces from this kind of subcultural chest-pounding. In *Citizen Youth*, I observed that this often took the form of competition over the question of "who is the most radical?" where being "radical" means various things to various players but generally circulates around notions of ultimate self-sacrifice,

---

1 There are self-declared activists on the political right as well, although it would seem the term is not taken up with the same vehemence and self-righteousness as accompanies it on the left. Indeed, the political right has used the term "bleeding heart activist" as a way to discredit people with whom they disagree.

commitment to the cause, and recrimination against others who are failing to live up to these standards. As I have analysed in *Citizen Youth* and elsewhere, the ability to display such a specific form of capital is unsurprisingly entrenched in classed, gendered, and raced forms of behaviour that, if left unchecked, actually create more injustice and exclusion within activist spaces (see also Kennelly, 2009a, 2009b, 2014).

Despite the conflicts that emerge between activist subfields, traversing them is pretty easy for those "in the know." Noor (Australian activist, age nineteen) narrates this quite clearly:

> One thing is the skills you learn from one campaign or one area of activism is very transferrable to another. Like, you know, in AYCC [Australian Youth Climate Coalition] we talked a lot about climate justice. Like, putting people of colour and Indigenous people at the forefront, you know, of the campaign. Coming to UN Youth, which is a very white space, it's quite elitist in a lot of ways, and being able to say, "hey, this is what I've learned from AYCC." It's really great and bringing that experience in and people being like, "wait, I've never thought of that!" And it's really interesting because, you know, it can bring like such deep ideas you thought would be in similar organizations but they're not. And it, yeah, it really allows people to grow into valid ideas and build off of them and I'd say it's been pretty inspiring seeing that happen.

The ability to symbolically work across activist subfields is excellent training for the shift required to move from an activist field to an homologous field located in more formal modes of political engagement. As described above, one field is homologous to another when the attenuated habitus of the first field has enough similar qualities to feel a sense of "fit" within the second field. One of the signifiers of a democratic disposition – or habitus – uncovered by the empirical work done for this project and described in chapter two, is the belief that "everything is political." This is one of the values that facilitates the transference of habitus across the related fields of activism and formal politics. We can see this happening in both directions; that is, young people entering the field of activism learn transferable skills that allow them to move into the world of formal politics, and young people entering into formal politics who then are able to better engage in activism.

Julia (age eighteen), in the United Kingdom, understood very clearly how her involvement in the Student Strikes for Climate helped her learn important leadership skills as well as increase her understanding of the role of formal politics in social change. As she told me,

> I kind of just picked up skills along the way. So talking to the press and talking to the police and giving speeches and facilitating and minute taking and doing all

these things, I've kind of just learned on the way. And I think that it's kind of the best way to do it because you've obviously learned from the stage you had last time. And you get used to learning all these skills and get used to doing these skills in that kind of setting. And I've definitely taken on leadership roles within the youth strike group. Even though it is non-hierarchical, it's kind of just like, so when we do meetings on Zoom, I usually facilitate, so I make sure everyone gets to speak. I make sure that the minutes are going to be taken. I make sure that we have the agenda, and we get through it, and we make sure everything's planned.

The concrete skills that Julia describes have obvious transferability into the realm of formal politics, where talking to the press, taking detailed notes, and facilitating meetings are all directly applicable. But Julia also narrates a shift in habitus – that is, a shift in her beliefs and dispositions regarding herself and her relation to others – that is less easily taught:

Learning these skills have actually changed my life, because if you would come to me a year and a half ago, I wouldn't have been able to speak to a stranger. I wouldn't be able to speak to somebody that I didn't know. I was so shy before the youth strikes. I was cowering, and I hated speaking to people, even people I knew vaguely, and I never just stuck my neck out for anything. But since the youth strikes, I've become a bit more outspoken, which some people have said is a bad thing, but I personally love it. I'm letting my opinions be known. And I think that's important for when I go into the real world and meet all these people. I can say, "You know what, I don't think that is a good idea. Can you please, do something else?" And I've learned these leadership skills and honestly, it's been the best experience of my life going through this, going through the motions, and just learning these new skills.

Recall that Julia is one of only a few young activists to come from a working-class background in this study. The life-changing skills she has learned through the Student Strikes for Climate can thus also be read through a class lens. Before moving into the middle-class world of activism, Julia had absorbed an anxious and self-deprecating political habitus forced upon the working class in neoliberal Britain, who have learned that their views are not valued and that "sticking one's neck out" could be a precarious endeavour. This is also arguably a gendered habitus, where women continue to be socialized to keep their opinions to themselves; as Julia notes, some have suggested that her being "outspoken" is a "bad thing." Being exposed to an activist habitus – which overlaps significantly with what I describe as a "democratic disposition" – has given Julia not only the skills, knowledge, and social networks to have her views be amplified and make an impact, it has also shifted her sense of entitlement about having her views heard and expressing them loudly to anyone who will listen. This dispositional transformation is required to be able to meaningfully engage with formal liberal democratic structures. Bourdieu identifies this as part of the "economy of linguistic exchanges," whereby learning both the language of a specific field, and feeling entitled to use it, is a competence that is "acquired in a social context and through practice" (1991, p. 82). As he notes, "The sense of the value of one's own linguistic products is a fundamental dimension of the sense of knowing the place which one occupies in the social space" (Bourdieu, 1991, p. 82).

Involvement in the youth strikes also gave Julia exposure to others who were already well-versed in the world of formal politics, who could educate her explicitly about how the activism they were doing might lead to formal political change:

> So one of my coordinators is a youth council member, so youth parliament member. So she kind of explained a little bit to me when I didn't understand. I was like, "Okay, so this is happening within the government. What does that mean because I'm really confused?" And she always used to come back to me, "Right, okay. So this is what's happening and everything." I was like, "Oh, right. Okay. I got it now." So I definitely learned it through other people within the youth strikes. Obviously, I had to learn about the government in action, which governments are promising, who's promising to go zero carbon by 2030 or something. I just kind of learned which political party that I aligned with, and I kind of had to learn about politics for the youth strikes. Definitely, during the near elections because I knew I was turning eighteen soon. I want to vote, but I don't feel educated enough, so I definitely accumulated that, and I post it on our social medias. We definitely try and keep our followers educated about politics and everything and what the government's doing and things, which is really helpful. And I've just learned through the youth strikes what the government has done, what it hasn't done.

The explicit recognition of the skills learned through activism was more likely to be commented upon by those few activists from working-class or working-poor backgrounds, like Julia. This is not surprising, as it speaks to the earlier acquisition of an activist habitus and its associated skills for middle-class kids, especially those who came from activist or politically engaged families. In other words, the young people who already had a democratic disposition, acquired through families of origin, would be less likely to notice a specific acquisition of skills and knowledge through activist worlds, since they had them to begin with. For young people like Julia, from a non-activist working-class family, the skills and knowledge she acquired through her involvement in student strikes were very apparent to her.

Karen (age twenty-four) was similarly able to recognize the skills she learned through activism and then apply them to homologous political fields. Born in the United Kingdom but raised in New Zealand, Karen grew up in poverty and went into the foster care system at age thirteen. Like Julia, Karen became involved in activism through climate justice movements, which led to her being able to attend one of the large UN climate summits as a youth representative. This remarkable opportunity was transformative for Karen's understanding of political actors and political change:

> I think one of the earliest and most striking things was at the Rio+20 conference, there's prime ministers in the room and being sixteen, me and the other delegate, we weren't shy. We went up and talked to them. It felt the most direct democracy, being in that environment where the leaders are there and just some crazy situations like heading up to them, talking to representatives about the outtake and things like that. Because I think the UN is usually such an amorphous concept. But actually having seen it in action and seeing what its aims are and what its weaknesses and then bringing that back to New Zealand, suddenly, MPs and their whole system wasn't as unapproachable as it was before. And that helped inform me – the activist strength of being able to speak truth to power, and doing what needs to be done to get in front of who is making the decision and things like that.… And also seeing no matter how big the decision-maker is, whether it's the UN secretary general or prime ministers and things, they are just people and you can talk to them and they're approachable to different extents. But having seen that gave me a very open view to what democracy is and also what you can achieve with it.

Karen's involvement in climate justice activism gave her direct experience of having unfettered access to those holding power. As for Julia, this generated an important and needed sense of entitlement for Karen, that her views were worthy of attention from the powerful. Her experiences at the UN summit also demystified the process, and the people involved, giving Karen the confidence to approach other decision-makers in other contexts. The acquisition of skills, knowledge, and, perhaps most importantly, a sense of entitlement to voice her views and expect that they will be listened to, led Karen to activist engagement with another issue of importance to her: the foster care system.

> Because, basically, once I saw the change that can be brought about from my environmental experience.… Just having issues that you care about and actually rallying and organizing. Foster care has always been something that I kept quite private and didn't tell anyone about. And so when I was nineteen, twenty, in 2016, I think, I actually thought, "Maybe I should go about trying to apply some of the lessons that I learned in climate organizing to this space." And so we founded a group called Foster Child Support Network. And we started trying to connect kids in care and also reach out to the government agencies and start a conversation with them about improving policies and putting the child at the center of care. And then the government set up a whole funded agency to do just that. So I was happy. Because it was just completely run by volunteers and other students that were happy to

help. And so it was really cool to see the government create this independent body now. And so I could come in and kind of advise at a high level without having to spend all my time organizing people.

For some young activists in my study, the transference of skills and knowledge between the homologous fields of political activism and formal politics happened in the other direction. Matt (age nineteen) first joined the youth wing of a national progressive political party in the United Kingdom; when I asked him about the biggest influences on his activism, he replied: "I think pre-joining the party and post-joining the party, the young people I've met within the party. And, they kind of like, the network that I've built up through that which like matched my politics pretty entirely. And it's also maybe interesting to note, I guess, the kind of youth wing of the party have a politics that's definitely different from like, the national party, the kind of adult party. It's definitely more radically focused." The networks and knowledge Matt developed through his involvement with the party led him into activist organizing both within and outside of the confines of the party itself. In Canada, Gregory (age eighteen) also began in formal politics, supporting the campaign of a local candidate, which led to other opportunities that opened into more direct forms of advocacy and activism. Edward (age nineteen), in the United States, drew a direct line between watching Donald Trump win the presidential election in 2016, becoming more involved in the local Democratic Party as a result, and then shifting into activism that both blended into and emerged from his formal involvement with the Young Democrats.

The homologous relationship between the field of formal politics and that of activism exists in every Anglo-American liberal democracy included in this study, making it relatively straightforward to take the skills and attitudes developed in one and apply these to the other. This does not mean that these fields are identical; they can be quite antagonistic to one another, for obvious reasons. Angie, for instance, narrates a condescending encounter she had with a politician in Canada, reinforcing her disdain for certain elements of formal politics:

> So Diane Finlay was my MP [Member of Parliament]. Um, and this was sort of the height of like the Omar Khadr issue [Canadian child soldier being held in Guantanamo Bay throughout the 2000s by the US Armed Forces]. And I found out she was going to be at this like Kinsmen event in Port Dover, like a small-town business leader type thing. So, I bartended the Kinsmen event sometimes as a teenager [laughs] for some cash. And I have a very distinct memory of seeing that she was going out for a smoke, going, "I'm going to go talk to this lady," and saying, "I don't understand why you're doing this. Like, why are you violating the international, like it's a child soldier, like don't we have a responsibility? It's not what Canada is supposed to be." And I just remember her specifically patting me on my cheek, and

saying, "I'm so happy you're interested, sweetie." And I [said], "Well, I'm glad that you're glad that I'm interested, but you know, this is wrong." And she goes, "No, sweetie, what you have to understand is there are actually three sides to every story. And, the media doesn't like to tell you. There's the truth, there's the lies, and then what the media tells you and the media doesn't want to tell you the truth. But I'm just so glad you're interested and please stay interested."

Having been raised by working-class activists in a strong tradition of trade unionism, this encounter did not turn Angie away from formal politics, but actually *towards* it. She took her anger at Diane Finlay, a Conservative MP, and funnelled it into getting involved with the campaign of the New Democratic Party (NDP) candidate in the area during the next election, "Because I was like, what's this? Like, how dare you!" However, Angie also recognized how off-putting this kind of encounter could be for a young person: "And like, that's a really common thing and one of the reasons why I would never judge anyone for not engaging with electoral politics. It's a really common thing for elected officials to do [that] to young activists, to say, 'it's so good you're interested! I'm so proud of you!' I don't want you to be proud of me. You have power, use it."

Antagonisms between these homologous fields does not lessen the degree to which they are similar. Their similarities lie not only in the dispositions needed to work within them, but also in the shared *illusio* that makes their logic discernible to one another, even if some players disagree with the details of that logic taken up by other players. As I describe in chapter two, the illusio refers to the "tacit recognition of the value of the stakes of the game and ... practical mastery of its rules" (Bourdieu & Wacquant, 1992, p. 117). In order to recognize the stakes of the game, one must first be capable of *seeing* that there is a game being played, and what kind of game it is. I use "game" here in the same sense as Bourdieu: not to belittle the process nor suggest that the players within it are being disingenuous or deceitful, nor even to suggest that players are particularly conscious of their alignment with the rules of the game which occur at the level of dispositions and embodied or affective responses. "Game" is an analogy that applies to every field in which all social beings find themselves, not only within politics.

In political fields, whether activist or formalist, players share an understanding that the game being played requires political engagement at a much deeper level than mere voting. Political fluency in the structure of government is needed, as is the capacity to engage media in a manner that can shift the public story; applying pressure at key junctions is required, as is swaying the beliefs of people around you. Being confident in your own views and your ability to speak them is necessary, as is being connected to a network of like-minded others who reinforce and amplify your perspectives. The stakes of successfully playing the game in political fields include changing laws, influencing behaviour, shifting policy, and raising public awareness about issues that are of vital importance to everyone. Under current conditions of inequality, everyone might be subject to political decisions but very few are able to appreciate the underlying logic that renders such decisions possible, nor do they have the skills and knowledge to influence political decisions in meaningful ways.

Barriers to Democratic Engagement

For those without a democratic disposition, who cannot make sense of the illusio that exists across the homologous fields of activism and formal political engagement, the stakes of the game are not at all clear. Indeed, the stakes can appear quite different, understood as being simply about corrupt interests working against them, or seem irrelevant to their everyday lives. Yet the stakes of the game, the illusio, of the formal political field IS relevant to their everyday lives – everyone is affected by this game, whether they know it or not. This is the nexus of what makes (neo)liberal democracies antidemocratic under current contexts of extreme inequality – whether a person does or does not have the disposition to recognize the illusio of the political field, they are still affected by it.

Amaia (age twenty-four) provides a clear example of how this plays out for people who are excluded from the political game, either activist or formal. Born to mixed Māori–Pakeha (white) parents in a remote Māori community in New Zealand, Amaia is the middle of eight children. At the time of our interview, she was sharing a flat with two of her younger siblings in a small city about a five hours' drive away from the rural community where she was born. That small city itself is between a six and seven hours' drive away from Wellington, the capital of New Zealand, and is inhabited by a much higher proportion of Māori people than is typical in New Zealand cities. Affected by a series of complex health conditions, compounded by a car accident, Amaia was living on government benefits with plans to attend the local polytechnical college and acquire a one-year diploma in the health sciences. Amaia did not feel that she fit the category of having experienced homelessness, but as I learned more about her backstory I ascertained that she had indeed experienced housing deprivation and instability for significant parts of her life, made worse by her poor health and resulting inability to do paid work. As described in the Introduction, Amaia's experience fits within the broad definition of homelessness that informs this study, developed by the Canadian Observatory on Homelessness. Thankfully, Amaia had never experienced street homelessness, or absolute homelessness, arguably the most traumatizing form of homelessness.

Despite her experiences of housing precarity, Amaia had grown up within, and continues to be surrounded by, a rich community of extended family who look out for one another and provide for each other as much as they are able. Graham Hingangaroa Smith (2005, p. 37) describes this as "some alleviation of the impact of debilitating socioeconomic circumstances" by the Māori's "collective cultural structures and practices of *whanau* (extended family)." New Zealand is the only country among those in this study to have established a parallel public schooling system for Indigenous peoples, in their Indigenous language. This emerged directly from the political struggles of Māori communities to establish alternative and critical schooling options for their children in the 1980s, as New Zealand was embracing neoliberal reforms (Smith, 2005). Amaia attended Māori public schooling from primary to secondary; her first school was a "decile 1" school (meaning it served the part of the community where the poorest 10 per cent of New Zealand residents live), followed by a "decile 3" school (serving the third poorest 10 per cent of New Zealand residents – see chapter one for a description of the decile system for schools in New Zealand). Although a decile 3 school is not considered to be from a particularly wealthy area, Amaia noticed marked class differences between these two schools: "So the decile one [school], you know, had a lot of parents on like a [state] benefit or yeah. Like, all don't work or whatever. And then you had decile three. At that school, we had a lot of parents who were like lawyers or doctors or teachers, you know? You had I guess this different career path." Thanks to being in the Māori public school system, Amaia did receive some critical education about histories of colonialism and their impact on Māori communities. However, as was true for most participants in this study – particularly for those from poorer or more marginalized backgrounds – Amaia remembers little in the way of civics or democratic education from her public schooling:

> I don't really see how it affects me. Like the legislation and all that. I think, like you know, in school we were taught about Māori history and you know legislation and laws that were put in place to, well I guess discriminate, or to, you know, take away our ability to live as we did and everything. I think, yeah, but like other than all that history stuff.... I don't necessarily see how the government – I want to say the government but like, you know, the whole voting system and um, you know, how these people in power kind of affect me, I guess. Especially living in a small, rural secluded place.

Without the political knowledge or skills to make sense of the rules of the game – meaning the game of changing legislation that is relevant to her community – Amaia and her community found their best resort was to make it appear that they were complying with legislative strictures that came down from above, without necessarily changing their own practices. Amaia provides a very clear example of this in relation to her family's child care centre:

> AMAIA: I guess a way I found legislation and you know government shenanigans did affect me was like the – I don't know if you call it the administration thing? Or, you know, you have different legislation that came into policies, say like working in a

school and early childhood centre back home where, like, so for example, the policy came in about the ratios of having so many kids to an adult. And because you know we live right by the beach and it's our backyard, so because the policy is, "you need to have this many people – one on one [adults to children] or something – by water." It really, like, dictated our way of living because like all these kids, well most of these kids swim by themselves anyway. Or you hear, you know, this one auntie who has seven kids and they're all swimming just with her. You know?

JACKIE: Right. Sure. Yeah, I imagine with eight children [in Amaia's family], right? If you're out with your mum.

AMAIA: Yeah, yeah. So that legislation and government laws and that does affect us in rural towns because it's, you know, if there's a rule put in place for everybody, but it doesn't suit some of us who live a certain way and have a different lifestyle to a city centre –

JACKIE: Yeah. And would you see those kinds of rules being enforced? Like, a little bit – you know, once it came into play, was anyone tracking and enforcing?

AMAIA: Yeah, well I found you had a lot of like elderly teachers who were like, well, we've done it this way for so long. You know, no one's drowned, no one's died. So why change? But then, it was like when we'd have an audit or like the Ministry of Education come and, well, depending on who it was, like it depended mostly on the background of the auditor. So if they were Māori, [they'd say], "well, this is how they live and they've always done it this way." They were a bit more like, they gave us a bit more leeway on that. But then you had other ones who were very strict, like to the book, like, "No. You're not meant to do it like that." And yeah, we had to, like we kind of kept things hush-hush. Like, you don't want to tell them that you're going against the law because the next thing you're going to get stung. You know?

Amaia and her community knew enough about the legal system that had been imposed upon them to understand the consequences of not following the rules. Under liberal democratic structures, they technically had an opportunity to voice their dissatisfaction with these rules through either voting and/or attending consultations. Amaia witnessed these formal machinations with an understandable sense of distaste and mistrust, seeing sufficiently through the veil of democracy to recognize that domination was clearly at play, but without knowing how else this political game might be played:

AMAIA: And then obviously, when it was coming up to election time, you'd hear all the, well I want to say jargon – but you know all the promises and blah, blah, blah that certain parties would put to the table and then you'd, you know, soon see or hear that they actually haven't fulfilled their promises. And then you heard like certain ones who, especially when I was about to come of age to vote, just the amount of people who would say, "oh, you should vote for this person because they're the best." So you know, it was kind of like you heard about the so-called importance to vote and you know, it might be your vote that saves us and blah, blah. It was just, I guess again, like not necessarily seeing what they actually did for me. As a young Māori female who lives in a rural town. I was kind of just like, "oh, it just sounds like a whole lot of jargon to me." And I don't necessarily see these people come and talk with me or come and see how it is to live here and the lifestyle we live. You know? They just send out their little minions and they have a conversation with us and then they go back and they tell people how we so-called "live our lives" you know, according to their views and what the minority of us who got together to attend those meetings said.

JACKIE: Yeah. Would it be fair to say, I'm going to paraphrase a bit – like, it feels like the views of yourself or your community are not really represented?

AMAIA: Yeah, and because even like council meetings and all that kind of stuff. And I guess it even goes back to like the schools and different meetings in general, where you have, you know, a minority get together and have this meeting that represent all of us. You know? So if you were to have a meeting where the population in that town is like 10,000 or whatever and only you know twenty people or thirty people show up and say these people are the hierarchies, you know? The um, the big kahunas or the business owners so they say, "we need more businesses" or whatever then it – because you know, well I don't know if it's democracy but I feel like it is. But correct me if I'm wrong, like it's the voting system and everything, you're overruled because, one, you didn't attend the meeting and two, because some of you didn't even know the meeting was happening.

JACKIE: Yeah.

AMAIA: And then it's like you're out-voted because all these, well, I don't want to say educated people, but you know all these um, I guess, I don't know – not necessarily money hungry but, you know, just all these people who live a certain way that isn't the way you did, the way you were raised or whatever. And then you're kind of just unheard. But, what the community needs – that isn't [just] an alliance with the economy – isn't heard because it's all about money.

JACKIE: Yeah. Ok, I'm going to paraphrase again and I want you to tell me if this is right or wrong: But, what I hear you may be saying is, like, say in the community there are going to be people who are higher status or like –

AMAIA: Yeah, yeah. Or power, yeah.

JACKIE: More power, maybe more income, more affluent perhaps, or more authority who are speaking for everyone but then the people with less status or less money or less authority –

AMAIA: Yeah.

JACKIE: Are not being heard.

AMAIA: Yeah.

In this example, Amaia and her community know how the liberal democratic system is *supposed* to work. They know they are meant to vote for someone to represent their interests, and they are supposed to come out to town halls to have their views heard, which then are taken back to parliament to inform the policymaking process. But Amaia also knows, at the level of experience, that this system does not work for her or her rural Māori community. The difference between Amaia and, say, Kanoa, a Māori–Pasifika activist in New Zealand, is their respective exposure to the *actual* rules of the game. Where Kanoa has learned the *illusio* of the political field to such an extent that she was actually able to run for elected office with a left-leaning national party in the last general election, Amaia sees nothing of relevance in the current system. This means she must work around it, rather than with it or against it, leaving herself and her community at risk of sanction for breaking the laws that have been set without reference to their priorities or needs.

Even those young people who try to work *within* the liberal democratic system as they are supposedly meant to do – by voting, for example – may face substantial structural barriers to such engagement when they are homeless or impoverished. Beyond the cultural and knowledge barriers I have been describing here and in chapter four, there are sometimes major *practical* barriers to engaging with the political field in the only way that most young people learn they are allowed to engage. This was particularly remarked upon by both activists and homeless young people from the southern US states, such as Georgia, Florida, or Texas. Isabella (age twenty-one) was one of the few young people who had experienced homelessness who was extremely committed to voting and believed that it could make a difference politically. This had been modelled for her by a politically engaged Mexican-American family, and it was reinforced when she was able to attend university for a year before her financial situation led her to homelessness and dropping out of college (discussed in more detail in chapter four). As I learned through our discussion, Isabella faced major barriers to voting, but she did not, at first, articulate them as such:

JACKIE: Are there any barriers to voting for you that you've encountered that makes it hard in any way?
ISABELLA: I'm pretty lucky. As long as you're in line before six, then you're good to go.
JACKIE: Six p.m.?
ISABELLA: Yeah. So, the only thing that's tricky is transportation and work. So I guess those are barriers, yeah.
JACKIE: How far away is it to vote?
ISABELLA: Well, the thing is, I'm busing home after. It's already dark half the time because it's in winter and I just get nervous busing home in the dark.
JACKIE: Of course. But it's a bus ride away?
ISABELLA: Yeah, thank God. Yeah.
JACKIE: So, let me give you some perspective on why I'm querying you on this. When I have voted in every place I've lived in, in Canada, it's less than a five-minute walk away.

ISABELLA: Oh!!
JACKIE: Because that's how many polling stations we have. Like, they're always set up in local schools and yeah.
ISABELLA: It's less here [polling stations]. Yeah.

Isabella had grown up in Texas, and so presumably had always been exposed to the state logic of polling stations being few and far between. Without a car, the only way for Isabella to access the polling stations when not attending university (where polls were also set up) is by bus. Once I told her about the close proximity of polling stations in Canada, she began to reflect on other challenges to voting in Texas:

ISABELLA: But now in Texas it's illegal to give out water or food. It's explicitly illegal to give out water or food to people in line. It's ridiculous. It just passed this year.
JACKIE: Why? What's the rationale for that?
ISABELLA: That's a good point! I don't agree with it obviously, but it just passed, just in Texas.
JACKIE: Can't even give out water. So how long, in your experience, how long do you have to wait in line to vote? Do you have a sense that the lineups are, that it can be a long wait?
ISABELLA: They're pretty long. I have friends who waited for hours outside.
JACKIE: Wow.
ISABELLA: Yeah. Yeah.
JACKIE: And have your parents talked about that? Like, when they vote? Does it take a long time?
ISABELLA: Yeah, it's hard, it's hard getting off work to go there because everybody wants to take off work at the same time to go vote and I understand but it's hard scheduling that.
JACKIE: Yeah. How late are the polling stations open typically?
ISABELLA: You have to be in line, there's like people monitoring it. There's like cops. You have to be in line by six [p.m.] or else they block you off.
JACKIE: Oh. So it's not just that you're like, "I've got to get there for six so the line up isn't too long, it's that –
ISABELLA: No –
JACKIE: You must or the police will stop you from getting in line.
ISABELLA: Yeah. Yeah.
JACKIE: These are lots of barriers actually.
ISABELLA: Well that's another reason a lot of people don't vote for small, how do you say it? In quotations – like "smaller" elections like city council because it's a hassle getting off work.

Barriers to voting for low-income and racialized communities in the United States are well documented, and have often been equated with intentional voter suppression (e.g., Scholars Strategy Network, 2019; Carnegie Corporation of New York, 2019). These kinds of barriers are not as prevalent in the other four countries of this study, although each have issues with lower turnout for Indigenous, racialized (especially recent immigrants), impoverished, and/or homeless individuals (Page, 2019; Galicki, 2018; Uberoi & Johnston, 2021; Larkin, 2021). The relevance of Isabella's experience for the overall argument here is that even if young people accept the terms of democratic participation offered through (neo)liberal democracies, wealth inequality may still affect their ability to engage in even this limited manner.

The Race and Class Biases of Political Fields

As the types of skills and knowledge required to navigate both activist and formalist political fields are similar, so too are the forms of classed and raced exclusions that function across both.[2] In other words, the isomophism between activism and formal democratic participation extends to the implicit (and sometimes explicit) biases contained within each. This functions to exclude people who are also systematically marginalized in other domains, for instance, those from poor and/or racialized backgrounds. This then serves as a multiplier to preventing meaningful political engagement, adding to the barriers described above and in chapter four.

Unsurprisingly, it was the activists from poor and working-class and/or racialized backgrounds who were able to see these aspects most clearly within their own encounters with political and activist organizing. Several activists from these domains had an uneasy relationship with claiming the term "activist." As Alejandro (age twenty, United States) told me, "I didn't really consider myself an activist. I think I consider myself an advocate." I asked him whether he pictured someone when he thought of activists, and whether they had a race, class, and gender:

> Yeah. White. Someone white, because for me, I couldn't be attending those things with my immigration status. I cannot risk, anything like that could be used against me and stuff. And that's why I was so very cautious.... So for me, what I always thought as an activist was someone that was white, or maybe, typically, I would say maybe female. Female and white, never usually male. And I never knew why, and it's kind of just that's what I pictured. And it wasn't until college where I realized there are other.... That's when I started realizing there's people of colour that are activists, and it's not just a white thing.

---

2 There are gender dynamics at play in both activist and formal political spaces, but they are not as straightforward as exclusion or inclusion based on gender. See Kennelly (2014) for an in-depth analysis of the gendered dynamics of youth activism in Canada.

In Canada, Gregory (age eighteen) was similarly ambivalent about claiming the category of "activist":

> When people call me that word I don't vibe with it as much. I obviously laugh when I hear that word. Honestly, I feel like the work I'm doing, whether it can be defined under activism I see it as just, I mean, from a Christian perspective, I can say doing the work of God. Like from a society perspective, I can say you're doing the work of humanity, to be honest. That's what I would say. I don't mind the word but usually when you hear activists.... I mean, well, most of these politicians like to claim that they were activists. Maybe they were activists whether it's for food and security, whatever issue it may be, but I feel like people just want to draw round the word, "I'm an activist. Oh, my Lord, that thing bothered me." I feel like that word has been overused and people just love the title. Like if I'm at an event, I don't want anyone to call me an activist. When they ask me my title, mostly I would acknowledge the work I'm doing is advocacy but don't call me an activist.

Although Gregory does not explicitly draw connections between the term "activist" and a race or class position, it is noteworthy that Gregory is a Black man who grew up poor in a working-class neighbourhood of Toronto. He acknowledges the relationship between activism and formal politics with the comment "most of these politicians like to claim that they are activists," an indirect reference to the homological relationship between these white and middle-class fields.

Cadence's (age nineteen, United States) experience of being raised in a family of Black civil rights activists and being embedded within that community from birth meant that she did not see activism as an exclusively white phenomenon – until she attended university. Her white-dominant campus has what she described as "the biggest college Democrat chapter in the country," which is also "our biggest student organization." When she began attending those meetings, she got her "first glimpse into white activism and white liberalism especially." She told me she found the difference in the activist cultures difficult to explain, but she described it as follows: "I could tell that they were doing it for a very different reason than I was doing it. It was far more personal [for me]. And I'm regularly impacted by it every day, and even just navigating through campus. When they left those meetings, they were still able to just exist normally. But when I had to leave the meetings and if I went to CVS [an American pharmacy chain], I'd get followed around the store to make sure I wasn't stealing. It's very, very different." In the United Kingdom, Julia (age eighteen) also found herself personally implicated in the activism she was doing in a way that her middle-class peers were not. As a white woman, her class origins could not be read easily by others, unlike for many racialized activists, who may be wearing that aspect of their identity on their skin.[3] As such, Julia's activist peers would often assume she shared a middle-class background with them, an assumption Julia discovered when discussing political decisions that impacted poor and working-class Britons:

> And I was talking to this girl once. Because I was upset about the Tories, the Conservative party had got into power again because of their austerity [platform]. I was quite upset on the day after election, and I was talking to this girl, and she was like, "Well, you've probably never experienced the cuts that the Tories have made, and you probably won't even experience the cuts that they're going to make." I was like, "I've already experienced it, and it's horrible." And I gave her a list of things that they've done and how it's made my life really difficult. And she was actually in shock that the government has such an impact on working-class people. And I was like, "I can't believe you didn't know anything about this." It just showed that it's very much not talked about.

Julia's main activist organizing has happened within the climate justice movement, which is often critiqued for being uninformed about class and race politics. In New Zealand, Karen (age twenty-four), who also grew up poor, noticed immediately the class hierarchies structured into the climate justice and environmental movements she became involved with in secondary school:

> One of the examples that really came up for me a lot with environmental activism and, particularly at the UN level, it's all unfunded. And particularly UN Youth. And some other organizations like actually make money off funding delegations from private schools. So they're paying $7000 to go to conferences that are free to attend if you're accredited. I think it's great that people have that experience regardless of background. But I think in doing that, it does isolate the opportunities or reflects that only the UN and places like that are for the elite in the society or people who are funded and can ask their parents for money to go to these things. I definitely found that leadership, at least in the formal sense, is very much built upon previous experience. And so if someone has [leadership] experience before, even through internships and things like that, it creates this cycle. And only now are we recognizing that in a lot of activist circles. But that was something, to me, that always stuck out. And I stood out and always stood out. It's really unfair. And I think a lot of the assumptions around what your demographic is, if you're involved in this kind of work, reinforces to others, who don't fit into that category, that they aren't welcome at the table.

It was actually my interview with Karen that first alerted me to the importance of the theme explored within this chapter, that of the homology between activist and formal political fields. As she so astutely notes, "leadership, at least in the

---

3 Racialization is a complex process and is applied and experienced differently for people who are "read" in different ways by others.

formal sense, is very much built upon previous experience," which generates a cycle of inclusion for those who can access those opportunities, and exclusion for those who cannot. Recognizing these classed dynamics led Karen to organize alternative points of entry and accommodations that would not reinforce class exclusions:

> Working at an international level, I'm really trying to get everyone, anyone with an Internet connection can have a voice at the UN in a different way. Because the UN doesn't have participation costs and things like that for everyday people.... I think that [my] upbringing [in poverty] and seeing how much a variable money can be is what really annoyed me about this UN stuff later on. That's why I keep trying to create more opportunities for them. And honestly, volunteering and activism always takes energy. With [organization she works with], we really try to ensure that whatever activism people want to do, they could fit it around their lives and not make it, "Oh, you cannot work. Just stay." If it's the cost for a bus, reach out. Because I think until you have those kinds of insights where things are difficult, then the environmental movement and other movements won't ever be where they should be.

Karen recognizes that it is not only money but also energy and time that can create barriers for non-middle-class young people to get involved in activism. In the United Kingdom, Rochelle (age twenty-eight) organizes with an activist group that made a conscious and strategic decision to not hire a staff member to run campaigns, but rather to keep it as grassroots and non-hierarchical as possible. While hiring a staff member would resource one person to devote their time to the cause, Rochelle's group decided to instead distribute any financial resources they get to anyone who needs them in order to more fully participate:

> It's a bit tricky because obviously most of the people in the campaign, like we're working full time or we're struggling with the chaos of benefits, which feels like a full-time job sometimes. But it feels like that's how we've managed to keep going because we've gone on for seven years, that's a really long time and any money that we get we use on like an inclusivity fund instead. So rather than somebody being given more [paid] time, we want to give more people the ability to organize through paying transport costs and food costs if they haven't got access to food or internet, childcare, and things like that. Like yes and that, I think that's really significant.

For Kanoa (age eighteen), also in New Zealand, the raced exclusions that occur within the climate justice movement were mediated by the pre-existence of Māori–Pacifika organizations working on climate issues, from which she was able to draw mentors:

> When I joined School Strike [for Climate], I was one of two brown people I guess you could say that were in the room, the other girl, who I love dearly, she was

Filipino and we were always some of the only two people who were of colour in the room, which is very difficult. But we always had people like Pacific Climate Warriors [a climate activist group made up of Pacific Islanders] who were there to sort of know how it felt to be in a very white-dominated space. The [political party she became involved with] is quite dominated by white people; however, in our top twenty we've got some really good people of colour who are in electable positions and that's really good and it's the beginning of a shift in whose running the show really, which is great.

Unfortunately, it appears that the efforts of Rochelle's group and Kanoa's experience of growing racial diversity remain the exception rather than the norm. As attested to by other working-class and/or racialized activists, activism as a political field tends to be white and middle class in these Anglo-American (neo)liberal democratic nations. If we consider the close homological relationship between the fields of activism and formal political engagement, this has the unfortunate consequence of potentially closing off access to poor and racialized young people from acquiring the skills and knowledge available within activist fields. These are the skills and knowledge that can then be transferred into meaningful engagement with formal political fields, whether that means running for office or simply knowing how to affect systems of power to generate more just outcomes.

Darius (age twenty) and Gregory (age nineteen), both young Black men living in the United States and Canada, respectively, eloquently describe the dynamics of political exclusion that they see playing out in their own poor and racialized communities. They both link these to political decisions that have been made which have worsened inequality. When I asked Darius about the most important influences on his activism, he said:

> DARIUS: Hmm. [pauses] I would say [sighs], seeing how my people live. That's very vague. Um, so, seeing how hard Black individuals have to work to make ends meet and kind of understanding that that also is a reason why they aren't necessarily as politically involved just because I mean, if you've worked forty plus hours a week the last thing you care about is Donald Trump on TV. So kind of just seeing how different the Black world is from the actual world and how it's intentional, you know?
> JACKIE: Yeah, totally. Um, and by intentional, you mean? I won't guess. [laughs]
> DARIUS: Sure. Yeah. I would say government, society as a whole, the fact that we don't invest in Black communities enough, Black schools enough. It's kind of intentional because we know that if they don't have the right education, if they don't have the resources to do something else other than education, they're going to be working a nine to five their entire life – or multiple nine to fives their entire lives – so we can keep them down. Then they won't be the ones marching in DC or, or voting at the polls, maybe. You know? They're just surviving.

Gregory says something very similar, succinctly summing up the core argument of this book at the same time:

> I feel like all in all, looking at public participation, we have to recognize that people do not have the same opportunity to partake. Like we talked about mothers, most single mothers, or just the mothers in general, individuals have to work multiple jobs basically to make ends meet, to pay their bills. I've spoken to so many individuals in my riding whose children have to go to a job early or to basically push hard just to ensure that there is a roof over their heads. So I feel like it's important just thinking about people in society, democracy. Just thinking of society as a whole and democracy and citizenship, it's all just for nothing if inequality is continuing to be on the rise and if you aren't striving to make it better. Inequality is continuing to be on the rise. Democracy, citizenship, public participation: let's throw all that away if things are continuing to be the same. It's kind of useless. I can use the phrase, "it's not fair." I guess it's even beyond being unfair. It's just a matter of we can't keep on the path of "oh, I'm in it for everyone. I'm in it for everyone, da-da-da." Our politicians can keep on with the "we represent this whole community." What you tend to see is everyone loves to say "Oh, we're in it together." The truth is we are not in it together because people's experiences are totally different. Obviously, in society, people's experiences are going to be different, but we are talking about drastically different. That's where the problem lies. People are literally suffering.

Conclusions

The focus of this chapter has been on establishing the existence of a strong homological relationship between the fields of activism and formal political engagement. This helps explain how young people engaged in activist politics are able to transition into formal political spaces with relative ease, either in the sense of being able to run for office or in being able to understand how the formal political system works and thus advocate more effectively for justice. Conversely, the systemic barriers that function across both of these fields, most notably in terms of class, and also in relation to race in white-dominant societies, serve to further cement the inaccessibility of a democratic disposition for those positioned at the very bottom of the opportunity structure. As Wang (2016, p. 358) notes in his overview of Bourdieu's use of the concept, "The seemingly 'miraculous homology' across cultural, economic, educational, religious, athletic, and political fields, is more or less explained by an appeal to agents' class backgrounds."

How has this come to be? In chapter one, I traced the growth of inequality, due largely to neoliberal policymaking, across all five of the study countries. Are the effects of inequality on democracy an accidental and unintended consequence of these political decisions? Thinking with Bourdieu, the answer is a definitive *no*. It is not a coincidence that neoliberal political strategies which have enriched the dominant have further disenfranchised the marginalized. State strategies tend to work towards dominant interests, if left unchecked. As Wang (2016, p. 359) points out, for Bourdieu, "educational institutions play a decisive role in legitimating social domination, in that they obscure the homology between 'social origins' and the field of power." In the next and final chapter before the Conclusions, I trace how dominant interests are represented through state-mandated educational systems, with a specific focus on civics education. Both the explicit and hidden curriculum of public schooling in Anglo-American (neo)liberal democracies serve to symbolically and materially reinforce messages about who is entitled to have a say in political decisions and who is not.

6 Belonging to the State: Citizenship as Symbolic Power

> The survival of democracy depends upon a broadly and deeply educated people resisting the neoliberalization of everything, including themselves.
> – Wendy Brown (2011, p. 36)

Liberal democracies are quite preoccupied with linking the concept of "citizenship" to that of "democracy." This linkage is neither natural nor necessary. When thinking of democracy in the sense offered by many of the activists in this study – for example, "democracy should mean that the people collectively have control over what happens to them and their communities" (Angie, Canada) – whether one is a citizen or not of a given country is irrelevant. The importance placed by states on "citizenship" as a concept linked to democracy can be discerned by the presence of "citizenship education" in the state-mandated curricula of all five liberal democracies. Every country in this study has its own version of citizenship education in their public school system, either as a separate course or embedded within other social studies curricula. The definition of a citizen is never made explicit, but implicitly citizenship is aligned with formal democracy (through voting), (limited) rights, and duties to the state and local community. The latter is particularly emphasized, in keeping with the neoliberal political culture that has engulfed each of the countries within this study. The first part of the chapter will provide a brief analysis of these curricula in order to discern the priorities of liberal democratic states when it comes to educating their citizens to participate in their democracies.

In at least two of the study countries (the United States and the United Kingdom), there are extra-curricular or co-curricular offerings of citizenship education that are also made widely available to public school students. These are broadly aligned with the curricular goals laid out in formal civics classes, whether they are offered via separate not-for-profit organizations (as in the United States) or as a state-funded program (as in the United Kingdom). In the second part of the chapter, I will draw on the stories of UK participants who had varying experiences with this extra-curricular option, called the National Citizen Service, in order to further illustrate the opportunities and obstacles that such approaches to citizenship offer to young people seeking meaningful engagement in the polity.

State efforts to connect citizenship to democratic participation notwithstanding, the first response of the vast majority of participants in this study, whether they were youth who had experienced homelessness or young activists, was to link citizenship to a sense of belonging (or not) to the state. A very close and inter-related second response was to see citizenship as access to the rights and entitlements that come with a passport or other forms of formal recognition in each of these globally dominant Western liberal democracies – where the passport has come to represent the bureaucratic version of an affective sense of belonging. These two forms of citizenship – as belonging and as bureaucracy – do not always align easily. Some young people could feel they had one without the other, and this dissonance could be quite distressing. Consistent with the dominant characteristics of the political field, as explored in chapter five, young people experienced citizenship as a racial category (associated with whiteness) and a classed one (linked to being middle class and stably housed). The only young people to comfortably make the link between citizenship and political participation, as per civics curricula, were those who did not have to worry about either belonging or bureaucracy: white, middle-class, English-speaking youth who were born within their country of citizenship.

At first, I found the extreme disconnect between notions of citizenship offered in formal curricula and those described by young people to be puzzling. Participants who had completed a civics course (i.e., those who had finished secondary schooling) could generally recall some content related to the structure of government and how to vote – in other words, the formal modes of individual participation in liberal democracies that are emphasized through civics classes. Yet they had not retained the strong association made within the curricula between these forms of democratic participation and the meaning of the word citizenship. This signals that there is another, stronger, form of curriculum circulating for young people in all five of these countries. This hidden curriculum (which we could also call doxa), both within and outside of the school, generates a powerful affective charge for the word citizenship, linking it to belonging and to formal recognition by the state.

As discussed in the Introduction, it is Pierre Bourdieu's theory of the state that informs my analysis. To reiterate briefly, the three fundamental qualities of the state according to Bourdieu (2014) are: (1) that it generates social classifications and slots people into them, producing a "state identity" for all individuals – citizen versus non-citizen being one of the most fundamental classifications the state produces; (2) it is an arbiter of legitimacy, including everything from professional certifications to the use of violence; and (3) it is a "well-founded illusion," meaning that it is not a "thing" we can lay our hands upon or tackle directly but rather a constellation of "acts of state" that together produce doxa or the "point of view of the dominant, which … imposes itself as a universal point of view" (Bourdieu, 1998, p. 57).

Taken together, the evidence from youth participants and state civics curricula suggest the following:

1. The state has a strong interest in classifying *citizens* as the sole legitimate participants in formal liberal democratic structures. Curricular documents implicitly define citizens as requiring specific qualities and characteristics in order to be considered deserving of state involvement: namely, to be the informed, active, consuming, and responsible neoliberal citizen of liberal democracies whose social welfare systems have been decimated over the past forty years. The good and deserving citizen of civics curricula does not make claims of the state, nor demand entitlements. They might be the bearer of rights, but their duties to the state and sub-state (which typically takes the form of local community) are given the highest precedence.
2. The state has a parallel but non-explicit interest in classifying some individuals as "belonging" to the state (whether they carry official citizenship or not); such belonging is most clearly marked by race and class, although other social markers such as gender, disability, and sexuality also mediate individuals' subjective feelings of belonging. These feelings of belonging (or not) are embodied and affective, and as such are among the deepest forms of doxa generated by the state.
3. Contemporary liberal democracies competing for dominance within the globalization of capital seek to maintain their distinction on the basis of an exclusive club of "citizens" who are granted the bureaucratic privilege of formal citizenship and the passport that comes with it. This "golden ticket," as UK participant Khalil describes it, legitimates these Western liberal democracies as beneficent sites whose membership must be closely guarded. Being granted membership thus means one must be eternally grateful – and therefore not demand more of the state than it already offers.

I first developed similar ideas in my 2011 monograph and a 2011 journal article in the *British Journal of Criminology*, in which I identified citizenship as "governance," following Foucault (Kennelly, 2011a , 2011b). The arguments I present here are compatible with those, but are using Bourdieu's concepts more thoroughly and leaving aside the Foucauldian concept of "governmentality," which he was unable to develop to completion before his death (Brown, 2005). Instead, I rely on Bourdieu's concept of *symbolic power*, "the power that is exercised in such an invisible way that people are unaware of its very existence, and those subject to it are the first among these, since the very exercise of this power depends on this lack of awareness" (2014, p. 163).

The Symbolic Power of Citizenship Education

Schooling is one of the major ways in which the state ensures the reproduction of doxa, according to Bourdieu, "by inculcating common cognitive structures" via the school system (2014, p. 168). "The state is the principal producer of instruments of construction of social reality" (2014, p. 168), he notes. Keeping in mind that the state is also a "well-founded illusion," making it difficult to pin it down as a specific "thing," we need some means by which to discern the intentions and priorities of the state and the doxa it seeks to produce and sustain. State-mandated curriculum offers a tool by which we can "read" the state, particularly when it comes to educating its citizens. By analysing state-mandated curricula across all five liberal democratic countries that are part of this study, we can observe the patterns that recur within citizenship education; from here, we can draw some conclusions about the shared meanings of "citizenship" being offered by neoliberal/liberal democracies and the limits and potentials thereof.

I build here upon work begun with my colleague Kristina Llewellyn, with whom I published a paper in *Citizenship Studies* that discussed the findings from our critical discourse analysis of three provincial civics curricula in Canada from the mid-2000s (Kennelly & Llewellyn, 2011). Our analysis revealed that "the formation of the 'active' citizen [is] a fundamentally neoliberal project" (p. 903). We based this conclusion on the constant coupling of "active citizenship" with "cautions about the importance of compliant behaviour (i.e., ethics, duty and responsibility)" and the relative silence on collective acts of solidarity or civic dissent (p. 903). As we noted then, "The documents either do not contain or give passing note to 'activism', 'activists' or 'protest'" (p. 903). We identified the strong emphasis on formal and individual engagement with liberal democracy, via voting or political parties, and the degree to which "[e]xclusive rights-based claims to citizenship pale in comparison to citizens' responsibilities within these curricula" (p. 906). We conclude that these curricular documents signal a "discursive shift of the burdens of citizenship onto the individual and away from the collective, onto the self-regulating and self-perfecting person and away from the protesting, rights-based group" (p. 907).

Using curricular documents from a decade or more later, and sampling across all five liberal democracies, it appears that our analysis and conclusions remain relevant (also see Erdal and Kennelly under review, for a more detailed analysis of these curricular documents). Australia's civics curricula for Years 7 and 8 (with students between the ages of twelve and fourteen) emphasizes "active" citizens only inasmuch as they are also "informed" and "responsible." The term "freedoms" is always paired with "responsibilities" – that is, the freedoms and responsibilities of citizenship – which is essentially the same semantic pairing as "rights and responsibilities" from the Canadian curricula, both past and present. Australian civics does include one mention of "direct action" as an option for citizenship, "such as organizing a public demonstration or social media campaign"; but, consistent with our 2011 analysis, this was a single statement made within a longer document dominated by the need for knowledge of the formal political and legal systems. Noteworthy and somewhat unique to the Australian context was a preoccupation with "social cohesion" in the face of diversity, a discourse with a history dating back at least to the late 1990s when the Howard Liberal Coalition government rejected the term "multiculturalism" in favour of an emphasis "on social cohesion, national identity, community harmony, and obligations rather than rights or opportunity" (Carey, 2021, p. 3). This discourse continues to this day, and has been analysed as representing an "emphasis on assimilation into existing social order and to allegiance" (Carey, 2021, p. 3). Fiona Carey (2021, p. 3). notes that, "These policies have also been critiqued as representing Australia as culturally homogenous, [and as] more concerned with containing difference than fostering it."

Citizenship curricula in Britain was part of a larger document outlining the national curriculum for England in "Key Stages 3 and 4," which translates to students in Years 10–11, between the ages of fourteen and sixteen.[1] Like all of the curricular documents analysed, "responsible citizenship" was emphasized and paired with informed and active (students are required to present "reasoned arguments and take informed action" [UK Department for Education, 2014, p. 83] in order to be good citizens in England), and, unlike in Australia, no mention was made of anything remotely resembling collective action or activism. "Rights and responsibilities" was a common semantic pairing. The British curriculum requires that students recognize "the *precious liberties enjoyed* by the citizens of the United Kingdom" (UK Department of Education, 2014, p. 83; emphasis mine), which is included in a list of pedagogical aims that also incorporates "the operation of Parliament," and "the nature of rules and laws and the justice system" (ibid.). This particular phrasing, of *precious liberties enjoyed* by citizens, is congruent with production of the dutiful, responsible, and *grateful* citizen of Western (neo)liberal democracies – that is, citizens' freedoms are precious (i.e., rare) and thus must not be squandered, and also might be taken away should one not behave appropriately. They are not rights and entitlements owed to citizens from the state but must be earned through a citizen's good behaviour. England's citizenship curricula is also explicit in linking citizenship to economic productivity: its opening paragraph states that, "A high-quality citizenship education ... should also prepare pupils to take their place in society as

---

1   I did not look at Welsh, Scottish, or Northern Irish citizenship curricula in this review.

responsible citizens, manage their money well and make sound financial decisions" (UK Department for Education, 2014, p. 82).

The entire New Zealand Curriculum from Years 1 to 13 (ages six to eighteen) is encompassed in one sixty-seven-page document, which is meant to "set the direction for student learning and to provide guidance for [English speaking] schools" (there is a separate document for Māori schools) (New Zealand Ministry of Education, 2015, p. 6). As such, and unlike the curricula of other countries examined here, the document provides broad guidelines only. Noteworthy is that citizenship education is meant to be embedded throughout the curriculum, with both disciplinary areas of science and social science being flagged as developing "critical, informed, and responsible citizens" (New Zealand Ministry of Education, 2015, p. 19). Although there is no specific course designated as civics, throughout the social sciences guidelines are objectives that are similar to citizenship education curricula in other countries. The curriculum describes the social sciences as a whole to be about "how societies work and how people can participate as critical, active, informed, and responsible citizens" (ibid., p. 30), and includes such aims as "[to] learn about the ways in which people participate in economic activities and about the consumption, production, and distribution of goods and services" (ibid.), and to "understand how government policies and contemporary issues interact" (ibid., p. 63). New Zealand's guidelines include a promising commitment to teach students to "[u]nderstand how individuals, groups, and institutions work to promote social justice and human rights," but make no mention of social movements, activism, or collective organizing. By contrast, the document includes six references to enterprise/enterprising/entrepreneurial (each word appears two times), denoting the importance placed upon this neoliberal value for New Zealand students.

In Canada, I reviewed Ontario's 2018 Grade 10 Civics Curriculum, wondering whether anything had changed since our discourse analysis of the 2005 curriculum (Ontario Ministry of Education and Training, 2018). This is a required course for all Grade 10 students (ages fifteen to sixteen) in Ontario. Education is a provincial matter in Canada, and thus each province generates their own curricula; as Llewellyn and I argue in our 2011 paper, the similarities between provincial civics curricula at the time outweighed the differences. I opted only to review Ontario's curricula this time around, as it is the province where the majority of my Canadian participants were schooled and is also the most populous province in the country.[2] I found that the semantic pairing of "informed" with "citizen" as the key quality of a good citizen in Ontario persists, as does the pairing of "rights" with "responsibilities." The updated curricula did dedicate a

---

2 In the paper co-authored with Cihan Erdal, currently under review, we also analyse the Nova Scotia and Alberta provincial civics curricula.

section to exclusively exploring the rights that Canadians might claim of the state, particularly via the Charter of Rights and Freedoms; this section was followed immediately by one dedicated to the responsibilities of citizenship. "Protest" appeared four times, always within parenthetical examples of issues that students might explore within a given topic; other key words associated with collective organizing (e.g., activist, social movement) did not appear. While the bulk of the course focuses on formal government and policymaking as the primary means with which to engage in democracy, there is also a dedicated strand entitled "Civic Engagement and Action" that focuses on the civic contributions of a range of individuals and the ways in which students might contribute through non-formal civic action. I was pleased to see that the Ontario civics curriculum had lost some of its neoliberal intensity, perhaps due to the fact that it was developed under a provincial Liberal government which was known to actively engage with the scholarly education community to develop their new curricula (a trend that ended abruptly with the election of the current provincial Conservative government, whose first act was to cancel the integration of Indigenous content into the curriculum, despite the fact that the process was already well underway [Crawley, 2018]). Nonetheless, there are more similarities than differences between this course and its predecessor, and between Ontario civics and the curricula under review in other countries.

Analysing civics curricula in the United States proved to be more of a challenge. Like Canada, education is largely de-centralized, so that each American state autonomously develops its own social studies and/or civics curriculum. The American participants in this study attended K–12 public education in various states, including Georgia; Florida; California; Washington, DC; and New Jersey. It would take more than this entire chapter to thoroughly analyse the curricula of a representative sample of American states; instead, I offer here some comparative notes on the curricula of four American states: New York; California; Washington, DC; and Florida.

There are several similarities and some distinctive differences between the American approach to civics and that of the other countries analysed above. The semantic pairing of "rights and responsibilities" was consistent across all four state civics curricula, as was that of "informed" with the active citizen. There was no particular emphasis put on financial literacy or participation in the economy as a function of good citizenship, although the role of capitalism as "better" than other financial systems was a disputed point across different curricula. For instance, Florida's 2021 revisions to its Civics and Government Standards for K–12 Social Studies include a new benchmark for Grade 7 students (ages eleven to twelve) to "analyze the advantages of capitalism and the free market in the United States over government-controlled economic systems (e.g., socialism and communism) in regard to economic freedom and raising the standard of living for citizens" (Florida Department of Education, 2021, p. 13). Other states include capitalism as a topic of interest, but in a comparative manner that does not *a priori* privilege it over other economic systems (e.g., California: "Analyze the emergence of capitalism as a dominant economic pattern and the responses to it, including Utopianism, Social Democracy, Socialism, and Communism" [California Department of Education Sacramento, 2017, p. 53], and New York: "Economic policy makers face considerable challenges within a capitalist system, including unemployment, inflation, poverty, and environmental consequences" [The State Education Department, 2015, p. 50]). "Responsible" is paired not only with the rights of citizenship, but also with the role of government and media, an emphasis that was unique to the United States and likely reflects a republican history grounded in the American Revolution with its suspicion of colonial rule under Britain. Activism/protest/social movement appear sporadically throughout all four curricular documents, generally as parenthetical or one-off examples to be discussed by students (e.g., DC Social Studies curriculum: "Analyze the rise of social activism and the antiwar and countercultural movements" [District of Columbia Public Schools, n.d., p. 73] and Florida Civics curriculum: "Students will be able to discuss attempts to increase voter turnout (e.g., get out the vote campaigns, social movements)" [Florida Department of Education, 2021, p. 16]). Overall, the emphasis of all four curricular documents, like that of the other countries, was on formal government and its structures; civic participation was generally limited to formal political mechanisms, such as voting, lobbying Congress, or writing letters to state representatives; and the rights of individual citizens were repeatedly tempered by an emphasis on the citizen's responsibility to the state.

Taken together, this analysis suggests that the doxa being transmitted through schooling for citizenship in Anglo-American liberal democracies continues to be steeped in neoliberal logic. As the neoliberal state divests itself of social supports for its citizenry, its civics curricula shifts emphasis away from the rights and entitlements that individuals might claim of it, and towards the responsibilities of individuals to the state. The citizen must be informed and reasoned in his or her "active" participation, which is largely limited to individual, formal engagement with the infrastructure of government, such as voting. As Llewellyn and I argue in our 2011 paper, "[T]he pairing of 'informed and active' suggests that citizenship might only be taken up by those reasonable individuals who take the time to deliberate on all aspects of a social issue before taking action, continuous with liberalism's legacy of emphasis on the rational, rights-bearing individual" (Kennelly & Llewellyn, 2011, p. 903). To encourage students to be informed about issues is not, in itself, a problem; however, when this recurring refrain is contrasted with the relative lack of information about collaborative, group-based efforts for social change (such as occur through social movements and activism), it becomes clear that the good and active citizen of the (neo)liberal state is constituted as free from the constraints of social contexts and thus able to make reasoned, rational, *individual* choices. Two of the five countries (New Zealand and England) explicitly couple economic knowledge with positive citizenship attributes, while a third (the United States) privileges knowledge of capitalism within its civics education, whether viewed critically or not. This is evidence of the ongoing desire to cultivate ideal, active citizens who are capable of "the continual re-negotiation of one's skills and identity in light of the demands of global capitalism" (Kennelly & Llewellyn, 2011, p. 903).

Extracurricular Civics Education: The National Citizen Service (UK)

State-funded schooling is not the only site of transmission for doxa about citizenship and its meanings. Several of the countries under study have extra- or co-curricular citizenship programs funded directly or indirectly (via charitable organizations receiving government funding) by the state. The largest of these is the United Kingdom's National Citizen Service (NCS). Begun under David Cameron's Conservative government in 2008–9, Mills and Waite (2017, p. 69) observe that "this youth programme remains the centrepiece of the Conservative Party's youth policy and investment in young people's services," developed in a period of particularly intensive cuts to public services and local youth programming across the country. It was this context that likely prompted Matt (age nineteen, United Kingdom) to remark that the NCS was created, "on the back of shutting down all the youth centres so they could fund it." Despite changes to elected government, the NCS still exists, now organized by a cross-party-supported Royal Charter Body called the NCS Trust. The NCS has continued throughout the COVID-19 pandemic of 2020-2 via virtual programming (National Citizen Service Trust, n.d.).

I asked all but two of my UK participants whether they had heard of the National Citizen Service.[3] Of the six participants I asked (both young activists and youth who had experienced homelessness), five knew about it and two of these had participated. Their views of and experiences with the NCS provide a relevant supplement to experiences of formal civics education, described further below, and the modes of citizenship action promoted in formal civics curricula, as analysed above.

Although the title of the program and its origins are firmly rooted in the goal of transmitting the qualities of good citizenship to UK students, initial perceptions of the NCS among my research participants differed significantly

---

3   Of my UK participants, I did not ask Maggie (age twenty-four) or Daraja (age thirty) about the National Citizen Service. With Maggie, our wide-ranging discussion did not leave space for the question; for Daraja, I knew she was educated outside of the United Kingdom, in Nigeria, and so her experience with the NCS was not a relevant question to ask about her civics education background.

from this. Matt (age nineteen) learned about it in school and considered it to be "a really cheap program of going on a fun action holiday where you do a lot of kayaking and there'll be your friends in a house that you have to pay off by doing a week of volunteering." Julia (age eighteen) had friends who attended, and told me that "it was perceived as something of an employability thing. And it was meant to occupy teens over the summer." Elizabeth (age twenty-two) commented explicitly on the contradictory class dynamics embedded in the program: "[I]t was kind of mocked and looked at snidely, especially because of the whole angle of it was pushed really aggressively in our school at assemblies where, alongside things like 'don't do drugs' and 'don't get into a knife crime gang' and then the people who would actually have maybe benefited from that or who were meant to be the targets never took it up. It just became, because it was so heavily subsidized by the government, it just became a cheap way for middle-class parents to get rid of their kids for two weeks." Elizabeth's perception of the NCS as "a cheap way for middle-class parents to get rid of their kids for two weeks" is borne out by data on who the program attracts. Mills and Waite (2017, p. 70) note that, despite its origins as a program designed specifically for disadvantaged young people, "the 'social mix' of NCS graduates is primarily middle-class," with far more female than male participants.

Khalil (age twenty-three) and Tiffany (age twenty-three) were the two UK participants who took part in NCS. Despite the dominance of middle-class participation in the program, Khalil and Tiffany had both experienced homelessness and grew up in poor families and communities. Thus they were actually among the targeted demographic for the program. Khalil was a paid NCS mentor for five years, and Tiffany was a program participant at age seventeen. As far as I know, they had not encountered one another during the program. Khalil enjoyed his work there, which helped fund his university studies, but he was also quite critical of the program, which he saw as "the biggest propaganda machine in the world." As one example of this, he described an activity they would run with participants that had the youth trying to, "calculate or guess how much they think we spend on the [national government] budget":

> So, like, [we] would say, the UK budget is a hundred pounds. And then they break it down into sections of costs for [government expenses like] defence, etcetera. And then [we] say, what do you think you spend most on? Then the kids have a little guess etcetera. And then you show them the actual proof, and this is where the biggest lie is, it was ridiculous. [We] would say the biggest spending, the biggest expense should I say for British government was benefits. And benefit fraud, yeah? So the welfare state. When like the whole motive behind NCS is to become active citizens, etcetera. It's a very demonizing concept to think when things like tax avoidance, white-collar crime, nuclear defence cost so much more. Do you get it?

Convincing young people that the largest drain on government coffers is welfare fraud is clearly aligned with neoliberal ideologies. While other aspects of the program were not so overt in their ideological position, there is an obvious emphasis throughout the program on an individual's self-development and on supporting local, charitable, and community initiatives – without any critical assessment or analyses of injustices they might seek to remedy through collaborative work. The flow of the program, as described by Khalil, began with a four-day residential program: "They would call it personal challenges. So you'd do like white water rafting or whatever, like, essentially to overcome your personal stuff." During the second week of this eighteen-day program, participants would stay in university accommodation: "and you give them a taste of uni life. Like budgeting, cooking your own meals, etc." During the days, mentors like Khalil would lead team challenges: "So it was like how to build your team skills, etcetera." For the last two weeks of the program, participants would return to their home community and develop a project with a community partner, "because the project [of NCS] was about being active citizens" (Khalil). Participants would meet with the community partner, "like a care home or charity," and ask them what they needed. "You would do some kind of like maybe quick advertising for the day or you'd paint the room and make it better for the service users. Just something to benefit you, benefit the community, etcetera." When I asked Khalil whether they explicitly talked about democracy during the program, he said yes: "So the whole thing about NCS was to become active citizens. And a part, a huge part of that was vote, vote, vote. They even give them a sheet to register to vote." Khalil described another NCS activity that he would run:

> So they would do this thing called Bite the Ballot where they would let kids debate. And they'd do this whole thing where they said to the kids, "Stand over here if you think this. Stand over here if you think that," etcetera. And then, they'd give like half the people, like they say, "okay, in this round you don't speak." And then after, when the kids don't speak they're supposed to get frustrated and then it's like, "okay, how does it feel to not have a voice?" And then it's like, "oh," it's like "oh, that's how it feels." Okay. "So then you should vote." ... They literally, like, spoon-fed them this idea of democracy and like voting is good, etcetera, etcetera.

Tiffany's description of the NCS program was similar to Khalil's, with one important exception: she had no memory of being educated about democracy. When I asked her what she did in the program, she told me, "We would have like little challenges. Um. [pauses] We camped out somewhere, but we were in like lodges, we weren't in tents. And we would do group activities and then we'd all get together at the end of the day and like be in this massive hall and eat food and talk about our experiences. And like, 'Oh, what did we do today? What did we learn today?' So it was a lot of reflecting. And um, teamwork definitely built my confidence. Helped me find really cool friends." Tiffany was also encouraged to manage her own campaign after the official NCS program had ended. Given her experiences with family alcoholism, Tiffany decided to focus on alcohol and drug awareness:

> TIFFANY: You'd go to the office and you'd plan the campaign and they were working with this place called Free Space dot com, which is now, doesn't exist anymore. But, um, it was like free spaces for young people who need it for venues. It was really cool. And, I basically printed off a lot of information on local alcohol places like for help.
>
> JACKIE: Did you do that by yourself, or did you have a little team of people working together on the campaign?
>
> TIFFANY: My friends and my sister helped me. So. Well, they helped me to set up on the day, but I did the campaign by myself. I mean, I had help from the [NCS] people, like, I had guidance. Because I was young. But like, to actually be in charge of it was me.

Despite being encouraged to run her own campaign, which to me seemed like an actual pragmatic exercise in democratic participation, Tiffany understood the purpose of the NCS in completely different terms: "I think it, they advertise and it did – um – it was a place where you gained confidence. Where you make friends. And where you gain work experience for when you want to be, when you want to be anything. Like leadership skills and stuff like that. Independence." In response to this description, I asked, "Did they talk about democracy in that at all? Like as a concept?" to which Tiffany replied, "No."

In sum, the experiences of Khalil, Tiffany, Matt, Elizabeth, and Julia echo the findings of Mills and Waite (2017) in their much more comprehensive study of NCS participant experiences: "Our study has exposed the ... legitimacy given to certain types of community engagement and 'good' participation that reveal how this 'branding' of citizenship is being used by the neoliberal state to encourage a particular type of citizen-subject" (p. 74). This citizen-subject resembles that being promoted through formal civics training, although it sounds as if the NCS experience is at least fun for participants, unlike the uninspiring civics curricula on offer through formal schooling. Nonetheless, the "good citizen" of the National Citizen Service is interpellated by young people – both those who participated and those who did not – as being primarily a confident and employable worker who contributes to local community and charitable causes. Explicit references to democratic participation were unabashedly liberal and/or neoliberal in emphasis, and it seems, from Tiffany's experience, that even this was not a prominent feature in all NCS programs. Certainly, the good citizen of the NCS did not challenge the state, nor did they learn about the injustices and inequalities that shape the experiences and opportunities of young citizens.

In other words, like civics curricula, the NCS does not provide the skills and knowledge required to develop a democratic disposition, whereby young people learn how to mobilize in order to generate greater justice for themselves and their communities within the state. As discussed in previous chapters, learning these skills must happen through private encounters and/or postsecondary schooling, rather than through state-funded schemes for educating citizens. This perpetuates the existing inequality of access to democracy, keeping those skills and dispositions largely within middle-class populations who can acquire a democratic biography through family of origin and/or extra-curricular and postsecondary educational experiences.

"I Learned about Democracy so I Could Pass a Test": Experiences of Civics Education

I did not expect civics education to be particularly relevant to the political development of young activists in this study because of my experience asking similar questions of young Canadian activists over a decade earlier (Kennelly, 2011a). Then, as now, activists found formal civics courses to be essentially meaningless in developing skills they could use to actually effect change, "so much so that I began to feel embarrassed when I asked them about their experiences of citizenship education" (Kennelly, 2011a, p. 54). This time around, armed with more than a decade of research experience and the confidence that comes with it, I returned to questions about civics education – without embarrassment – in order to see whether anything had changed. As made clear in the above discourse analysis of civics curricula, the similarities far outweigh the differences between early aughts civics curricula and curricula of the late teens and early twenties. Perhaps not surprisingly then, I found that the experiences of civics curricula I first heard about from young Canadian activists appear to hold across all five liberal democracies. In other words, young activists' memories of civics education, if they have any, are dominated by lessons about formal structures of government, presented at a fairly superficial level, and/or lessons in patriotism and the positive values they are meant to associate with their specific country. Most of the young activists I spoke with experienced civics classes as boring and meaningless, unless they happened to have an unusually dynamic teacher. No matter which liberal democracy they lived in, civics courses did virtually nothing when it came to helping them develop the skills and knowledge they now had regarding how to create positive social change – the skills I include as part of the acquisition of a democratic disposition.

> I actually distinctly remember my ninth grade civics class when I was in high school. And I remember my very Southern white woman teacher teaching us about democracy and political parties. And she was definitely skewing which one

was better than the other one. And I learned about democracy in the way I was learning it for class so I could pass a test. But because of my parents and, I think, my community, I knew something very different. So what I was learning in class was just to get the grade (Cadence, age nineteen, United States).

We definitely didn't learn a lot about how the government works. I don't remember being taught how a bill gets passed into legislation or why we have two houses, what is the difference between the Senate and House of Reps. We also have this incredibly complicated preference voting system in Australia. It has never once been taught. I, honestly, still don't understand that fully, how it actually works. But they didn't even touch that at all (Joanna, age twenty-six, Australia).

We don't have civics education [as a separate] subject, we have social studies where we briefly talked about it maybe for a couple of weeks, but that was all stuff that was like, "democracy is great, New Zealand is democratic, that's fantastic." So yes, that's as far as that went (Kanoa, age eighteen, New Zealand).

I remember being told that British values are tolerance and democracy. And you know, like that sort of thing.... It wasn't a major part of schooling, but it was like, you got told it. And I guess even now I almost remember it being something teachers recognized we have to do but they weren't particularly interested in (Matt, age nineteen, United Kingdom).

I remember learning about the parliamentary system, the political parties, um, yeah, past prime ministers. I think to a certain extent we learned about social movements but um, for the most part the social movements that we learned about were rooted like well into the past – like the suffragette movement and the other big one that came up was the anti–Vietnam War movement but mostly like the way it manifested in the United States.... I think the textbooks mentioned the Vietnam War and like people protested it ... [but] they brought it up in a way that also made Canada look great because they were like, people were fleeing [the draft] and they were coming to Canada, so it was also a way to bring up social movements in a way that glorifies the state (Sanaya, age twenty-eight, Canada).

While young activists found that civics lessons provided the bare minimum of information about formal democratic systems and told them more about how to be loyal patriots than dissenting citizens, they at least gained the advantage of some basic knowledge about how formal liberal democratic structures function. It was not until I began interviewing homeless youth about the kinds of civics education they had received that I recognized that some formal civics training, however superficial, is better than none.

One of the major failings of (neo)liberal states is pushing vulnerable youth out of education systems, particularly those who are experiencing homelessness. A pan-Canadian survey of homeless youth in 2016 – the first of its kind – reported that 83 per cent of the 1,103 respondents from across forty-seven different communities in Canada had experienced bullying in school, and 50 per cent had been tested for a learning disability (Gaetz et al., 2016). Not surprisingly, secondary school drop-out rates for homeless young people are extremely high – a 2001 report from Canada Mortgage and Housing Corporation (CMHC, Canada's federal housing agency) states that homeless youth drop out of high school at a rate of between 63 per cent and 90 per cent (Kraus, Eberle, & Serge, 2001) – compared to a national drop-out rate of 5 per cent to 14 per cent (Pathways to Education, 2019). Every other country in this study sees similarly high rates of secondary school drop out, or early school leaving, for young people experiencing homelessness (Mackenzie, 2020; Centrepoint, 2016; Fitzgerald, 2016; Lifewise, 2015). Even those youth who are able to remain in school are at risk of receiving a lower-quality education, either because they are streamed into "basic" or non-university prep courses, they have missed a number of classes in order to deal with the complications of being homeless, and/or they attend alternative or "special needs" classes that provide a pared-down curriculum.

Caitlin (age nineteen, Canada), for instance, attended her Grade 10 civics class before she later dropped out of her mainstream high school, but she remembers nothing from it. This was one of the classes she skipped while couch-surfing with friends, as home life became too difficult to handle.

JACKIE: Do you remember a Grade 10 civics class?
CAITLIN: Yes.
JACKIE: Yes. What was that like?
CAITLIN: That's definitely one of the courses that I kind of skipped out on. [laughs] A lot.
JACKIE: Why did you skip out on it?
CAITLIN: I don't remember. I just, I feel like it was boring, I guess. It's kind of rude to say, but I think that was like three years ago. But yeah, I definitely skipped out on that class the most. Like, I can't pinpoint what I did, what we learned in that class, but I definitely was in that class. [laughs] But I definitely skipped the exam or like the, some of that. Yeah.
JACKIE: Yeah. And you don't remember anything that they talked about?
CAITLIN: I'm sorry. I really don't. [laughs]

It was common for homeless young people to miss out on high school civics courses, and the impact on their general knowledge of the political system was shocking. Felix (age nineteen, Canada), who had a neurological disability and an unstable home life, attended several different special needs schools before dropping out at age sixteen. When I asked him what came to mind when I said the word "democracy," he told me he had never heard the word. Later, he called Justin Trudeau the "president" of Canada (in Canada we do not have a president, only a prime minister). Tamara (age twenty-six, Canada), whose story I shared in part in chapter four, thought that the Canadian province of British Columbia was a different country requiring a distinct passport to enter. This lack of knowledge was particularly marked among Canadian participants, most likely because in Canada I was able to attend a drop-in at a local youth-serving agency, and so interviewed young people who happened to be attending that day. This means, I strongly suspect, that my Canadian sample is made up disproportionately of young people who have been most vividly failed by the liberal democratic state – the most impoverished, the least educated, and the most vulnerable. By contrast, as my interviews with homeless youth in Australia, New Zealand, the United Kingdom, and the United States required participants to self-select by replying to an advertisement or the recruitment efforts of a local RA, they tended to be somewhat more stable, with higher on average access to postsecondary schooling, and less overall self-reported trauma and disruptions in their biographies than the Canadian participants who had experienced homelessness.

Many homeless youth filled the gaps in their knowledge through mainstream and/or social media, learning predominantly about American politics in the process. Dominic (age eighteen, Canada) told me that he gained a lot of his political information through YouTube. When I asked whether the YouTube channels he watched were American or Canadian, he responded:

> DOMINIC: Um, some were Canadian. Mostly American. Yeah. It's funny how we know, I know more about American politics and their views compared to Canada's.
> JACKIE: It's so easy to learn about the US. It's just everywhere.
> DOMINIC: Yeah. And everyone talks about it.
> JACKIE: Yeah, totally. And it's pretty sensational at the moment.
> DOMINIC: Yeah. Like, you hear Joe Biden, you hear Donald Trump, you hear ah Hillary Clinton, but the only um, um, what do you call it, like the people who are trying to become prime minister?
> JACKIE: Yeah. Like the candidates?
> DOMINIC: Yeah, the candidates. Um, I only know about [Canadian Prime Minister and Liberal Party leader] Justin Trudeau.
> JACKIE: Okay. You don't know the leaders of the other political parties?
> DOMINIC: Like, I know what the political parties are. Like the Green Party, the Liberals, the [pauses] – I think that, I forget the rest.

In late 2020 and early 2021, American formal politics were often at the forefront of young homeless people's minds when I asked them about democracy, no matter which country they lived in. During this period, then American President Donald Trump was running for re-election against Joe Biden; after losing the vote, Trump instigated multiple lawsuits to re-count the vote and incited a riot on Capitol Hill. These spectacular and sensational examples, cast on repeat through global media in all five study countries, set a specific tone for homeless young people about what politics means and encompasses. Alison (age eighteen), who had been born and raised in Canada, relayed her enthusiasm for, and knowledge of, US politics when we met in November of 2020 at the drop-in centre:

> ALISON: So, I can get very heart-to-heart with people about politics. I get very mad. Like, the fucking Donald Trump. Bruh. That's just stupid. Like, I'm actually very surprised he didn't get elected because of the gun[s] and shit. Because like me, I don't like him. I just like the shit that he says, it's funny to me. I just laugh because it's fucking stupid. Like you're a president, man. And, I don't know, but like I thought Biden was going to lose the whole time. So I was like, fuck. Biden. But like the only reason I thought Trump was going to win was because of the gun law because Biden basically wants to have the same gun law as Canada. And Trump was just like, yeah, like, "I don't give a fuck. Keep your guns." So that's why I thought he was going to win. Like, when it was Biden, I was like voting for Biden. I was like, oh, Biden. I don't know, like, especially when Trump was getting elected, when he first was getting a run for it. I was so cheesed. Even if Hillary Clinton was bad, like, bruh, at least get Hillary. At least she caught some bodies, you know?
>
> JACKIE: Do you ever get that way about Canadian politics?
>
> ALISON: Uh, sometimes. Well, Canadian politics is boring. [laughter] It's not deep like the States. Like the States is just [makes laser noises] zhh, zhh, zhh. They're always going at it.

On the other side of the world, in Australia, Rachel (age eighteen) was also avidly following American politics. I interviewed Rachel on 11 November 2020: eight days after the US presidential election, and nine days before my interview with Alison in Canada. Unlike Alison, Rachel felt that her interest in American politics had opened up avenues of understanding about Australian politics:

> RACHEL: If anything, I've learned more about politics and democracy in the last couple of weeks from TikTok. Because like, everything about the election was on there.
>
> JACKIE: The US election?
>
> RACHEL: Yeah. And then also I kind of got into about like Australian democracy from that as well.
>
> JACKIE: Okay. What kinds of things were you learning on TikTok?
>
> RACHEL: Well, just how voting works because this was my first year to vote as well. And like, yeah, like just how to do that and um, I suppose like how one leader can change, like affect so many people. It just opened my eyes about the people, like with letting one person lead a whole country. I just can't really understand that sometimes. Yeah. I was just learning about that and also a lot about how different countries took on the, obviously we have a state of emergency, like health emergency [due to COVID-19]. I was just learning about how the rules have to pass through different stages of government and things like that.

For both Rachel and Alison, the US election was a form of civic pedagogy, educating them about a specific subset of political activity within a country that was not their own. Unfortunately, this did not seem to translate into direct knowledge of their own political system and ways in which to participate within it. For Alison, Canadian politics seems too boring to be worth engaging with. Rachel claims that her interest in US politics helped educate her about Australian politics; yet the examples she gives leave me wondering how this worked in practice. For instance, she suggests that she learned "how voting works," yet the Australian voting system is a mixed-member proportional (MMP) system, which requires citizens to be knowledgeable about both their local candidates (for whom they vote "above the line") and their political parties (for whom they vote "below the line"). This is very different than the "first past the post" system that exists in both the United States and Canada. It is possible that her interest in US election coverage on TikTok led her to other videos that provided education for her about Australian politics, but it is hard to ascertain that from her comments.

In New Zealand, where no formal civics course exists, Monica (age sixteen) recalls that there were student councils that were meant to be democratic, but they were clearly class-stratified, excluding poor kids like herself from participating.

> MONICA: We always had like the student council and stuff but it [democracy] wasn't that much of a thing that was acknowledged. Like even the classes that should have been based around it. I sort of stayed clear a little bit of it because, I don't know, schooling's a little bit poop here.
> JACKIE: Yeah? So there was a student council at school but it didn't seem –
> MONICA: Yeah. They [the student council] were the ones who got to do all of that [democracy]. They got to have all that and you could try and get into it, but it was the stuck-up sort of people and I had tried to kind of like smudge myself into it, but they just kind of – Yeah, you have to be like the top people to actually be able to have a chance to voice any opinions, because classes didn't really do it as much. And it's like, oh, here's the theory [of democracy] you're learning about [in class]. You don't get to have any opinions or look any further into it.
> JACKIE: When you say the top people, are we talking about those with the highest grades? Which often –
> MONICA: The highest grades. Which are the ones who have the most money.
> JACKIE: Yes. That's kind of what I was driving at, but I didn't want to put the words in your mouth. So you could see that link, eh? Between high grades, lots of money, and could be on student council. Versus less money –
> MONICA: [They were] the ones with the stable lives.

Monica points precisely to one of the major differences between her experience and that of her affluent peers who participated in student council: their lives were stable. By contrast, Monica's life was disrupted by poverty and the loss of housing she experienced with her mum, forcing them into a friend's back room, and then into a motel paid for by a state benefit that would only be renewed if they had viewed enough rentals that week. The affordable rental market was incredibly tight, and it took them seven months to finally secure a spot in a Housing New Zealand rent-geared-to-income home, located in the poorest neighbourhood in her small town. Such order that was maintained in the area came from the local gangs, which protected hers and her mum's house from rival gang violence, a situation that Monica described as "not normal" for New Zealand, particularly that "it's so concentrated in this little tiny town." When I asked her why she thought it was particularly bad where she lived, she promptly replied "housing." I asked her to explain further:

> MONICA: They've upped the housing prices. And so that's left a lot of people kind of just like selling drugs and like people just getting angrier and pushed together and like making less opportunities and it's making it harder for anyone who's not got the steady income and not got like the best start of life to be able to do it without doing illegal things.

The precarity and instability that Monica experienced throughout her schooling life, before dropping out of school at age sixteen, can be traced directly to the expansion of neoliberalism and the loss of the welfare state in New Zealand, particularly its impact on social and affordable housing (as discussed in chapter one). Monica very astutely links her poverty and the instability it created to a classed hierarchy in school that mimics classed access to civic participation outside of school: those with sufficient income to be stable and receive higher grades are the ones who get to practise democracy in school. Those without such income and stability, do not.

One week later, Tiffany (age twenty-three) from the United Kingdom echoed Monica's comment about the instability generated by poverty and how this impacts one's access to citizenship rights and entitlements. When I asked her whether she feels like a citizen, she responded:

> Um. I have some of the rights. [pauses] But I think, I wouldn't even – maybe it's just what I think rights should be [laughs], where it's like, you know, my friends that I went to secondary school with, they would class themselves as poor but they would never imagine. Like, when I go to their houses, I'm like, what? People have rooms this big? Like, people have extra living rooms? And stuff like that, so. That's just down the road. So the differences in even little things like housing and things like parenting, um, like, people who grow up in stable situations are more likely to be stable and then have stable situations in the future. Right? It just affects everything. So I don't know, I feel like although I am a citizen, I do always feel like there

are higher-class citizens and there are lower-class citizens and there's real disparity between the two.

Tiffany had received very little explicit training in citizenship, despite participating in the National Citizen Service program (as described above). When I asked her about whether she had been taught anything about citizenship in school, she replied:

> TIFFANY: We had this thing called citizenship class. Which, well we only had it for half a year. So this was, yes, in secondary school. Um, our school tried to do it because you're able to get half a GCSE, which is like a credit kind of thing. So they're like, okay, let's do citizenship. All we learnt was about, we learnt consumer rights, some of the like, that if you buy something they have to refund you in a certain amount of time. And we learnt a little bit about um, STDs [sexually transmitted diseases].
>
> JACKIE: What? In citizenship? [laughter] I mean, those are important things to learn about, but as citizenship?
>
> TIFFANY: [laughter] Yeah. And we were taught by random teachers. It wasn't always the same teacher. I think it was more like who had the time. And no one was actually qualified. They were all different teachers, like one of them was a Spanish teacher, maths teacher. Um, and most of the time, the lessons were just, they were just extra playtime basically. I think it would have been so cool if they used those lessons and taught people how to drive or how to do their taxes. Like, that would be a good use of that amount of time. But also some intelligence and self-reflection skills. Anything.

The experience of civics education as described by both young activists and youth who had experienced homelessness suggests that public school systems in all five countries are failing to provide an even remotely accurate and effective version of citizenship education. At best, young people came away with a vague sense of how formal systems of government and voting work; at worst, they were taught to mimic their teacher's political beliefs in order to "pass the test" or learned irrelevant topics, such as how to prevent sexually transmitted diseases (a topic students should certainly learn about in school, but not in civics classes!). Interviewing homeless youth about their experiences with civics education, particularly in Canada, sensitized me to the necessity of providing that bare minimum of knowledge about the formal liberal democratic systems that are captured within the curricular documents analysed at the beginning of the chapter. But this is clearly insufficient for generating thoughtful citizens with the skills and knowledge to actually advocate for their own interests within our current opaque political systems. The consequence is that young people must gain this knowledge elsewhere, which generates systemic barriers to engaging meaningfully in democracy for those who do not have access to such (class-bound) knowledge systems.

Citizenship as Belonging and Bureaucracy

Despite state efforts to couple citizenship with democracy through formal civics training, when asked what they associate with the word "citizenship," both young activists and homeless young people typically spoke first of exclusion or belonging, felt within themselves and also as experienced through the bureaucracy of the state. Despite the fact that we had just been discussing democracy, when I asked the question, "When I say the word 'citizenship,' what comes to mind?" I typically received variations on the following comments:

> Belonging to a country. That feeling of belonging to a country (Julia, age eighteen, UK activist).
>
> The piece of paper that dictates if you get to have certain rights in a country or not. And it should be a feeling of belonging. It should be a feeling of belonging (Mahala, age twenty-five, New Zealand activist).
>
> Citizenship is someone that lives in Canada. And like has the citizenship to be in Canada.... I don't know because they always ask me for my citizenship when I do stuff, so. Because when I applied for housing, they ask for citizenship. At first I thought they thought I was an immigrant because they sent it back and I was like, wait, I live in Canada, like, I have a birth certificate. And I had to call them and be like what do you need? I need my proof of citizenship. They're like, oh, you need like a birth certificate or something. So I just like photocopied my birth certificate (Alison, age eighteen, Canadian homeless youth).
>
> So I would say, essentially, citizenship is acceptance from the state (Khalil, age twenty-three, UK formerly homeless youth).
>
> I think being legally in a country, like legally in the sense of in the government's eyes. And probably um documentation as well, I suppose.... Citizenship is probably like the legal documentation of coming into a country and being like, technically Australian (Rachel, age eighteen, Australian homeless youth).

"Belonging" is a powerfully emotive word, and its association with citizenship has been analysed by several other scholars (e.g., Yuval-Davis, 2007; Stella et al., 2015; Wood & Black, 2018). What interests me is how this emotionally charged association has been so strongly linked to a concept that educational curricula is trying very hard to connect with formal democratic participation. Likewise, I am interested in the common leap made by young people between this feeling and the formal state mechanisms that grant them rights (or not) within the country in which they live. Put differently, I am working outwards from what young activists and youth who have experienced homelessness in liberal democracies have told me to piece together a picture of the "common sense" or doxa with which they (and the rest of us) live when it comes to interpreting the term "citizenship."

To "belong" without contradiction within all of the liberal democracies in this study is to be white, housed, and to speak "without an accent" (the accent in question differs, but this is always about speaking English in the way that native-born speakers do). This was made clear both by the experiences of people who did not fit these categories, and the experiences of those who did. Those who were *not* white, housed, and/or speaking English without an accent (which stands in for foreign birth) could at times feel quite keenly the disjuncture between their sense of belonging and their legal status within the state. Alejandro (age twenty), who crossed into the United States illegally from Mexico with his parents and grew up as an impoverished, undocumented migrant in California, is confronted with the racialized and classed conditions of citizenship-as-belonging every time he reveals to someone that he is not an American citizen:

> Most people that meet me, whenever I tell them like, yeah, I can't apply for that because of my citizenship status, they're like, "Oh, really? You're not a citizen? You just seem so American," because I don't have an accent, I dress more American-style, I guess. I have a particular mannerism that's not considered Mexican and stuff. I used to watch movies, I guess, American films, and it would be like, you know, those fancy dinners that they would have, so I would always kind of mimic them and learn etiquette and the proper class sense of how to eat.

Alejandro has been able to mimic class and race privilege not only by carefully watching American films, but also by growing up in an extremely affluent corner of California and negotiating his way into a private university (see chapter three for more on Alejandro's story about how he got into university). He recognizes this unique juncture, highlighted for him in particular by a book he read during his studies entitled *The Privileged Poor* (Jack, 2019):

> So it's a book that really talks about kids that come from low socio-economic class and low income but grew up in a high socio-economic class [neighbourhood]. And I didn't know what advantages [that gave me]. So like, when you go to an institution, a private school, that's predominantly white, to me, that's normal, but someone coming from LA that has 95 per cent of their students being Latino, they get things like culture shock, imposter syndrome. I do get imposter syndrome at times, but it's very rare. And I demand things, like I demand to see the professor. I thought it was normal ..., and I didn't realize that that was a privilege that I carry, I guess.

Without a Mexican accent and with light-coloured skin, Alejandro can "pass" for white; his education in an upper-class public secondary school and then in

Belonging to the State: Citizenship as Symbolic Power 189

a private high-profile university allows him to also "pass" as middle class. For some young people, "passing" as the dominant group is not possible, and this has direct implications for their felt emotions in relation to the concept of citizenship. Cadence (age nineteen), for instance, was born in the United States, and comes from several generations who were also born in the United States, dating back to slavery. She and her family thus have access to the bureaucratic markers of citizenship, that is, a passport or Social Security number. But their sense of belonging is more complicated. When I asked her whether she feels like a citizen – one of the questions I asked every participant – she responded:

> In the technical sense, in terms of I have a Social Security card, yes. But in the communal sense, no. I think I've always felt like I was just kind of stuck here. And in a way, I literally was. I did not intend to be here. And my parents did not intend to be here. My grandparents did not intend to be here.... I feel like a lot of Black Americans, we just don't have a sense of space in the US. There's a prolonged othering that takes place, which is painfully ironic because we didn't ask to be here in the first place. But I really don't feel like an American citizen. Because I think American citizenship is tied so deeply to patriotism and I'm not, in any way, patriotic at all.

These kinds of race-based exclusions were experienced in all of the study countries, although with variations relevant to the history and geography of their community. Gregory (age nineteen), who grew up in Toronto, Canada, shared the following story when I asked him whether he feels like a citizen of Canada:

> And living in Toronto do I feel like a citizen? I say, for sure, no. The answer would be no because looking at our whole society, all in all, is against I guess people who look like me or like our race all in all. Like I'll never forget the day, for example, I left City Hall to go to my research because I'm a co-researcher with the University of Toronto, [with] an Indigenous professor. So I was going there for a meeting and then I saw a police officer, I wanted to ask him a question. I gave him like a one-metre distance, and then I called him out. I was like, "Officer, officer," like getting his attention. He immediately turned around, put his hand on his gun and pulled out his gun and stepped back. And I was shocked. I was just like, "Whoa!" In my head, I was like. "Whoa? Why so quick?" And especially because it was daylight, it was right outside a government building, the courthouses all around us, so police officers are almost every day moving around. And that day specifically there were like four other police officers around. Just looking at the environment those seconds leading up to and after it, there was no reason for anyone to feel unsafe. But then he did that. He moved back.... But like if that was a white person in that situation, 100 per cent he wouldn't have reacted like

that. So I feel like when you talk about citizenship.... Like we have all these rights that are owed to us, but it's like it's not really given to us, sadly. It's given to us selectively, select people. It's choosy choosy, like we pick and choose who we want to [give those rights to].

The function of racism in generating a specific doxa about who belongs within white-dominant societies creates seemingly perverse consequences. This is because it is one's proximity to whiteness rather than one's country of birth that determines whether an individual is a "citizen" or not in the sense of belonging to the state. Mahala (age twenty-five), a Muslim woman from New Zealand, intentionally wears a hijab in part to defy the normative expectation that she assimilate to a particular notion of whiteness. She told me that although she feels like a citizen, she does not believe that she is *seen as* a citizen by others no matter what her passport says:

[T]he wider community, and I should say, the wider and *whiter* community, is just not.... They'll never see us as citizens. My mom has an accent when she speaks. I don't want to say broken English, but you can see the Arabic accent coming out. And honestly, people immediately assume that she's just recently come in as a refugee or something. But it's like, "Why do you have to assume things? Why do you have to assume my history? You don't know anything about me." I think it's a few stages. So if you're a European and you come into New Zealand today, if you're from the UK and you come into New Zealand today, you're seen as more of a New Zealander than I am even though we're second-generation, or my nephews are third-generation, New Zealanders.

One's proximity to whiteness is distinguished in various ways, not limited to skin colour but also by accented English, specific apparel (e.g., the hijab for women or turbans for men), and class markers, such as access to higher education and housing. These are all bundled together into the amorphous but also extremely specific signifier of "the citizen" in every one of the countries in this study. The citizen, the insider, the one who belongs and is accepted by the state stands in contrast to the foreigner, the outsider, the one who does not belong and is excluded by the state. This is not the curricula of school-based civics education: this is public pedagogy, or doxa, the common sense that permeates all aspects of being within the state, invisible yet pervasive and thus all the more difficult to identify and name.

Another key category of exclusion within the doxa of citizenship in liberal democracies is Indigeneity, particularly in Australia, Canada, and New Zealand. Many participants in these three countries remarked upon the contested dynamics between the settler-colonial state and Indigenous peoples; no mention was made of similar dynamics by participants in either the United Kingdom or the

United States.[4] For Indigenous participants, a sense of belonging within the state was fraught at the best of times, made more so when compounded by experiences of homelessness. Dominic (age eighteen), whose mother is Inuit, told me that he feels like a second-class citizen in Canada, and that this feeling was compounded when he entered a homeless shelter: "I don't really think that they treat us [Inuit and other Indigenous peoples] like actual citizens because citizens are heard and are helped. But Native people are not. They're pushed away into the north and like swept under the rug. Pretend that we don't exist.... [O]nce I went to that homeless shelter I, like, the idea of second class really stepped in. Like, I already knew that they [Indigenous peoples] were treated like that, and even worse if you're in the community or off reserve. But it really changes things when you experience it first-hand." For Michael (age eighteen) in New Zealand, born to and raised by a Māori father and Pakeha (white) mother, citizenship as a concept is troubling:

MICHAEL: You said citizenship, and I thought of our country and how little connection that I feel toward it. But it's an awkward position. Because I mean, on mom's side, we are citizens of this country type of thing.
MICHAEL'S MOTHER: Colonizing.
MICHAEL: I'm thinking about colonization as well and that, technically, the Parliament is not very legitimate of lots of our iwis [iwi = nation or tribe].... I've got all these other things that keep popping up. I'm just thinking about how our iwi never signed the treaty, our sovereignty.
MICHAEL'S MOTHER: And Māori fighting in World War II to get that citizenship and all that stuff.
MICHAEL: Yeah. It does bring up a whole bunch of things. Māori have fought in a bunch of wars with the idea being that "When we come back from war, we will have earned citizenship of New Zealand." When it was already our country. And then every time we've come back, instead of citizenship, we've found more of our land has been stolen while we were at war. And then we find the white soldiers, who we weren't allowed to fight alongside, being gifted, as a reward for fighting for the empire, our land. So citizenship, basically, has been a big scam for that side of me and worked out quite well for the other side.

I did not have any Indigenous participants in Australia, but my settler participants were generally aware of and would speak about the tense relationship

---

4   The relationship between Indigeneity and citizenship is a complex one, to which I do not do justice here. Sunera Thobani (2007) has written a very important book on the topic in the Canadian context, and Richard Iton's (2008) work touches on the relationship between Indigenous peoples and Black Americans in relation to whiteness and citizenship in the US context (I am indebted to Dr. Daniel McNeil for pointing out this latter connection).

between the state and Australian Indigenous peoples. For instance, Joanna (age twenty-six), a white activist who works on migrant justice issues, made explicit connections to these tensions in her response to my question about what she associates with the word "citizenship": "We should probably also acknowledge that if you ask any Aboriginal activist what they thought about that [citizenship], they would think about the referendum. We had a referendum in '67 where Aboriginal.... Literally, it wasn't even about making them citizens. It was about counting them in a census as people instead of animals. And so, citizenship, yeah, in that context, particularly for an Aboriginal activist, would have really different connotations as well. Because they would probably think of the referendum before they thought of refugees or ... yeah."

As proximity to whiteness and Indigenous–settler tensions shaped young people's ideas about citizenship, so too did social class. The powerful relationship between class and citizenship is most apparent when speaking with young people who have experienced homelessness. Youth who have been forced to rough sleep on streets or under bridges quickly experience a state pedagogy through policing about who belongs and who does not, and they readily make these links to citizenship (see also Kennelly, 2011b, 2018a, 2020). When I asked Alison (age eighteen) whether she feels like a Canadian citizen, she wanted to know what I mean by that. After I responded that it means whatever she thinks it means, she said: "Like, I don't know, but when it's an officer or something I don't feel like it's Canadian citizenship because like the way they talk to kids especially. It's like they try and use that, sort of, like back then when they used to use their tone of voice with me. I think some people will talk to you like you're stupid because you're younger." Scarlett's (age twenty-four) response to the same question in Australia also referenced her poor treatment by the police before she was housed: "I don't really feel like a citizen of Australia because I get treated less than and I get discriminated against and my lack of rights, um, and like the way I've been treated by police. Yes, I was a criminal, when I was younger, but that does not excuse police brutality. I got bashed by police officers for not becoming an informant like some of the other sex workers." Chloe (age nineteen) told me that she currently feels like she is seen as a citizen by others in Canada, but she did not when she was homeless: "Even though I was obviously still a citizen, it seems when you're homeless that the kind of rights that every Canadian citizen has, people don't really, what's that word? Um. [pauses] Care that homeless people are still citizens and they still have the same rights as everybody else.... Like the police treat homeless, at least from my experience, treat homeless people with a lot more violence than they do the general population.... They're [homeless people] viewed as more of a burden. Like, an economic burden. You know, they're treated, just very violently and not really treated with respect." Chloe's insight about homeless people being viewed as an economic burden is particularly salient when considered in light of the implicit, and often explicit, focus of civics education on producing the fiscally responsible consumer. As neoliberalism increasingly conflates citizenship with consumerism, homeless individuals become the ultimate anti-citizens (see also Feldman, 2004). This ideology is also apparent in Isabella's (age twenty-one) experience of being seen as a non-citizen while homeless and travelling to her part-time evening job by public transit in a Southern US state: "It felt very much like [you're] a citizen if you're able to have a nine to five or be able to have reliable transport or be able to afford groceries. And that felt very much like a citizen's dream situation. I just felt very out of place. I couldn't afford any of that stuff. And I felt like this job wasn't worth all the pain that I was taking for it, but I didn't want to admit to my family how hard that it was."

Although other aspects of identity have been analysed by scholars as also mitigating individuals' access to the rights of citizenship – gender, sexuality, and disability, for instance (e.g., Lister, 2003; Weeks, 1998; Waldschmidt & Sepulchre, 2019) – it was clear from young people's responses that race, Indigeneity, and class are the most prominent in their felt experiences of citizenship as belonging and bureaucracy. For instance, Angie (age twenty-four), a Canadian white activist with a visible disability who identifies as queer and non-binary, named none of these potentially marginalizing identity markers when I asked whether she felt like a citizen: "Yes, I mean, yeah. Like, I'm very aware of my relative privilege, right? For all of the many things in my life, like I am an English-speaking, native-born [Canadian]. Never a foreigner, it's never a question in the eyes of the government that I am a citizen." This is not to suggest that sexuality, gender, and/or disability are irrelevant to the experiences of citizenship; delving more deeply with Angie into these intersections would likely have revealed the ways in which these aspects of her everyday life collide with the expectations, rights, and opportunities of citizenship. But the most readily available dynamics of belonging and bureaucracy remarked upon by young people in relation to citizenship were race, Indigeneity (in three of the study countries), and class. This signals that the public pedagogy concerning who falls within the state category of "citizen" in all five of these liberal democracies continues to be strongly aligned with whiteness and middle classness.

The stories of those who feel that innate sense of belonging to the state are as telling as the stories of those who do not. Karen's experience in New Zealand is the flip side of a coin to that of Alejandro's in the United States. Alejandro (age twenty) grew up knowing that he was an undocumented migrant and learning implicitly to mimic white, middle-class norms in order to garner a sense of belonging within the state, even without the formal recognition of a passport. Karen (age twenty-four), on the other hand, born in the United Kingdom to white parents with middle-class professions, spent her childhood in New Zealand without formal citizenship, unknown to her. Although her home life eventually came apart and she went into foster care at the age of thirteen, she was lucky enough never to experience homelessness (which is another common failure of the state for young people coming out of care). When she discovered she was not in fact an official citizen of New Zealand, she told me that she was "surprised to find out that I wasn't because, for apparent reasons, I was treated exactly the same. So, yeah, it was interesting to me to do the formal ceremony and be welcomed to the country that I already felt was my home."

Young people who grew up feeling simply that they belonged – because they are white, speak non-accented English, and grew up in middle-class homes – were the ones most likely to respond to my questions about citizenship by making the link that civics education is trying to make: that is, of citizenship as political involvement in a democratic state. Leila (age nineteen) connected her sense of being a citizen with her political organizing work with School Strikes for Climate: "I feel like I'm ... a citizen of New Zealand. I know that I feel a lot more like it now because I've been able to play a role in School Strike for Climate and activism and that's allowed me to kind of, like again, know my role a little bit more. And as a citizen, the power that I have to influence our democracy and to be able to influence the change that I want to see." Leila does not remember learning about citizenship as a concept in school, although she does remember winning a "citizenship award" at age twelve and being unclear about what that meant:

> I remember being quite confused by what it was, and I was like, so what does it mean to be a good citizen? What does citizenship mean? Because, like, I'd heard of it in the context of like when you move to New Zealand from another country you can get citizenship. And I was like, well what does that...? I just couldn't understand whether it was kind of linked to that. So I was very confused. But we didn't learn about it, like, no one's ever sat me down and said "this is the definition of citizenship." I feel like I've just created my own definition through watching people being good citizens and, yeah, kind of seeing how other people do citizenship and how other people help others around them and play a role in the world and kind of figuring out how I can do that myself.

As a white, non-accented English-speaking, cisgender woman growing up in a comfortably middle-class home, Leila's experience with doxa about citizenship did not leave her wondering whether she belonged or not. She simply belonged. This left her free to learn by "seeing other people do citizenship" that citizenship is a concept linked to political engagement. Her extra-curricular education as an activist, through the School Strikes for Climate movement, meant that she included activism as a legitimate means by which to engage in the polity, a lesson she would not have learned through formal civics curricula. Although she recognized that "many people in New Zealand ... wouldn't feel that same sense of citizenship," she still links this feeling to democracy: "Whether that's because they feel like the democracy isn't accessible to them, or they feel like they haven't quite found the role that they play in democracy and how they can influence it." For Leila, citizenship is about democratic participation, not about belonging to the state, because her belonging is a given.

Brendan's (age twenty-seven) take on citizenship in Australia is more complex than Leila's, but he nonetheless also positions citizenship in relation to political activity rather than belonging. A white, cisgender man born to professors in the United States who moved to Australia during his childhood to take up academic positions there, Brendan went through the formal process of attaining citizenship in Australia at age seventeen, "Largely so I could get the government subsidy for higher education [laughs]." Brendan is pursuing a doctoral degree in history and had an academic interest in the research topic I was exploring with him; he was intrigued by what he described as the inherent contradictions of citizenship, articulating a phenomenon that I have identified in my earlier work as the "good citizen/bad activist" dichotomy that faces young people trying to engage in political work within a state that does not want to be challenged (Kennelly, 2009a, 2011a): "Um, and yeah, so I'm, I'm not a good citizen. I don't see myself and my actions – well I am a good citizen – in that, particularly the ideal of you're meant to participate in the, whether it's the Greek sort of idea of democracy or whatever, but I definitely, well I don't think of my own activist and political activity as related to citizenship. Anti-citizenship in a sense that I am against the state." Although Brendan's political analysis means that he does not "see his political activity as related to citizenship," his ruminations on citizenship and its meaning make it clear that he connects the concept very tightly to politics and participation, even if not the politics he practises. When I first asked him about the concept, with the question "When I say the word 'citizenship,' what comes to mind?", his response was: "Um, nationalism. Um, civic responsibility and civic duty. Um, voting. Um, [pauses] participation. The notion of participation. But, those ideas that I'm, the way I'm doing word relationship in that sense is a lot of the way in which you're educated about what citizenship means, the general liberal ideas of participation and so forth." A highly educated man with many years of activist practice under his belt, Brendan immediately connected his own word association process with the formal education system, with critical insight about its bias. Like Leila, however, and unlike most of the other participants, Brendan's strongest association with the word was the one conveyed through civics curricula, linking citizenship to democratic participation. The public pedagogy that was so apparent in the responses of the majority of participants, about citizenship as a raced and classed category signalling a sense of belonging to the state, was not a lesson he faced. His political analysis means that he understands, analytically, that the state is racist and exclusionary, but he does not have to live that reality on a daily basis and so does not experience citizenship as an affective category denoting belonging or exclusion.

Conclusions

The civics curriculum currently in use in all five of the study sites makes apparent the investment of the state in producing compliant citizens with limited knowledge of formal liberal democratic structures, and no understanding of collective organizing or other ways in which to effectively advocate for justice. In some cases, this is reinforced by other forms of pedagogy made broadly available to school-aged young people, for instance the National Citizen Service in the United Kingdom. Even more powerful than the efforts of the state to link formal democratic participation to citizenship is the informal curriculum that has generated persistent affective associations between "citizenship" and "belonging." Such belonging is felt both in terms of identity – most particularly in relation to class and race or Indigeneity – and in terms of the bureaucratic access to state protections that come with formal citizenship. When these two forms of belonging collide, where a young person has one but not the other, the dissonance is felt with particular ferocity for those who may have formal state recognition but do not feel that they "belong" due to raced and classed exclusions.

In the next and final chapter of the book, I bring together the themes explored across the preceding six chapters in order to consider the implications of these findings for democracy under current conditions of extreme inequality.

Conclusions: When I Say the Word "Democracy," What Comes to Mind?

I think that in terms of symbolic domination, resistance is more difficult, since it is something you absorb like air, something you don't feel pressured by; it is everywhere and nowhere, and to escape from that is very difficult.
– Pierre Bourdieu (in Eagleton & Bourdieu, 1992, para. 10)

When reviewing the chapters I have written for this book, I think it is fair to say that they offer a reasonable level of insight into what democracy is *not*: it is not about individuals acting rationally through discrete decisions made separately from their communities of others. It is not about hopelessly voting for one elite versus another, in a last-ditch effort to avert the worst possible outcome. It is not about being responsible to the state, particularly when the state has ceased to take responsibility for its citizens.

The more difficult question, not surprisingly, is to explain what democracy *is*. The empirical evidence offered by young activists of their own homological transitions from activism to the realm of politics is helpful: democracy is, as Hannah Arendt asserted over fifty years ago, a relational process. Within liberal democratic structures, it requires specialized knowledge and access to specific social networks in order to meaningfully effect change. Under neoliberalism, such specialized knowledge and networks have increasingly come to be clustered among those with a specific class history, one that typically includes access to postsecondary schooling, alongside politicizing influences from family or other mentors.

Where Hannah Arendt tells us that everyone has the *potential* to participate in the public realm, simply by being born, Pierre Bourdieu helps us understand how such potential is nurtured in some and left undeveloped in others, not randomly but systematically and structurally. This happens through patterns of symbolic capital acquisition and the emergence of diverse dispositions that can be traced through sociological inquiry. Across all five liberal democracies, it was class background that best predicted a person's relationship to democracy and the state. Homeless youth in Australia, where voting is mandatory, were more similar in attitudes and behaviour to Canadian homeless youth, who are not legally obliged to vote, than to their middle-class Australian counterparts. Homeless youth in New Zealand, with their proportional representation system, were closer in practices and beliefs to homeless youth in the United Kingdom, who have a first past the post system. In the United States, with their complex layers of government and their Electoral College, homeless youth described their relationship to the state in terms that most closely resembled homeless youth in the Commonwealth countries of Canada, Australia, and New Zealand. Likewise, activist youth in each country resembled each other more closely than they did youth in their own countries who share nationality but not social class.

So what does this mean for democracy?

Let us return here to the work of Wendy Brown, whose quotation about inequality and democracy opened the Introduction to this book. In her essay entitled "The End of Educated Democracy," she states the following:

> Democracy: rule (*cracy*) of the people or poor (*demos*). Democracy is the name of a political form in which the people are sovereign, in which the whole, rather than merely a part, rules the polity and hence itself. How this sovereignty is best achieved, and through what complementary economic, social, cultural, and theological conditions and practices, is contestable and historically variable. Consequently there are many theories and modalities of democracy – direct, representative, liberal, socialist, libertarian, republican, social, anarchic, plebiscite, and more. At a minimum, however, democracy requires that the people authorize their own laws, whether directly or through elected representatives, and also that they share modestly in other, nonlegal powers governing their lives. Anything less means the people do not rule.
> (Brown, 2011, p. 19–20)

Like Brown, I am not seeking to theorize a specific form of democracy. Rather, I am demonstrating the ways in which our current dominant model – liberal democracy, particularly when influenced by neoliberalism – has become demonstrably *non*-democratic. It is not good enough to assert that everyone has equal access to participate in the polity, if a substantial subsection of the population is effectively blocked from any such participation due to lack of knowledge, social capital, and/or deep mistrust of the current systems. It is particularly unjust that those who are being most substantially and systematically failed by the state are also those with the least access to democratic means of changing those systems.

Struggling against Doxa

As will be clear to anyone who has read through this book from the beginning, Pierre Bourdieu's work has been hugely influential on my thinking about democracy, inequality, and resistance. Bourdieu's sociology has been described as "closely connected with democratic ideology." This is "not because Bourdieu was a naïve defender" of democracy, "but because this political ideal can be treated as a kind of pure theoretical model, sociology then taking up the task of showing the distance to realization of this model – that is to say, uncovering the specifically social obstacles to its accomplishment" (Champagne, 2005, p. 111). This precisely encapsulates my goal for this book. *Burnt by Democracy* represents my effort to deepen our collective understanding about the "specifically social obstacles" to the realization of democracy. Bourdieu (2014, p. 167) remarks that, "You can never be too excessive in struggling against doxa." I take this to signify the important recognition of how deeply doxa – or the "common sense" ideas that are in fact the views of the dominant – shapes all of our sensibilities, whether we be researchers, activists, or young people who have experienced homelessness. It is exceedingly difficult to peer through and beneath the multiple layers of misinformation and mythologization about democracy and its manifestations, particularly when such misinformation and mythologization benefit the state. This is why I have approached this study through the words and experiences of two distinct groups of young people, across five different liberal democracies. As I noted at the very beginning of the book, the study is neither about activism nor is it about homelessness, although I imagine that readers have gleaned some insights about each through the stories enclosed here. Rather, it is about getting a glimpse into the functioning of liberalism and neoliberalism and how they impact democracy *as actually lived and experienced* by young people born around the turn of the new millennium.

Understanding how contemporary young people experience democracy is also to get a closer look at the effects of inequality. Over the past twenty-five years, youth (ages eighteen to twenty-five) have replaced the elderly as the group most at risk of income poverty across all OECD countries (OECD, 2014). Millennials (those born in the 1980s and early to mid-1990s) in every country in this study are less likely to own a home, more likely to carry higher debt levels, and are less capable of accumulating wealth than the generations before (Gale, Gelfond, & Fichtner, 2019; Heisz & Richards, 2019; Roberts & Lawrence, 2017; Workman, 2020; Cokis & McLoughlin, 2020). While intergenerational wealth gaps are expanding, inequality *between* young people is also high; in fact, it is often higher between poor young people and affluent young people than it is between poor adults and affluent adults (Davidson, Saunders, & Phillips, 2018; Gale, Gelfond, & Fichtner, 2019; Heisz & Richards, 2019; Roberts & Lawrence, 2017). This is part of the general trend towards rising wealth inequality across all OECD nations, including all five study countries (OECD, 2015).

Burnt by Democracy emerged in part as I sought to make sense of findings from previous research projects with young activists and with homeless youth, which contradicted ideas I had absorbed as doxa about how democracy, marginalization, and social movements function. It began with fieldwork for *Citizen*

Youth (Kennelly, 2011a), where I uncovered empirically the strongly classed constraints in place for who can become an activist. This ran directly counter to the notion of activists as uniquely moral agents who come to social movement organizing due to their own direct experiences of injustice. I later came to recognize this in itself to be a deeply liberal idea that conceives of the individual as rational, acting in isolation, and freely able to engage in whatever political response they wish, whether that be voting or protesting, without reference to social contexts or constraints. Reckoning with my own absorption of liberal doxa continued through a later project called "Encountering Democracy," where I conducted fieldwork with Canadian homeless young people to learn their ideas and beliefs about democracy (Kennelly, 2018a, 2018b). I had designed the project to be a Youth Participatory Action Research (YPAR) project, which both the funder and the staff/gatekeepers at youth centres found appealing. The idea was to develop an understanding of the civic issues facing the youth and work with them towards implementing some sort of democratic response. As I reflected on the project afterwards (Kennelly, 2018b), I came to recognize to what extent the project had been infused with liberal and neoliberal assumptions about young people and their capacities to engage democratically, despite my training in critical analyses of this very phenomenon: "The neoliberal citizen is a phantom accompaniment to many participatory community projects, including my own: the self-directed and responsibilized individual who can move in a straightforward manner from insight to action" (p. 35). I also came to appreciate how this doxa generates another problematic assumption, also discussed by Janes (2016) in her critical reflection on community-based participatory action research; that is, believing the perspectives of marginalized people to be somehow more "authentic" and truthful than that of elites or other non-marginalized folks. As I note in my reflective piece: "The notion of community participants as unproblematically 'authentic' in their perspectives maps onto the rational, liberal individual inasmuch as it strips participants – and researchers – of their embodied and affective embeddedness in historical, political, and social contexts that obscure relations of inequality. In other words, participants are expected to 'see through' conditions of systemic marginalization and oppression, rather than reproduce them" (Kennelly, 2018b, p. 36).

The two aspects of neo/liberal democratic doxa that I described above – of marginalized folks having uniquely pure insights into their own marginalization, and of activism as a space of moral righteousness that can be accessed by anyone with the appropriate passion and will to action – are shared across the political spectrum. How this doxa is mobilized politically differs, however. For the right, marginalized people, particularly the most impoverished, are seen and represented as uniquely cunning in their ability to navigate the welfare state to advantage themselves – the notion of "welfare fraud" and how it is robbing decent citizens of a given liberal democracy is an example of this doxa at work.

For the left, the most marginalized are romanticized as the bearers of unadulterated truth about the systems within which they are caught; they only need to be organized and "given voice" in order to keenly and accurately fight back against the systems that oppress them. If only it were so. The reality is far more complex, and thus much more difficult to counter.

Unsurprisingly, it is the elite who reap the rewards of both of these narratives about the poor. As long as those resisting neoliberalism continue to labour under the liberal misapprehension about who gets to be an activist – that is, without essential insight into the extremely classed, as well as raced and gendered, dynamics of access to such spaces within contemporary liberal democracies – then progressive social movements will continue to exclude those who ought to be included, weakening our strategies and playing into the hands of the elite. The elite – or the dominant, to use Bourdieu's term – generate doxa to benefit themselves. The dominant control the state; the state controls education; education contributes to the myth of meritocracy and the reproduction of an extremely thin version of democracy modelled on the liberal notion of one person/one vote. At the same time, the hidden curriculum of the state dictates who belongs and who does not, which becomes a proxy for who can make legitimate claims of the state and who cannot. This is the affect that has been attached to the concept of "citizenship" for everyone except the white, middle-class, straight and non-"foreign" individuals who are freed to see citizenship as the formal curriculum tries to portray it, as linked to democracy.

The Death of Democracy

With the growth of inequality and thus of marginalization, the danger is that our political systems are becoming less and less capable of hearing and addressing the needs of the most marginalized. The cultural gulf that this then entrenches between classes results in distinct groups being unable to even speak the same political language, begging the question of what politics and democracy actually mean. The embedding of a democratic disposition within the middle classes shapes politics and what is possible within the formal political space, by constraining who is in it and therefore whose interests are being represented. We see in the homologous relationship between the political field of activism and that of formal politics the manner in which the (currently middle-class) democratic disposition generates further opportunities for middle-class actors, which in turn entrenches the barriers to poor and working-class actors – an inequality which has only widened under neoliberal policies since the 1980s.

Let us return to the other key theorist who has shaped my thinking in this book. Hannah Arendt conceived of the public sphere as the space of "who-ness," a uniquely human experience of being able to meet at a metaphorical "shared table" within the "web of relations" that makes up the political world. Being able to express one's "who-ness" as opposed to one's "what-ness" is akin to being recognized in one's full humanity, as a unique individual able to contribute to and participate in the shaping of our collective social and political worlds. Under (neo)liberalism, the space of expressing one's full humanity is reserved only for the middle classes and up. Thus, not only do we face the loss of truly democratic societies, where everyone's interests are heard and everyone's needs are met, we also reinforce a system which actively strips people of their humanity. In other words, current liberal democratic formal systems are inherently dehumanizing those who are not able to come to Arendt's "shared table" – neoliberalism makes this worse, with the complicity of civics curriculum, by mystifying democracy as something belonging only to formal politics and enacted by individuals through individual means (such as voting).

There is an important clue about how to educate more broadly for democratic participation within the empirical fieldwork for this project. The qualitative data demonstrated that the belief that "everything is political" is powerfully correlated with the development of a democratic disposition. This is a key insight. Its opposite is not that "nothing is political," but rather that only *formal politics* is political. This was how the majority of young people who had experienced homelessness saw it. Because they also saw formal politics as opaque, corrupt, or meaningless, this essentially blocks them from seeing a place for themselves in the political realm. The difference between thinking of oneself as political versus not is to see the possibility for making change and to feel a sense of agency and entitlement about generating a world that better meets one's needs. Unfortunately, without exposure to an alternative notion of what counts as political – that is, *everything* – young people are left only with the dominant idea that confines politics to formal systems, a doxa that is strongly reproduced through current civics curricula in all five countries. This in fact entrenches the helplessness and sense of nihilism and despair for young people who have not learned to see beyond that narrow definition. Under current systems of class stratification, this essentially means that those who are being most substantially failed by the state have little or no recourse to communicating their needs and their insights to the systems that might be able to serve them better.

The Role of the Democratic Disposition

The fieldwork I conducted for this book has helped me better understand and theorize what I have called a "democratic disposition." I interviewed young activists because past experience told me they almost universally carried the qualities and capacities that I associate with this category: the ability to strategize within current liberal democratic systems to challenge, overturn, resist, and mobilize the resources needed to generate positive and socially just outcomes.

As I illustrate empirically in chapter three, the biographies that lead to such a disposition are disproportionately grounded within middle-class families and exposure to postsecondary education and the social movements that are often associated with university campuses. This highlights the current classed disparities that exist when it comes to effective engagement under liberal democracies, generating barriers for those coming from non-middle-class families and/or those who are unable to attend postsecondary schooling.

The hopeful news, however, is that the classed disparities are incidental, not fundamental, to the acquisition of a democratic disposition. In other words, there is no reason that the knowledge and skills required to meaningfully engage in democracy should be limited to the middle classes or to postsecondary schooling. It has come to be that way in part because of our collective lack of understanding about how democracy actually functions. As long as we continue to labour under the myth of the rational, individual citizen who is cast as equal due to having an equal vote, then we will not put in place the institutions and supports that are required to truly level the playing field for all members of a society to meaningfully participate. Indeed, such an institution already exists, despite the many layers of retrenchment that have undermined its ability to truly level classed inequalities. I am speaking, of course, of public education, which all five of these liberal democracies continue to fund and support, if more thinly and following increasingly corporate models in some cases (particularly in the United Kingdom).

How to Stop Burning People by Democracy

A renewed and honest commitment to educating for democracy could emerge from public education systems. They would need to completely overhaul their current individualistic and excessively formal focus within civics curricula, and instead develop curricula that modelled itself on collective decision-making, providing deep dives into the actual foundations of inequality, including reckoning with colonial and white supremacist pasts and the ongoing legacies of neoliberal policymaking. Such curricula would provide students with examples from youth-led and other social movements past and present that have actually created social change, and would stop equating charitable work and financial literacy with citizenship. Effective civics curricula would start with the issues that young people are passionate about and help them understand both how those issues have come to exist and what they might do to change them. For such schooling to be successful, it would also need proper public reinvestment, with a particular focus on supporting the young people who are continually failed by current education systems, most notably young people living in poverty and/or experiencing homelessness. Among these young people are disproportionate numbers of Indigenous, racialized, and LGBTQ2S+ youth; schools thus need to reckon with internalized racism, colonialism, and homophobia, in addition to the ongoing effects of classism which remain deeply embedded within public education systems.

I opened this book with Stephanie's experiences as an example of how young people are being burnt by democracy. I close it with the words of Gregory, who has a knack for summarizing my own arguments more articulately than I can (also see the final quote in the previous chapter!). Gregory was responding to my question about whether he saw his views and experiences represented in current formal politics and mainstream media:

> No, no. No.... My views and perspectives can't be represented if they aren't even understood. And you can tell that, clearly, they are not understood. Like, people are really stuck in their ways and on their own mindsets and that's why I'm so keen on educating people at such a young age, that's why we need to have Black and Indigenous history in there yo, you know, because our education system is breeding ignorant individuals and that's not going to help anyone. So yeah, I do not feel like we're represented in politics for our views and perspectives.... Even when there is evidence-based research that's been conducted, that itself doesn't get to people. You have a man like Doug Ford [premier of Ontario, Canada] saying you need to arrest people to solve the gun violence problem, but evidence shows we need to invest in social housing, communities need more education programming, etcetera, etcetera. So it's like it's not understood. It's not welcomed through official channels. No, no, no.

As Gregory says, his views cannot be represented if they are not even understood. And they cannot be understood unless (1) people have received a broader and more historically accurate education about how inequality and injustices have been generated, and (2) those who are being most disadvantaged by current systems are able to relay their experiences and critiques back to the decision-makers with the power to affect those systems.

Lest the above come across as too glib or utopian, allow me to return to an important caution from Pierre Bourdieu, who acknowledges that, "while making things explicit can certainly help, only a thoroughgoing process of countertraining, involving repeated exercises, can, like an athlete's training, durably transform habitus" (Bourdieu, 2000, p. 172). A democratic disposition, which is an aspect of habitus, will not be generated through one civics course, although this could certainly be a start. This is, however, only one piece of the larger puzzle about how to create deeply democratic and equitable societies. The larger piece has to do with the ongoing reproduction of inequality by the state. This must stop. The role of the state in a democratic society ought to be levelling the playing field, not making it more steep. To truly level the playing field, liberal democracies need to reinvest in affordable and publicly managed housing, roll back tuition costs so that postsecondary education becomes broadly available to all, institute a fair and reasonable social benefits system that does not further entrench poverty and provides a minimal level of basic dignity and access to required goods for all. This is how we protect and strengthen democracy.

Appendix 1: Youth Participants by Country (All Names Are Pseudonyms)

Australia

    Armin (age twenty-two) – experienced homelessness
    Brenden (age twenty-seven) – activist
    Joanna (age twenty-six) – activist
    Noor (age nineteen) – activist
    Rachel (age eighteen) – experienced homelessness
    Rima (age eighteen) – activist
    Saanvi (age eighteen) – experienced homelessness
    Scarlett (age twenty-four) – experienced homelessness

Canada

    Alison (age eighteen) – experienced homelessness
    Angie (age twenty-four) – activist
    Caitlin (age nineteen) – experienced homelessness
    Chloe (age nineteen) – experienced homelessness
    Darryl (age twenty-nine) – activist
    Dominic (age eighteen) – experienced homelessness
    Felix (age nineteen) – experienced homelessness
    Gregory (age nineteen) – activist
    Jenny (age twenty-five) – experienced homelessness
    Joseph (age twenty-four) – experienced homelessness
    Sanaya (age twenty-eight) – activist
    Sandra (age twenty) – activist
    Tamara (age twenty-six) – experienced homelessness

New Zealand

Amaia (age twenty-four) – experienced homelessness
Jillian (age twenty-two) – experienced homelessness
Kanoa (age eighteen) – activist
Karen (age twenty-four) – activist
Leila (age nineteen) – activist
Mahala (age twenty-five) – activist
Michael (age eighteen) – activist
Monica (age sixteen) – experienced homelessness
Shane (age seventeen) – experienced homelessness

United Kingdom

Daraja (age thirty) – experienced homelessness
Elizabeth (age twenty-two) – experienced homelessness
Julia (age eighteen) – activist
Khalil (age twenty-three) – experienced homelessness
Maggie (age twenty-four) – activist
Matthew (Matt) (age nineteen) – activist
Rochelle (age twenty-eight) – activist
Tiffany (age twenty-three) – experienced homelessness

United States

Alejandro (age twenty) – activist
Cadence (age nineteen) – activist
Darius (age twenty) – activist
Dylan (age twenty-one) – activist
Edward (age nineteen) – activist
Isabella (age twenty-one) – experienced homelessness
Rebecca (age twenty) – activist
Stephanie (age twenty-two) – experienced homelessness

Bibliography

Agamben, G. (1998). *Homo sacer: Sovereign power and bare life*. Stanford University Press.

Amore, K., Viggers, H., & Howden-Chapman, P. (2021). *Severe housing deprivation in Aotearoa New Zealand, 2018* (2021 update). Housing & Health Research Programme, Department of Public Health, University of Otago. https://www.hud.govt.nz/assets/News-and-Resources/Statistics-and-Research/2018-Severe-housing-deprivation-estimate/Severe-Housing-Deprivation-2018-Estimate-Report.pdf

Andrew, M. (2017). Effectively maintained inequality in U.S. postsecondary progress: The importance of institutional reach. *The American Behavioral Scientist (Beverly Hills), 61*(1), 30–48. https://doi.org/10.1177/0002764216682809

Arendt, H. (1963). *Eichmann in Jerusalem: A report on the banality of evil*. Penguin Books.

– (1971). *The life of the mind*. Harcourt Brace & Company.

– (1998). *The human condition* (2nd ed., M. Canovan, Ed.). The University of Chicago Press.

Beer, A., Bentley, R., Baker, E., Mason, K., Mallett, S., Kavanagh, A., & LaMontagne, T. (2016). Neoliberalism, economic restructuring and policy change: Precarious housing and precarious employment in Australia. *Urban Studies, 53*(8), 1542–58. https://doi.org/10.1177/0042098015596922

Beer, A., Kearins, B., & Pieters, H. (2007). Housing affordability and planning in Australia: The challenge of policy under neo-liberalism. *Housing Studies, 22*(1), 11–24. https://doi.org/10.1080/02673030601024572

Béland, D., & Waddan, A. (2012). *The politics of policy change welfare, medicare, and social security reform in the United States*. Georgetown University Press.

Bing, A. (2021). *Extrinsic learning, corporate streaming, and ungrounded voting: The role of STEM schooling in the political socialization of Asian Canadian youths* [Unpublished doctoral dissertation, Carleton University].

Birot, M. (28 July 2022). *What is the average grocery bill?* Canstar Blue.

Bogan. (31 July 2022). *Wikipedia*. https://en.wikipedia.org/wiki/Bogan

Boliver, V. (2011). Expansion, differentiation, and the persistence of social class inequalities in British higher education. *Higher Education*, *61*(3), 229–42. https://doi.org/10.1007/s10734-010-9374-y

The Borgen Project. (2020). *10 facts about homelessness in New Zealand.* https://borgenproject.org/tag/homelessness-in-new-zealand/

Boston, J. (1993). Reshaping social policy in New Zealand. *Fiscal Studies*, *14*(3), 64–85. https://doi.org/10.1111/j.1475-5890.1993.tb00487.x

Bourdieu, P. (1984). *Distinction: A social critique of the judgement of taste*. Routledge & Kegan Paul. (Original work published 1979)

– (1991). *Language & symbolic power* (J. Thompson, Trans.). Harvard University Press.

– (1998). *Practical reason: On the theory of action*. Stanford University Press.

– (1999). *Acts of resistance: Against the tyranny of the market*. The New Press. (Original work published 1998)

– (2000). *Pascalian meditations* (V. Nice, Trans.). Stanford University Press.

– (2003). *Firing back: Against the tyranny of the market 2*. The New Press. (Original work published 1998)

– (2014). *On the state: Lectures at the Collège de France, 1989–1992* (D. Fernbach, Trans.). Polity. (Original work published 2012)

Bourdieu, P., & Wacquant, L. (1992). *An invitation to reflexive sociology*. University of Chicago Press.

Braver, T., & Jenvey, V. B. (2012). Lifetime risk factors associated with level of housing among Australian poor. *Poverty & Public Policy*, *4*(1), 1–30. https://doi.org/10.1515/1944-2858.1204

Brown, W. (2005). *Edgework: Critical essays on knowledge and politics*. Princeton University Press. https://doi.org/10.1515/9781400826872

– (2011). The end of educated democracy. *Representations (Berkeley, Calif.)*, *116*(1), 19–41. https://doi.org/10.1525/rep.2011.116.1.19

– (2017). *Undoing the demos neoliberalism's stealth revolution* (First paperback ed.). Zone Books.

– (2019). *In the ruins of neoliberalism: The rise of antidemocratic politics in the West*. Columbia University Press. https://doi.org/10.7312/brow19384

Butler, J., & Athanasiou, A. (2013). *Dispossession: The performative in the political*. Polity Press.

California Department of Education Sacramento. (2017). *History social science framework for California public schools, kindergarten through grade twelve*. https://www.cde.ca.gov/ci/hs/cf/

Canada Mortgage and Housing Corporation. (2020). *Rental market report – Ottawa-Gatineau CMA (Ontario)*. https://publications.gc.ca/collections/collection_2020/schl-cmhc/NH12-77-2020-eng.pdf

Canadian Alliance to End Homelessness. (2021). *What budget 2021 means for ending homelessness*. https://caeh.ca/budget-2021-analysis/

Carey, F. (2021). "Our shared values": The liberal coalition government's framing of Australia's national identity and multiculturalism. *Social Work & Policy Studies: Social Justice, Practice and Theory*, 3(2), 1–19.

Carnegie Corporation of New York. (2019). *11 barriers to voting*. https://www.carnegie.org/our-work/article/11-barriers-voting/

Carroll, W. K., & Little, W. (2001). Neoliberal transformation and antiglobalization politics in Canada: Transition, consolidation, resistance. *International Journal of Political Economy*, 31(3), 33–66. https://doi.org/10.1080/08911916.2001.11042863

Cellini, S. R., & Turner, N. (2019). Gainfully employed? Assessing the employment and earnings of for-profit college students using administrative data. *Journal of Human Resources*, 54(2), 342–70. https://doi.org/10.3368/jhr.54.2.1016.8302R1

Centrepoint. (2016). *Is prevention cheaper than cure? An estimation of the additional costs of homelessness for NEET young people.* https://centrepoint.org.uk/media/1702/is-prevention-cheaper-than-cure.pdf

Chamlin, M. B., & Denney, J. E. (2019). An impact assessment of the personal responsibility and Work Opportunity Reconciliation Act of 1996. *Journal of Crime & Justice*, 42(4), 382–92. https://doi.org/10.1080/0735648X.2019.1580603

Champagne, P. (2005). Making the people speak: On the social uses of and reactions to opinion polls. In L. Wacquant (Ed.), *Bourdieu and democratic politics*. Wiley.

City of Ottawa. (n.d.). *Subsidized housing.* https://ottawa.ca/en/family-and-social-services/housing/subsidized-housing#section-15b7b9c5-0760-4585-a716-95b184a94f47

Cokis, T., & McLoughlin, K. (2020). *Demographic trends, household finances and spending.* Reserve Bank of Australia. https://www.rba.gov.au/publications/bulletin/2020/mar/demographic-trends-household-finances-and-spending.html

Collins, D. (2010). Homelessness in Canada and New Zealand: A comparative perspective on numbers and policy responses. *Urban Geography*, 31(7), 932–52. https://doi.org/10.2747/0272-3638.31.7.932

Connell, R. (2015). Australian universities under neoliberal management: The deepening crisis. *International Higher Education*, 81, 23–25. https://doi.org/10.6017/ihe.2015.81.8740

Crawley, M. (10 July 2018). Ontario cancels curriculum rewrite that would boost Indigenous content. *CBC News*. https://www.cbc.ca/news/canada/toronto/ontario-education-truth-and-reconciliation-commission-trc-1.4739297

Croxford, L., & Raffe, D. (2015). The iron law of hierarchy? Institutional differentiation in UK higher education. *Studies in Higher Education (Dorchester-on-Thames)*, 40(9), 1625–40. https://doi.org/10.1080/03075079.2014.899342

Dahl, R. A., & Shapiro, I. (2015). *On democracy* (2nd ed.). Yale University Press.

Davidson, P., Bradbury, B., Wong, M., & Hill, T. (2020). *Inequality in Australia 2020 part 1: Overview.* Australian Council of Social Service and UNSW. https://

povertyandinequality.acoss.org.au/wp-content/uploads/2020/09/Inequality-in-Australia-2020-Part-1_FINAL.pdf

Davidson, P., Saunders, P., & Phillips, J. (2018). *Inequality in Australia 2018*. Australian Council of Social Services and University of New South Wales. https://www.acoss.org.au/inequality-in-australia-2018-html/

Dearden, L., Fitzsimons, E., & Wyness, G. (2011). *The impact of tuition fees and support on university participation in the UK* (Report No. 0126). Centre for the Economics of Education, LSE. https://ideas.repec.org/p/cep/ceedps/0126.html

Denniss, R. (22 July 2020). The Australian government's decision to cut benefits is based on feelings, not facts. *The Guardian*. https://www.theguardian.com/commentisfree/2020/jul/22/the-australian-governments-decision-to-cut-benefits-is-based-on-feelings-not-facts

District of Columbia Public Schools. (n.d.). *Social studies standards, grades 9–12 &economics* (p. 76). https://osse.dc.gov/sites/default/files/dc/sites/osse/publication/attachments/DCPS-horiz-soc_studies.pdf

Dodson, J. (2006). The "roll" of the state: Government, neoliberalism and housing assistance in four advanced economies. *Housing, Theory, and Society, 23*(4), 224–43. https://doi.org/10.1080/14036090601043540

Dutta, R. (5 December 2019). Point of view: I face sexism as a young, female engineer, but I have hope. *CBC News*. https://www.cbc.ca/news/canada/montreal/i-study-engineering-montreal-polytechnique-1.5382596

Eagleton, T., & Bourdieu, P. (1992). Doxa and common life. *New Left Review, 191*(1), 111–21.

Erdal, C., & Kennelly, J. (under review). Educating for active compliance, redux: (Neo) Liberal democratic citizenship education in the twenty-first century. *Citizenship Studies*.

Erdal, C. & Kennelly, J. (under review). The disorientation of democracy and civic life: (Neo)Liberal democratic citizenship education in the twenty-first century. *Curriculum Inquiry*.

Esser, I. (2009). Has welfare made us lazy? Employment commitment in different welfare states. In A. Park, J. Curtice, K. Thomson, M. Phillips, & E. Clery (Eds.), *British social attitudes* (pp. 79–106). Sage.

Evans, E. J. (2004). *Thatcher and Thatcherism* (2nd ed.). Routledge, Taylor and Francis Group.

Fergus, D. (2 September 2014). My students pay too much for college: Blame Reagan. *The Washington Post*. https://www.washingtonpost.com/posteverything/wp/2014/09/02/my-students-pay-too-much-for-college-blame-reagan/

Fitzgerald, D. (2016). *Youth experiencing homelessness*. American Youth Policy Forum. https://www.aypf.org/youth-populations/homeless/

Florida Department of Education. (2021). *Next generation, sunshine state standards – social studies, grades 6–12* (pp. 9–19). https://www.fldoe.org/core/fileparse.php/19975/urlt/5-3.pdf

Foucault, M. (2008). *The birth of biopolitics: Lectures at the Collège de France, 1978–1979*. Palgrave Macmillan.

Frenette, M. (2008). University access amid tuition fee deregulation: Evidence from Ontario professional programs. *Canadian Public Policy, 34*(1), 89–109. https://doi.org/10.3138/cpp.34.1.089

Gaetz, S., Barr, C., Friesen, A., Harris, B., Hill, C., Kovacs-Burns, K., Pauly, B., Pearce, B., Turner, A., & Marsolais, A. (2012). *Canadian definition of homelessness*. Canadian Observatory on Homelessness. https://www.homelesshub.ca/sites/default/files/COHhomelessdefinition.pdf

Gaetz, S., Donaldson, J., Richter, T., & Gulliver, T. (2013). *The state of homelessness in Canada 2013*. Canadian Homelessness Research Network Press. https://www.homelesshub.ca/SOHC2013

Gaetz, S., O'Grady, B., Kidd, S., & Schwan, K. (2016). *Without a home: The national youth homelessness survey*. Canadian Observatory on Homelessness Press. https://homelesshub.ca/sites/default/files/WithoutAHome-final.pdf

Gale, W. G., Gelfond, H., & Fichtner, J. (2019). *How will retirement saving change by 2050? Prospects for the millennial generation*. The Brookings Economic Studies. https://www.brookings.edu/wp-content/uploads/2019/03/How-Will-Retirement-Saving-Change-by-2050.docx.pdf

Galicki, C. (2018). Barriers to voting and the cost of voting among low socioeconomic, young and migrant voters in New Zealand. *Political Science, 70*(1), 41–57. https://doi.org/10.1080/00323187.2018.1473014

Giano, Z., Williams, A., Hankey, C., Merrill, R., Lisnic, R., & Herring, A. (2020). Forty years of research on predictors of homelessness. *Community Mental Health Journal, 56*(4), 692–709. https://doi.org/10.1007/s10597-019-00530-5

Glavin, C. (11 March 2019). *History of tertiary education fees in Australia*. K12 Academics. https://www.k12academics.com/Higher%20Education%20Worldwide/Higher%20Education%20in%20Australia/Tertiary%20Education%20Fees%20in%20Australia/histor

Government of Australia. (2021). *1.1.M.160 mutual obligation requirements*. Social Security Guide. https://guides.dss.gov.au/social-security-guide/1/1/m/160

Government of Canada. (2020). *Half of recent postsecondary graduates had student debt prior to the pandemic*. Statistics Canada. https://www150.statcan.gc.ca/n1/daily-quotidien/200825/dq200825b-eng.htm

– (2022). *Progress on the national housing strategy*. National Housing Strategy Initiatives. https://www.placetocallhome.ca/progress-on-the-national-housing-strategy

Government of New Zealand. (2019). *School leaver destinations: What happens to school leavers?* Education Counts, Ministry of Education, Te Tāhuhu o Te Mātauranga. https://www.educationcounts.govt.nz/statistics/what-happens-to-school-leavers

Granwal, L. (2022). *Median weekly house and unit rent prices in Australia as of June 2021, by capital city*. Statista. https://www.statista.com/statistics/1110866/australia-weekly-rent-for-houses-and-units-by-capital-city/

Hamilton, L., Wingrove, T., & Woodford, K. (2019). Does generous welfare policy encourage dependence? TANF asset limits and duration of program participation. *Journal of Children & Poverty, 25*(2), 101–113. https://doi.org/10.1080/10796126.2019.1638731

Harris, A., Wyn, J., & Younes, S. (2010). Beyond apathetic or activist youth: "Ordinary" young people and contemporary forms of participation. *Young (Stockholm, Sweden)*, *18*(1), 9–32. https://doi.org/10.1177/110330880901800103

Heath, N. (2017). Can Australian students actually afford to pay more for their university degrees? *SBS TV*. https://www.sbs.com.au/topics/voices/culture/article/2017/05/05/can-australian-students-actually-afford-pay-more-their-university-degrees

Heisz, A., & Richards, E. (2019). *Economic well-being across generations of young Canadians: Are millennials better or worse off?* Statistics Canada. https://www150.statcan.gc.ca/n1/pub/11-626-x/11-626-x2019006-eng.htm

Hemelt, S. W., & Marcotte, D. E. (2011). The impact of tuition increases on enrollment at public colleges and universities. *Educational Evaluation and Policy Analysis*, *33*(4), 435–457. https://doi.org/10.3102/0162373711415261

Henrique-Gomez, L. (30 December 2020). Australians on welfare face $100-a-fortnight income cut as Covid supplement is further reduced. *The Guardian*. https://www.theguardian.com/australia-news/2020/dec/30/australians-on-welfare-face-100-a-week-income-cut-as-covid-supplement-is-further-reduced

Hodkinson, S., Watt, P., & Mooney, G. (2013). Introduction: Neoliberal housing policy – time for a critical re-appraisal. *Critical Social Policy*, *33*(1), 3–16. https://doi.org/10.1177/0261018312457862

Holloway, B. (2018). *Methods briefing: Removing the benefits freeze a year early*. Joseph Rowntree Foundation. https://www.jrf.org.uk/report/methods-briefing-removing-benefits-freeze-year-early

Housing Authority City of Austin. (n.d.). *Public & subsidized housing*. https://www.hacanet.org/residents/public-housing/

Human Rights Watch. (2019). *Nothing left in the cupboards: Austerity, welfare cuts, and the right to food in the UK*. https://www.hrw.org/report/2019/05/20/nothing-left-cupboards/austerity-welfare-cuts-and-right-food-uk

Iton, R. (2008). *In search of the Black fantastic: Politics and popular culture in the post-civil rights era*. Oxford University Press. https://doi.org/10.1093/acprof:oso/9780195178463.001.0001

Jack, A. A. (2019). *The privileged poor: How elite colleges are failing disadvantaged students*. Harvard University Press.

Jackson, A. (20 July 2015). This chart shows how quickly college tuition has skyrocketed since 1980. *Insider*. https://www.businessinsider.com/this-chart-shows-how-quickly-college-tuition-has-skyrocketed-since-1980-2015-7

Jackson, M., & Holzman, B. (2020). A century of educational inequality in the United States. *Proceedings of the National Academy of Sciences – PNAS*, *117*(32), 19108–15. https://doi.org/10.1073/pnas.1907258117

Janes, J. E. (2016). Democratic encounters? Epistemic privilege, power, and community-based participatory action research. *Action Research*, *14*(1), 72–87. https://doi.org/10.1177/1476750315579129

Joint Center for Housing Studies of Harvard University. (2020). *America's rental housing*. https://www.jchs.harvard.edu/sites/default/files/Harvard_JCHS_Americas_Rental_Housing_2020.pdf

Joyce, R., & Xu, X. (2019). *Inequalities in the twenty-first century: Introducing the IFS Deaton review*. The Institute for Fiscal Studies. https://ifs.org.uk/inequality/wp-content/uploads/2019/05/The-IFS-Deaton-Review-launch.pdf

Junor, S., & Usher, A. (2004). *The price of knowledge: 2004 access and student finance in Canada*. Canada Millennium Scholarship Foundation.

Kennelly, J. (2009a). Good citizen/bad activist: The cultural role of the state in youth activism. *Review of Education, Pedagogy, and Cultural Studies, 31*(2-3), 127-49. https://doi.org/10.1080/10714410902827135

– (2009b). Youth cultures, activism, and agency: Revisiting feminist debates. *Gender and Education, 21*(3), 259-72. https://doi.org/10.1080/09540250802392281

– (2009c). Learning to protest: Youth activist cultural politics in contemporary urban Canada. *Review of Education, Pedagogy, and Cultural Studies, 31*(4), 293-316. https://doi.org/10.1080/10714410903132865

– (2011a). *Citizen youth: Culture, action, and agency in a neoliberal era*. Palgrave Macmillan. https://doi.org/10.1057/9780230119611

– (2011b). Policing young people as citizens-in-waiting: Legitimacy, spatiality, and governance. *British Journal of Criminology, 51*, 336-54. https://doi.org/10.1093/bjc/azr017

– (2014). "It's this pain in my heart that won't let me stop": Gendered reflexivity, webs of relations, and young women's activism. *Feminist Theory, 15*(3), 241-60. https://doi.org/10.1177/1464700114544611

– (2016). *Olympic exclusions: Youth, poverty, and social legacies*. Routledge.

– (2017). "This is the view when I walk into my house": Accounting phenomenologically for the efficacy of spatial methods with youth. *Young, 25*(3), 1-17. https://doi.org/10.1177/1103308816680437

– (2018a). Envisioning democracy: Participatory filmmaking with homeless youth. *Canadian Review of Sociology, 55*(2), 190-210. https://doi.org/10.1111/cars.12189

– (2018b). Troubling PAR: Institutional constraints, neoliberal individualism, and the limits of social change in participatory action research with homeless youth. In K. Gallagher (Ed.), *The methodological dilemma revisited: Creative, critical, and collaborative approaches to qualitative research for a new era* (pp. 32-50). Routledge.

– (2020). Urban masculinity, contested spaces, and classed subcultures: Young homeless men navigating downtown Ottawa, Canada. *Gender, Place & Culture, 27*(2), 281-300. https://doi.org/10.1080/0966369X.2019.1650724

– (7 October 2022). Kennelly: Turkey must release Carleton University PhD student on legal grounds. *Ottawa Citizen*. https://ottawacitizen.com/opinion/kennelly-turkey-must-release-carleton-university-phd-student-on-legal-grounds?fbclid=IwAR1hMwpycExTIqkAHFpC6jxXsnS7DytUg8I9YLVhtuIE4IlYkOsBQWQJ2JM

Kennelly, J., & Llewellyn, K. (2011). Educating for active compliance: Discursive constructions in citizenship education. *Citizenship Studies, 15*(6–7), 897–914. https://doi.org/10.1080/13621025.2011.600103

Kennelly, J., & Watt, P. (2011). Sanitizing public space in Olympic host cities: The spatial experiences of marginalized youth in 2010 Vancouver and 2012 London. *Sociology, 45*(5), 765–81. https://doi.org/10.1177/0038038511413425

– (2012). Seeing Olympic effects through the eyes of marginally housed youth: Changing places and the gentrification of East London. *Visual Studies, 27*(2), 151–160. https://doi.org/10.1080/1472586X.2012.677496

Knueven, L., & Houston, R. (26 May 2022). The average stock market return over the past 10 years. *Insider*. https://www.businessinsider.com/personal-finance/average-stock-market-return

Kraus, D., Eberle, M., & Serge, L. (2001). *Environmental scan on youth homelessness*. Canada Mortgage and Housing Corporation. https://publications.gc.ca/collections/collection_2011/schl-cmhc/nh18-1/NH18-1-22-2001-eng.pdf

Kulz, C. (2021). Everyday erosions: Neoliberal political rationality, democratic decline and the multi-academy trust. *British Journal of Sociology of Education, 42*(1), 66–81. https://doi.org/10.1080/01425692.2020.1861928

Laidley, J., & Aldridge, H. (2020). *Welfare in Canada, 2019*. Maytree Foundation & Caledon Institute of Social Policy. https://maytree.com/wp-content/uploads/Welfare_in_Canada_2019.pdf

Laidley, J., & Tabbara, M. (2023) Welfare in Canada, 2022. Maytree and Caledon Institute of Social Policy. Retrieved 25 July 2023 from https://maytree.com/wp-content/uploads/Welfare_in_Canada_2022.pdf

Lang, D. W. (2005). Financing higher education in Canada. In S. O. Michael & M. Kretovics (Eds.), *Financing higher education in a global market* (pp. 71–118). Algora Publishing.

Larkin, D. (7 November 2021). Why voter ID requirements could exclude the most vulnerable citizens, especially First Nations people. *The Conversation*. https://theconversation.com/why-voter-id-requirements-could-exclude-the-most-vulnerable-citizens-especially-first-nations-people-170797

Larner, W. (1997). "A means to an end": Neoliberalism and state processes in New Zealand. *Studies in Political Economy, 52*(1), 7–38. https://doi.org/10.1080/19187033.1997.11675320

Lathouris, O. (18 July 2020). The origins of the Aussie Bogan and what the word "Bogan" means today. *9News*. https://www.9news.com.au/national/origins-of-aussie-bogan-and-what-the-word-means-today/e5e4b184-dbc6-4d37-89da-874a21c58bb5

Laughland, O., & Beckett, L. (25 March 2018). March for our lives: Thousands join anti-gun protests around the world. *The Guardian*. https://www.theguardian.com/us-news/2018/mar/24/washington-march-for-our-lives-gun-violence

Li, S. X., & Jones, G. A. (2015). The "invisible" sector: Private higher education in Canada. In J. M. Joshi & S. Paivandi (Eds.), *Private higher education across nations* (pp. 1–33). B. R. Publishing Corporation.

Lifewise. (14 April 2015). Go study. *Lifewise.* https://www.lifewise.org.nz/2015/04/14/go-study/

Little, M., & Marks, L. (2006). A closer look at the neo-liberal petri dish: Welfare reform in British Columbia and Ontario. *Canadian Review of Social Policy (1987), 57,* 16–45.

Losurdo, D. (2014). *Liberalism: A counter-history.* Verso Books.

Lucey, H., & Reay, D. (2002a). Carrying the beacon of excellence: Social class differentiation and anxiety at a time of transition. *Journal of Education Policy, 17*(3), 321–36. https://doi.org/10.1080/02680930210127586

– (2002b). A market in waste: Psychic and structural dimensions of school-choice policy in the UK and children's narratives on "demonized" schools. *Discourse: Studies in the Cultural Politics of Education, 23*(3), 253–66. https://doi.org/10.1080/0159630022000029768

Luxton, M. (2010). Doing neoliberalism: Perverse individualism in personal life. In M. Luxton & S. Braedley (Eds.), *Neoliberalism and everyday life* (pp. 163–83). McGill-Queen's University Press.

Lynch, J. (4 July 2021). Revealed: Wait times for state houses balloon as those most at risk face lengthy delay. *Newshub.* https://www.newshub.co.nz/home/politics/2021/07/revealed-wait-times-for-state-houses-balloon-as-those-most-at-risk-face-lengthy-delay.html

Mabhala, M. A., Yohannes, A., & Griffith, M. (2017). Social conditions of becoming homeless: Qualitative analysis of life stories of homeless peoples. *International Journal for Equity in Health, 16*(1), 150. https://doi.org/10.1186/s12939-017-0646-3

Mackenzie, D. (2020). *Youth homelessness: Making a difference! Inquiry into homelessness in Australia* (Submission 196). House of Representatives Standing Committee on Social Policy and Legal Affairs.

Macrotrends. (2021). *Walmart gross profit 2006-2021 | WMT.* https://www.macrotrends.net/stocks/charts/WMT/walmart/gross-profit

Maldonado, C. (24 July 2018). Price of college increasing almost 8 times faster than wages. *Forbes.* https://www.forbes.com/sites/camilomaldonado/2018/07/24/price-of-college-increasing-almost-8-times-faster-than-wages/

Martin, A. J. (2012). *Young people and politics: Political engagement in the Anglo American democracies.* Routledge. https://doi.org/10.4324/9780203112274

Mason, R., & Adams, R. (30 May 2019). May urges Tories to cut tuition fees and revive student grants. *The Guardian.* https://www.theguardian.com/education/2019/may/30/may-urges-tories-cut-tuition-fees-revive-student-grants

McDonald, C., & Chenoweth, L. (2006). Workfare oz-style: Welfare reform and social work in Australia. *Journal of Policy Practice, 5*(2–3), 109–28. https://doi.org/10.1300/J508v05n02_08

McKeen, W., & Porter, A. (2003). Politics and transformation: Welfare state restructuring in Canada. In L. F. Vosko & W. Clement (Eds.), *Changing Canada: Political Economy as Transformation* (pp. 109–34). McGill-Queen's University Press.

McKeever, G., & Walsh, T. (2020). The moral hazard of conditionality: Restoring the integrity of social security law. *The Australian Journal of Social Issues*, *55*(1), 73–87. https://doi.org/10.1002/ajs4.101

Met Office. (2020). *A look back at the weather and climate in 2020*. https://www.metoffice.gov.uk/about-us/press-office/news/weather-and-climate/2020/2020-round-up

Meyer, B. D., & Sullivan, J. X. (2004). The effects of welfare and tax reform: The material well-being of single mothers in the 1980s and 1990s. *Journal of Public Economics*, *88*(7), 1387–1420. https://doi.org/10.1016/S0047-2727(02)00219-0

Mills, S., & Waite, C. (2017). Brands of youth citizenship and the politics of scale: National citizen service in the United Kingdom. *Political Geography*, *56*, 66–76. https://doi.org/10.1016/j.polgeo.2016.11.007

Murphy, L. (2003). Reasserting the "social" in social rented housing: Politics, housing policy and housing reforms in New Zealand. *International Journal of Urban and Regional Research*, *27*(1), 90–101. https://doi.org/10.1111/1468-2427.00433

– (2020). Neoliberal social housing policies, market logics and social rented housing reforms in New Zealand. *International Journal of Housing Policy*, *20*(2), 229–251. https://doi.org/10.1080/19491247.2019.1638134

Nairn, K. M., Higgins, J., & Sligo, J. (2012). *Children of Rogernomics: A neoliberal generation leaves school*. Otago University Press.

National Citizen Service Trust. (n.d.). *About NCS trust*. https://wearencs.com/about-ncs

Neill, C. (2015). Rising student employment: The role of tuition fees. *Education Economics*, *23*(1–2), 101–21. https://doi.org/10.1080/09645292.2013.818104

New Zealand Ministry of Education (2023). "The Equity Index." Retrieved 20 August 2023 from https://www.education.govt.nz/our-work/changes-in-education/equity-index/

New Zealand Ministry of Education – Te Tāhuhu o te Mātauranga. (2015). *The New Zealand curriculum for English-medium teaching and learning in years 1–13*. https://nzcurriculum.tki.org.nz/The-New-Zealand-Curriculum

Nicholls, S. (2014). Perpetuating the problem: Neoliberalism, commonwealth public policy and housing affordability in Australia: Neoliberalism. *The Australian Journal of Social Issues*, *49*(3), 329–47. https://doi.org/10.1002/j.1839-4655.2014.tb00316.x

Nissen, S., Hayward, B., & McManus, R. (2019). Student debt and wellbeing: A research agenda. *Kōtuitui*, *14*(2), 245–56. https://doi.org/10.1080/1177083X.2019.1614635

Nunns, P. (2021). The causes and economic consequences of rising regional housing prices in New Zealand. *New Zealand Economic Papers*, *55*(1), 66–104. https://doi.org/10.1080/00779954.2020.1791939

OECD. (2014). *Rising inequality: Youth and poor fall further behind*. Insights from the OECD Income Distribution Database. https://www.oecd.org/social/OECD2014-Income-Inequality-Update.pdf

– (2015). *In it together: Why less inequality benefits all*. https://www.oecd.org/social/in-it-together-why-less-inequality-benefits-all-9789264235120-en.htm

– (2020). *Social housing: A key part of past and future housing policy.* Employment, Labour and Social Affairs Policy Briefs. http://oe.cd/social-housing-2020
Oliphant, M., & Slosser, C. (2003). *Targeting the most vulnerable: A decade of desperation for Ontario's welfare recipients.* Canadian Centre for Policy Alternatives.
Ontario Ministry of Education and Training. (2018). Civics (politics). In *The Ontario curriculum grade 10: Canadian and world studies* (pp. 149–66). http://www.edu.gov.on.ca/eng/curriculum/secondary/canworld910curr2018.pdf
O'Toole, T., & Gale, R. T. (2013). *Political engagement amongst ethnic minority young people: Making a difference.* Palgrave Macmillan.
Page, A. (17 December 2019). *Breaking barriers: Factors that kept some Canadians out of the polls.* The Elizabeth Fry Society of Calgary. https://elizabethfrycalgary.ca/2019/12/17/why-barriers-to-voting-kept-some-canadians-out-of-the-polls/
Parker, S., & Fopp, R. (2004). The mutual obligation policy in Australia: The rhetoric and reasoning of recent social security policy. *Contemporary Politics, 10*(3–4), 257–69. https://doi.org/10.1080/1356977042000316718
Pathways to Education. (24 September 2019). Canada's high school dropout rates are staggeringly high, according to studies – Narcity. *Pathways to Education.* https://www.pathwaystoeducation.ca/in-the-press/canadas-high-school-dropout-rates-are-staggeringly-high-according-to-studies-narcity/
Pawson, H., Milligan, V., & Yates, J. (2020). Housing policy in Australia: A reform agenda. In H. Pawson, V. Milligan, & J. Yates (Eds.), *Housing policy in Australia: A case for system reform* (pp. 339–58). Palgrave Macmillan. https://doi.org/10.1007/978-981-15-0780-9
Piketty, T. (2017). *Capital in the twenty-first century* (A. Goldhammer, Trans.). The Belknap Press of Harvard University Press. (Original work published 2013)
Pizarro Milian, R., & Hicks, M. (2014). *Ontario private career colleges: An exploratory analysis.* Higher Education Quality Council of Ontario. https://heqco.ca/wp-content/uploads/2020/03/PCC-ENG.pdf
Pizarro Milian, R., & Quirke, L. (2017). Alternative pathways to legitimacy: Promotional practices in the Ontario for-profit college sector. *Journal of Marketing for Higher Education, 27*(1), 77–98. https://doi.org/10.1080/08841241.2016.1212450
Pomeroy, S. (2017). *Envisioning a modernized social and affordable housing sector in Canada.* Carleton University Centre for Urban Research and Education (CURE). https://carleton.ca/cure/wp-content/uploads/Envisioning-a-strengthened-social-housing-sector-FINAL-Oct-2018.pdf
– (2020). *Why Canada needs a non-market rental acquisition strategy.* Focus Consulting Inc. https://www.focus-consult.com/why-canada-needs-a-non-market-rental-acquisition-strategy/
Punwasi, S. (22 January 2021). Canadian real estate prices grew over 25x faster than U.S. prices since 2005. *Better Dwelling.* https://betterdwelling.com/canadian-real-estate-prices-grew-over-25x-faster-than-u-s-prices-since-2005/

Quirke, L., & Davies, S. (2002). The new entrepreneurship in higher education: The impact of tuition increases at an Ontario University. *Canadian Journal of Higher Education (1975), 32*(3), 85–109. https://doi.org/10.47678/cjhe.v32i3.183420

Radio New Zealand. (11 October 2016). *Pasifika need to be considered in any homeless solution* [Radio broadcast]. RNZ. https://www.rnz.co.nz/international/programmes/datelinepacific/audio/201819528/pasifika-need-to-be-considered-in-any-homeless-solution

Rashbrooke, M. (31 August 2020). New Zealand's astounding wealth gap challenges our "fair go" identity. *The Guardian.* https://www.theguardian.com/world/2020/aug/31/new-zealands-astounding-wealth-gap-challenges-our-fair-go-identity

Rashbrooke, M., Rashbrooke, G., & Molano, W. (2021). *Wealth disparities in New Zealand: Final report* (Working Paper 17/02). Institute for Governance and Policy Studies, Victoria University of Wellington, Te Heranga Waka. https://www.wgtn.ac.nz/__data/assets/pdf_file/0008/1175246/WP17-02-Wealth-Disparities-in-NZ-Final-2017.pdf

Reagan, R. (15 February 1986). *Radio address to the nation on welfare reform.* Ronald Reagan Presidential Library & Museum. https://www.reaganlibrary.gov/archives/speech/radio-address-nation-welfare-reform

Reitan, E. E. (2003). *The Thatcher revolution: Margaret Thatcher, John Major, Tony Blair, and the transformation of modern Britain, 1979–2001.* Rowman & Littlefield.

Rent Café. (2022). *San Antonio, TX rental market trends.* https://www.rentcafe.com/average-rent-market-trends/us/tx/bexar-county/san-antonio/

Roberts, C., & Lawrence, M. (2017). *Wealth in the twenty-first century: Inequalities and drivers.* IPPR Commission on Economic Justice. https://www.ippr.org/publications/wealth-in-the-twenty-first-century

Rolfe, S., Garnham, L., Godwin, J., Anderson, I., Seaman, P., & Donaldson, C. (2020). Housing as a social determinant of health and wellbeing: Developing an empirically-informed realist theoretical framework. *BMC Public Health, 20*(1), 1138. https://doi.org/10.1186/s12889-020-09224-0

Rorris, A. (2021, March 23). The Australian "school funding wars" may be over – but kids at public schools are still losing out. *The Guardian.* https://www.theguardian.com/commentisfree/2021/mar/23/the-australian-school-funding-wars-may-be-over-but-kids-at-public-schools-are-still-losing-out

Rose, N. (1993). Government, authority, and expertise in advanced liberalism. *Economy and Society, 22*(3), 283–99. https://doi.org/10.1080/03085149300000019

Rouillard, J., Frank, D., Palmer, B. D., & McCallum, T. (2006). Working-class history. *The Canadian Encyclopedia.* https://www.thecanadianencyclopedia.ca/en/article/working-class-history

The Salvation Army. (10 October 2017). *Brendan walks into Canberra.* https://www.salvationarmy.org.au/about-us/news-and-stories/media-newsroom/brendan-walks-into-canberra/

Samuel, C. (2017). *Conform, fail, repeat: How power distorts collective action*. Between the Lines.
Sassen, S. (2006). *Cities in a world economy*. Pine Forge Press.
– (2014). *Expulsions: Brutality and complexity in the global economy*. The Belknap Press of Harvard University Press.
Sawhill, I., & Pulliam, C. (21 October 2019). Amend the tax cuts and jobs act for more inclusive growth and better jobs. *AEIdeas*. https://www.aei.org/economics/amend-the-tax-cuts-and-jobs-act-for-more-inclusive-growth-and-better-jobs/
Scholars Strategy Network. (2019). *Securing fair elections: Challenges to voting in the United States and Georgia*. https://scholars.org/fairelections
Shahidi, F. V., Ramraj, C., Sod-Erdene, O., Hildebrand, V., & Siddiqi, A. (2019). The impact of social assistance programs on population health: A systematic review of research in high-income countries. *BMC Public Health*, *19*(1), 2. https://doi.org/10.1186/s12889-018-6337-1
Shildrick, T. (2018). Lessons from Grenfell: Poverty propaganda, stigma and class power. *The Sociological Review (Keele)*, *66*(4), 783–98. https://doi.org/10.1177/0038026118777424
Shore, C. (2010). The reform of New Zealand's university system: "After neoliberalism." *Learning and Teaching*, *3*(1), 1–31. https://doi.org/10.3167/latiss.2010.030102
Shotwell. (2016). *Against purity: Living ethically in compromised times*. University of Minnesota Press. https://doi.org/10.5749/j.ctt1hch845
Simon, C. A., James, C., & Simon, A. (2021). The growth of multi-academy trusts in England: Emergent structures and the sponsorship of underperforming schools. *Educational Management, Administration & Leadership*, *49*(1), 112–27. https://doi.org/10.1177/1741143219893099
Sisson, P., Andrews, J., & Bazeley, A. (1 March 2020). *The affordable housing crisis, explained: Blame policy, demographics, and market forces*. Curbed. https://archive.curbed.com/2019/5/15/18617763/affordable-housing-policy-rent-real-estate-apartment
Small, Z. (30 November 2020). Jacinda Ardern disagrees with child poverty action group's accusation of "unjustifiably slow" welfare reform. *Newshub*. https://www.newshub.co.nz/home/politics/2020/11/jacinda-ardern-disagrees-with-child-poverty-action-group-s-accusation-of-unjustifiably-slow-welfare-reform.html
Smith, G. H. (2005). Beyond political literacy: From conscientization to transformative praxis. *Counterpoints (New York, N.Y.)*, *275*, 29–42.
Smith, N., Lister, R., Middleton, S., & Cox, L. (2005). Young people as real citizens: Towards an inclusionary understanding of citizenship. *Journal of Youth Studies*, *8*(4), 425–43. https://doi.org/10.1080/13676260500431743
Stanford, J. (2014). *Canada's auto industry and the new free trade agreements: Sorting through the impacts*. Canadian Centre for Policy Alternatives. https://policyalternatives.ca/sites/default/files/uploads/publications/2014/05/canadas_auto_industry_and_the_new_free_trade_agreements.pdf

The State Education Department, The University of the State of New York. (2015). Grade 11: United States history and government; grade 12: Participation in government and civics; & grade 12: Economics, the enterprise system, and finance. In *New York State grades 9–12 social studies framework* (pp. 34–50). http://www.nysed.gov/common/nysed/files/programs/curriculum-instruction/ss-framework-9-12.pdf

Statista. (2022). *Average tuition fee for full-time Canadian undergraduate students in Canada in the 2021/22 academic year, by province*. https://www.statista.com/statistics/733512/tuition-fee-for-full-time-canadian-undergraduates-by-province/

Statistics Canada. (2017). *Dictionary, census of population, 2016, market basket measure (MBM)*. https://www12.statcan.gc.ca/census-recensement/2016/ref/dict/pop165-eng.cfm

Stats NZ. (2020). *The state of housing in Aotearoa New Zealand*. https://www.stats.govt.nz/infographics/the-state-of-housing-in-aotearoa-new-zealand

Stella, F., Taylor, Y., Reynolds, T., & Rogers, A. (2015). *Sexuality, citizenship and belonging: Trans-national and intersectional perspectives*. Routledge.

Stoesz, D., & Karger, H. J. (1993). Deconstructing welfare: The Reagan legacy and the welfare state. *Social Work (New York)*, 38(5), 619–28. https://doi.org/10.1093/sw/38.5.619

Suttor, G. (2016). *Still renovating: A history of Canadian social housing policy*. McGill-Queen's University Press.

Te Tāhuhu o te Mātauranga – Ministry of Education. (n.d.). *School deciles*. Education in New Zealand. https://www.education.govt.nz/school/funding-and-financials/resourcing/operational-funding/school-decile-ratings/

Te Tūāpapa Kura Kāinga – Ministry of Housing and Urban Development. (2020). *Experimental housing percentage measure*. https://www.hud.govt.nz/research-and-publications/statistics-and-research/housing-affordability-measure-ham/experimental-housing-percentage-measure/

Texas State Affordable Housing Corporation. (n.d.). *About us*. https://www.tsahc.org/about

Thobani, S. (2007). *Exalted subjects: Studies in the making of race and nation in Canada*. University of Toronto Press. https://doi.org/10.3138/9781442685666

Thornton, S. (1996). *Club cultures: Music, media, and subcultural capital*. University Press of New England.

Torres, M. A., Rizzini, I., & del Río, N. (2013). *Citizens in the present: Youth civic engagement in the Americas*. University of Illinois Press.

Uberoi, E., & Johnston, N. (2021). *Political disengagement in the UK: Who is disengaged?* (Report No. CBP-7501). House of Commons Library. https://researchbriefings.files.parliament.uk/documents/CBP-7501/CBP-7501.pdf

UK Department for Education. (December `2014). *The national curriculum in England, key stages 3 and 4 framework document, "citizenship"* (pp. 82–5). https://assets.publishing.service.gov.uk/government/uploads/system/uploads/attachment_data/file/840002/Secondary_national_curriculum_corrected_PDF.pdf

United States Government Accountability Office. (2020). *Federal social safety net programs: Millions of full-time workers rely on federal health care and food assistance programs* (GAO-21-45, p. 91). https://www.gao.gov/assets/gao-21-45.pdf

Villagrana, K. M., Mody, E. H., Lawler, S. M., Wu, Q., & Ferguson, K. M. (2020). Educational outcomes for homeless young adults with and without a history in foster care. *Children and Youth Services Review, 116*, 105–53. https://doi.org/10.1016/j.childyouth.2020.105153

Visentin, L. (17 October 2020). University fees are changing: How will it affect you? *The Sydney Morning Herald*. https://www.smh.com.au/politics/federal/university-fees-are-changing-how-will-it-affect-you-20201009-p563ib.html

Wacquant, L. (1993). From ruling class to field of power: An interview with Pierre Bourdieu on La Noblesse d'État. *Theory, Culture & Society, 10*(3), 19–44. https://doi.org/10.1177/026327693010003002

– (2004). Critical thought as solvent of Doxa. *Constellations, 11*(1), 97–101. https://doi.org/10.1111/j.1351-0487.2004.00364.x

– (2005). Pointers on Pierre Bourdieu and democratic politics. In L. Wacquant (Ed.), *Pierre Bourdieu and democratic politics: The mystery of ministry* (pp. 10–28). Polity.

– (2009). *Punishing the poor: The neoliberal government of social insecurity*. Duke University Press.

– (2013). Symbolic power and group-making: On Pierre Bourdieu's reframing of class. *Journal of Classical Sociology, 13*(2), 274–91. https://doi.org/10.1177/1468795X12468737

Wang, J., & van Vliet, O. (2016). Social assistance and minimum income benefits: Benefit levels, replacement rates and policies across 26 OECD countries, 1990–2009. *European Journal of Social Security, 18*(4), 333–55. https://doi.org/10.1177/138826271601800401

Wang, Y. (2016). Homology and isomorphism: Bourdieu in conversation with new institutionalism. *The British Journal of Sociology, 67*(2), 348–70. https://doi.org/10.1111/1468-4446.12197

Weatherley, R. (1994). From entitlement to contract: Reshaping the welfare state in Australia. *Journal of Sociology and Social Welfare, 21*(3), 153–73. https://doi.org/10.15453/0191-5096.2166

Webb, C. (2017). *Key graphs on poverty in New Zealand: A compilation* (Working Paper 2017/03). McGuinness Institute.

Welfare Expert Advisory Group. (2019). *Whakamana Tāngata: Restoring dignity to social security in New Zealand*. http://www.weag.govt.nz/assets/documents/WEAG-report/aed960c3ce/WEAG-Report.pdf

Western, M., Baxter, J., Pakulski, J., Tranter, B., Western, J., van Egmond, M., Chesters, J., Hosking, A., O'Flaherty, M., & van Gellecum, Y. (2007). Neoliberalism, inequality and politics: The changing face of Australia. *The Australian Journal of Social Issues, 42*(3), 401–18. https://doi.org/10.1002/j.1839-4655.2007.tb00066.x

Wickham, S., Bentley, L., Rose, T., Whitehead, M., Taylor-Robinson, D., & Barr, B. (2020). Effects on mental health of a UK welfare reform, universal credit: A longitudinal controlled study. *The Lancet: Public Health*, 5(3), 157–64. https://doi.org/10.1016/S2468-2667(20)30026-8

Wilkins, A. (2017). Rescaling the local: Multi-academy trusts, private monopoly and statecraft in England. *Journal of Educational Administration and History*, 49(2), 171–85. https://doi.org/10.1080/00220620.2017.1284769

Wilson, S., Spies-Butcher, B., Stebbing, A., & St John, S. (2013). Wage-Earners' welfare after economic reform: Refurbishing, retrenching or hollowing out social protection in Australia and New Zealand? *Social Policy & Administration*, 47(6), 623–46. https://doi.org/10.1111/spol.12035

Wood, B. E., & Black, R. (2018). Spatial, relational and affective understandings of citizenship and belonging for young people today: Towards a new conceptual framework. In C. Halse (Ed.), *Interrogating belonging for young people in schools* (pp. 165–85). Springer International Publishing. https://doi.org/10.1007/978-3-319-75217-4_8

Workman, M. (2020). *NZ insight: The intergenerational divide*. ANZ Research. https://www.anz.co.nz/content/dam/anzconz/documents/economics-and-market-research/2020/ANZ-Insight-Long-Run-20201208.pdf

The World Bank Data. (n.d.). *GDP growth (annual %) – United States (1961–2021)* [Data set]. https://data.worldbank.org/indicator/NY.GDP.MKTP.KD.ZG?locations=US

Yates, J. (2013). Evaluating social and affordable housing reform in Australia: Lessons to be learned from history. *International Journal of Housing Policy*, 13(2), 111–33. https://doi.org/10.1080/14616718.2013.785717

Young-Bruehl, E. (2009). *Why Arendt matters*. Yale University Press.

Yuval-Davis, N. (2007). Intersectionality, citizenship and contemporary politics of belonging. *Critical Review of International Social and Political Philosophy*, 10(4), 561–74. https://doi.org/10.1080/13698230701660220

Zon, N., & Granofsky, T. (29 October 2019). *Resetting social assistance reform*. Ontario 360. https://on360.ca/policy-papers/resetting-social-assistance-reform/

Index

Page numbers in *italics* indicates tables on the corresponding page.

activism, 5–7; clustering of middle-class, 79–80; community, 71; democratic biographies, *80*; democratic participation and, 160–5; habituation of language, 61; Maggie's story (UK), 112–18; political involvement and, 22; recruitment for operationalizing, 17–20; social movements, 13–15
activist(s): on being political persons, 58–62; democracy and young, 64–5; democratic dispositions and, 67–75; familial politicization of, 79; pathways of, 21; term, 61; title, 116
Acts of Resistance (Bourdieu), 24
acts of state, 10
adult mentors: influence on activism, 78, 101–4
advanced marginality, 25
Aid to Families with Dependent Children (AFDC), 35
American foster system, 3
American Revolution, 174
apartheid: South Africa, 72
Arab Spring, 14, 91
Ardern, Jacinda, 37, 41, 64
Arendt, Hannah: public space and democracy, 7, 8, 10–13, 53–5, 75, 197; public sphere as space of "who-ness," 201–2; relational agency, 93
Aristotle, 10
Athanasiou, Athena, 25
Australia: activist's influence by education, 90; Armin's education experience, 122–4; citizenship and belonging, 195; citizenship education, 170–1; civics education, 183–4; democracy, 64; education, 42–3; housing, 41–2; neoliberalism, 41–5; racism and, 67–8; Scarlett's story of democratic failure in, 118–22; Scarlett's welfare experience, 137–8; state failures in, 121–2; voting system, 184; welfare, 43–5
Australian Labour Party, 32, 119
Australian Youth Climate Coalition (AYCC), 71, 72, 148

bare life: term, 54
belonging: citizenship as, 187–95
benevolence, 146
Bentham, Jeremy, 16
Biden, Joe, 182, 183
biography matters, 82
Black Lives Matter, 3, 14, 62, 68, 73, 84, 93, 147

Blair, Tony, 29, 33
blame game, 7
bleeding heart activist, term, 147n14
boundaries, 54n5
Bourdieu, Pierre, 6, 8, 9, 24, 28, 47, 53–5, 75, 77, 106, 142, 143, 197; habitus, 204; public space and democracy, 10–13; sociology of, 198–9; theory of the state, 168
British Journal of Criminology (journal), 169
Brown, Wendy, 3, 23, 28, 53, 167, 198
bureaucracy: citizenship as, 187–95
burnt by democracy: example of Stephanie, 3–5
Burnt by Democracy, 199
Butler, Judith, 25

Cambridge University, 69, 72–3
Cameron, David, 140, 175
Canada: activist's biography, 84–6; activist's influence by education, 91, 92–4; Charter of Rights and Freedoms, 173; Chloe's education experience, 122, 127–8, 130–1; citizenship and belonging, 189–90, 192–3; citizenship curricula, 172–3; civics curricula, 170–1; civics education, 180–2; democracy in, 65–6; free trade agreements, 45–6; good citizen politics, 104–5; higher education, 48–9; housing, 46–8; neoliberal education system in, 128–30; neoliberalism, 45–51; political activism, 152–3; provincial civics curricula, 170; race and class biases in activism, 164–5; Tamara's story of democratic failure in, 107–12; welfare, 49–51
Canada Health and Social Transfer, 46
Canada Mortgage and Housing Corporation (CMHC), 47, 181
Canada Revenue Agency, 130
Canada-US agreement, 45

Canadian Alliance to End Homelessness, 48
Canadian Observatory on Homelessness, 18, 154
capitalism, 8–10; civics education and, 175; democracy and, 64; evil currents of, 14; role of, 173–4; understanding, 103
Carey, Fiona, 171
CHEO (Children's Hospital of Eastern Ontario), 108
Chicano Latino Youth Leadership Project, 103
Child Poverty Action Group, 41
Child Protective Services, 26, 138
Children's Aid, 138
Children's Aid Society (CAS), 26, 107
Chrétien, Jean, 46, 47
citizens: classifying, 169; state category of, 193
citizenship: as belonging and democracy, 187–95; concept of, 20, 195, 201; democracy and, 23, 167; experiences of civics education, 179–87; Indigeneity and, 191n20; mechanism of, 142; notions of, 168; term, 188. *See also* civics education
citizenship education, 167; Australia, 170–1; Canada, 172–3; multiculturalism, 171; New Zealand, 172; symbolic power of, 170–5; United Kingdom, 171–2; United States, 173–4
Citizenship Studies (Kennelly and Llewellyn), 170
Citizen Youth (Kennelly), 78, 93, 146–8, 199–200
civic life, participation in, 6–7
civics education, 22–3; Australia, 183–4; Canada, 180–2; experiences of learning, 179–87; National Citizen Service (UK), 175–9; New Zealand, 184–5; United Kingdom, 185–6; United States, 182–3
classism, 103, 104, 204

climate change, 59, 67, 71, 97, 103
climate justice activism, activist's involvement in, 150–1
Climate Strikes, 96, 105
Clinton, Bill, 32, 36, 50; administration, 33, 37
Clinton, Hillary, 183
colonialism, 104, 155, 204
common sense, 145, 188
Commonwealth Employment Service, 43
Commonwealth Supported Places (CSP), 42
Concordia University, 91
Congressional Joint Committee on Taxation, 33
consumer choice: education, 128
Consumer Price Index (CPI), 34
contemporary civics curriculum, 6
couch surfing: as form of hidden homelessness, 131
COVID-19 pandemic, 17, 18, 33, 41, 45, 70, 71, 74, 83, 96, 107, 127, 132, 183

Davis, Angela, 83
democracy, 5–7; Brown on, 198; capitalism, liberalism and, 8–10; categorizing, 63; citizenship and, 23, 167; death of, 201–2; as façade of equity, 3; freedom and, 116–17; how to stop burning people by, 203–5; liberal, 54; public education, 203–5; public space and, 10–13; relational process, 197; as relational process, 6; struggling against doxa, 198–201; what it looks like, 62–7
democracy sausage, phenomenon of, 70
democratic biographies: activism through higher education and/or student organizing, 78, 89–101; being mentored by trusted adults outside of family, 78, 101–4; class origin breakdown of activists, 80; influence of political family, 77–8, 83–9
democratic dispositions, 14, 21; Bourdieu on, 55; categorizing democracy, 63; classed origins of, 82–104; defining, 56–8; description of, 58; habitus, 148, 149; originating in a habitus, 89; on political persons, 58–62; role of, 202–3; skills through activism, 150; synthesis and obstruction of, 67–75
democratic engagement, barriers to, 154–60
democratic failures: Maggie's story (United Kingdom), 112–18; neoliberal education systems, 122–31; neoliberal housing, 131–7; neoliberal welfare benefits, 137–41; Scarlett's story (Australia), 118–22; Tamara's story (Canada), 107–12
democratic participation, 143; activism and, 160–5
democratic theory, 15–17
Demographic International Housing Affordability Survey, 38
dispositional priming, phenomenon of, 89
disposition to resist, Bourdieu on, 75
Distinction (Bourdieu), 146
dominance, term, 147
Douglas, Roger, 37
doxa, 10; dissolution of, 8; liberalism, 16

Earned Income Tax Credit (EITC), 36
education: neoliberal, 122–31; postsecondary, 9; public systems, 203–5. *See also* higher education
"End of Educated Democracy, The" (Brown), 198
equality of access, 6
Erdal, Cihan, 94

Facebook, 97, 120
failures. *See* democratic failures
Family Supports Ottawa, 108
feminism, 93
Feminist Club, 99
field: concept of, 144; of power, 14. *See also* political fields

Finlay, Diane, 152–3
Firing Back (Bourdieu), 24
Ford, Doug, 204
formal politics, 202
Foster Child Support Network, 151
freedom: association with democracy, 116–17; term, 170
free market, neoliberalism on, 28
Free Trade Area of the Americas protest, 24
Friedman, Milton, 28
Future Hope Adoptions, 108

game, 153
Generation Zero, 98
governance: citizenship as, 169
Government of Australia, 44
Gypsy/Roma/Travellers, 61, 112–13, 115–16

habitus: acquisition of, 75, 86; activist, 149–50; Bourdieu, 12, 57, 143–4, 204; democratic dispositions, 7, 57, 58, 61, 67, 79–80, 89, 148, 204; individual, 145; people with shared, 82; political, 149; social dispositions, 117; specific, 146
Harris, Mike, 32, 47, 50, 128
Hayek, Friedrich, 28
health care: equality in, 6
Health Sciences, 26
Health Services, Canada, 129
Heidegger, Martin, 10
higher education: Australia, 42–3; Canada, 48–9; influence on activism, 78, 89–101; New Zealand, 39; private, in Canada, 128–9; United Kingdom, 30–1; United States, 34–5. *See also* civics education
homelessness, 5–7, 119–20; activists and, 67; couch surfing as form of hidden, 131; experience of, 21–2; political people and, 60–1; recruitment for operationalizing, 17–20; shared stories of, 143; youth, 197–8, 200
homology, 142, 166; activist and formal political fields, 162; between political fields, 146–54; concept of, 146; miraculous, 165; political fields, 144–6
homophobia, 103, 204
housing: Australia, 41–2; Canada, 46–8; Daraja's experience in UK, 135–7; Isabella's experience in US, 133–5; Jillian's experience in New Zealand, 131–3; neoliberal, 131–7; New Zealand, 38–9; United States, 33–4
Housing Act (1980), Thatcher government, 29
Housing and Urban Development (HUD), 33
Housing Corporation of New Zealand, 38
Housing New Zealand Corporation, 38
Howard, John, 43
Howard Coalition government, 42
Howard Liberal Coalition, 171
Human Condition, The (Arendt), 13
human rights: democracy and, 25

Idle No More, 92
illusio, 7, 153; political field, 158; rules of the game, 57, 75
IMF, 8
Indigeneity: citizenship and, 191n20
Indigenous peoples: belonging and, 190–3; youth, 203
Internal Revenue Service: US Department of Education and, 129
IPPR Commission on Economic Justice, 29
Irish Catholics: in Scotland, 80
"Ivy League" universities, 69

Job Network, 43, 44
Job Seeker Payment (JSP), 43–4
Job Services Australia, 44

Kāinga Ora, 38
Kinder-Morgan Transmountain Pipeline, 92
King, Martin Luther, 70
Kulz, Christy, 126

Labour Party, 120; Blair, 29; New Zealand, 40
Lancet (magazine), 32
Lang, Daniel, 48
language: economy of linguistic exchanges, 150
Leeds University, 69, 70
legacy benefits: Universal Credit (UC), 31
legitimacy, 10, 14, 117, 168, 178
Lepine, Marc, 85
LGBTQ2S+, 85; issues, 120; movements, 147; rights, 9; youth, 203
liberal democracy, 54: exclusion within doxa of citizenship, 190–1; perception of, 57n6
Liberal Democrat-Conservative Coalition government: United Kingdom, 31
liberalism, 8–10; counter-history of development of, 95; democratic participation, 143
Liberal-National Coalition, Australia, 124
Liberal Party, Morrison, 64
literature, youth political participation, 15–17
Llewellyn, Kristina, 170
Locke, John, 16
Losurdo, Domenico, 8, 9, 95
Luxton, Meg, 47

McKeen, Wendy, 46
McNeil, Daniel, 191n20
Malcom X, 70
mandatory reporting rules: research project on, 4
Māori's culture, New Zealand, 154–60
Maple Spring, 91

March for Our Lives, 14, 89, 95, 99–101, 103
Marjory Stoneman Douglas High School, 99
markers of distinction, 61
Market Basket Measure (MBM), 50, 50n4
Martin, Paul, 46
May, Theresa, 31
meaning, searching for, 54
Medicaid, 37
meritocracy: benevolence and, 146; ideology of, 8, 145; myth of, 143, 201
Mike Harris Conservatives, 27, 50
Mills, John Stuart, 16
miraculous homology, concept of, 165
Monash University, 71
Montreal's École Polytechnique, 85
moral hazard, concept of, 44
Morrison, Scott, 64
Morrison centre-right Coalition government, 43
mortgage-interest tax deduction (MID), 33
Mulroney, Brian, 45
Multi-Academy Trusts (MATs), 126–7
multiculturalism: idea of, 68; term, 171
mutual obligation, 44

National Citizen Service (UK), 74–5, 168, 175n19, 196; citizenship training, 186; extracurricular civics education, 175–9; good citizen, 178
National Housing Strategy, 48
nationalism, citizenship, 195
National Party, 38, 40
neoliberalism, 8, 24, 106; ascendance of, 27–8; Australia, 41–5; Canada, 45–51; democratic participation, 143; knowledge and network, 197; liberal democracies and, 25–7; New Zealand, 37–41; rise of, 9; United Kingdom, 28–32; United States, 32–7

New Democratic Party (NDP), 153
Newstart, 43
New Zealand: activism influence of trusted mentor, 103; activist's biography, 83–4, 88–9; activist's influence by education, 93–4; barriers to democratic engagement, 154–60; citizenship and belonging, 190–1, 193–5; citizenship curricula, 172; civics education, 184–5; climate justice activism, 150–1; democracy in, 64–5; economic reform, 38, 39–40; higher education, 39; housing, 38–9; Jillian's housing experience, 131–3; Monica's welfare experience, 138–9; neoliberalism, 37–41; race and class biases in activism, 162–3; Rogernomics in, 29; welfare, 40–1
NIMBY (Not In My Back Yard), 116, 116n12
North American Free Trade Agreement (NAFTA), 45
Northern Gateway Pipeline, 92

Occupy (2011), 14
Occupy movement, 92
oeuvre, 146
Omnibus Budget Reconciliation Act (OBRA), 35
One Girl, 71
"one person-one vote" vision, 56, 57
Ontario Disability Support Program (ODSP), 50–1, 109, 111
Ontario Works (OW), 50, 51, 111
Opposition Labour Party, 120
Ottawa Community Housing, 26
Oxford University, 69, 72–3

Pacific Climate Warriors, 164
Palestinian rights, 93
Pateman, Carole, 16
Personal Responsibility and Work Opportunity Reconciliation Act (PRWORA), 36, 37
Piketty, Thomas, 24, 33, 53

political families, influence on activism, 77–8, 83–9
political fields: barriers to democratic engagement, 154–60; fields of activism and, 165–6; homologies between, 146–54; homologous, 144–6; public awareness, 153–4; race and class biases of, 160–5
political involvement, activism and, 22
political participation literature, youth, 15–17
political person, definition of, 58–62
political philosophy, 16
politics, voting and, 6–7
Porter, Ann, 46
potentiality, human, 56
poverty propaganda, 137, 138
private schools, 4; elite students in, 71–3, 188; term in UK, 112n11
Privileged Poor, The (Jack), 188
public education system: democracy and, 203–5
public school: citizenship education in, 167, 186; civics training, 22, 62; Māori in New Zealand, 155; progressive, 84; term in UK, 112n11; UK, 112, 121, 126
public space, democracy and, 10–13
public sphere, Arendt's concept of, 10, 12–13, 54, 201

Quebec Student strikes (Maple Spring), 14, 91

racism, 14, 103, 104; anti-, 93; Australia and, 65, 67–8, 71–2, 74, 123; internalized, 204; New Zealand, 190; structural, 72; systemic, 66, 72; United States, 87, 91
Reagan, Ronald, 32, 33, 46, 50; administration, 34, 35–6; welfare benefits, 139
Reaganomics, 29, 32, 37
recruitment: operationalizing homelessness and activism, 17–20

relational agency, Arendt on, 93
Rheostatics, 24, 51
Rogernomics, New Zealand, 29, 37
Rorris, Adam, 123
Rotary Youth Leadership, 103
Royal Charter Body, 175
Royal Commission on Social Policy (1988), 40
Royal Commission on Social Security (1972), 40
"Russell Group" universities, 69

Salvation Army, 119
Sassen, Saskia, 8, 25, 32, 53
schooling, 9
School Strikes for Climate (2019), 14–15, 98, 99, 163, 194
Scotland, tuition for residents, 80
self-identity, "political" as marker of distinction, 61
Sen, Amartya, 16
sex trafficking, 3, 4
shared table, Arendt's concept, 7, 11, 13, 201–2
Shildrick, Tracy, 137
Shorten, Bill, 119
Smith, Graham Hingangaroa, 154
SNAP (Supplemental Nutrition Assistance Program), 37
Social Justice Centre (SJC), 94
social movements, 9, 17, 199–200; Canada, 78, 92, 93, 173, 180; education and, 203; freedom and, 95; involvement in, 101; left-wing, 77; New Zealand and, 172; progressive, 201; speaking back to, 13–15; student-led, 121, 203; United States, 83, 174
social space, 144, 146, 150
South Africa, apartheid, 72
space of appearance, 7, 10–11
Stanford, Jim, 46
Steggall, Zali, 71
student organizing: influence on activism, 78, 89–101

Student Strikes for Climate, 14, 79, 89, 95, 96, 101, 103, 148, 149
subcultural capital, activist spaces as, 147
Sydney University, 90
symbolic power, 28, 55, 146; Bourdieu's concept of, 169–70; citizenship education, 170–5
symbolic violence, 12, 67, 144–5

Teaching and Higher Education Act, 30
temporary accommodation, 135
Tenancy Rights, Etc. (Scotland) Act, 29
terrorist: country, 123; label of, 68
"Texan Rent Relief" program, 133
Texas State Affordable Housing Corporation, 133
Thatcher, Margaret, 28; Conservatives, 31; Thatcherism, 24, 28, 30, 37
thinking: Arendt on, 8, 54–5, 201; Bourdieu on, 16, 165; critical, 129; democracy, 64, 167, 198; neoliberal, 43, 47; strategic, 107
Thobani, Sunera, 191n20
Thornton, Sarah, 147
Thunberg, Greta, 89, 96
transfer payments, 48
Trump, Donald, 24, 64, 99, 152, 182, 183
Trussell Trust, 32
Twitter, 18, 116

UK Labour Party: Blair, 33
UN Climate Action Summit, 96, 98
UN Climate Change, 96
UN Declaration on Human Rights, 131
UN Declaration on the Rights of the Child, 131
United Arab Emirates (UAE): activist's biography, 88–9; activist's influence by education, 93–4
United Kingdom: citizenship curricula, 171–2; citizenship education, 167–8; civics education, 185–6;

United Kingdom (*continued*)
Daraja's housing experience, 135–7; Elizabeth's welfare experience, 139–40; homologous fields of political activism, 152; Maggie's story of democratic failure in, 112–18; National Citizen Service (NCS), 74–5, 168, 175n19, 175–9, 186, 196; neoliberalism in, 28–32; political activism, 152; race and class biases in activism, 161–2, 163; Tiffany's education experience, 122, 124–7
United Nations, 34; UN Climate Action Summit, 96, 98; UN Climate Change, 96; UN Declaration on Human Rights, 131; UN Declaration on the Rights of the Child, 131
United States: activism influence of trusted mentor, 102; activist's biography, 86–7; activist's influence by education, 91–2; citizenship and belonging, 188–9; citizenship curricula, 173–4; citizenship education, 167–8; GDP growth, 32–3; Internal Revenue Service, 129, 130; Isabella's housing experience, 133–5; neoliberalism, 32–7; race and class biases in activism, 160, 161, 164–5; Reaganomics, 29
Universal Credit (UC) system, 31, 32
universal rights, 8–9
universities, tuition at American, 3
University of California campuses (UCs), 102

voting: Australian, 184; citizenship and, 167

Wacquant, Loïc, 12, 25, 55
Walk the Walk for the Homeless, Salvation Army, 119
web of relations, Arendt on, 7, 11, 54, 75, 201
welfare: Australia, 43–5; benefits of neoliberal, 137–41; Canada, 49–51; Elizabeth's experience in UK, 139–40; Monica's experience in New Zealand, 138–9; New Zealand, 40–1; notion of fraud, 200; Scarlett's experience in Australia, 137–8; United Kingdom, 31–2; United States, 35–7
Welfare Expert Advisory Group (WEAG), 40
whiteness: citizenship and, 191n20; education and, 147; privilege and, 85; proximity to, 190, 192; racial category, 168, 193; of school, 72, 91
"who-ness": public sphere as space of, 201–2
Wilkins, Andrew, 126
Women's March, 99
World Bank, 8, 32
World Health Organization, 17

Young, Iris Marion, 16
Young-Bruehl, Elizabeth, 13
Young Men's Shelter, 26
youth homelessness, 131, 154
Youth Participatory Action Research (YPAR), 200